THE CATHOLIC THING

THE
CATHOLIC
THING

Rosemary Haughton

Copyright © 1979
Rosemary Haughton

All rights reserved, including
the right of reproduction in whole
or in part, in any form.

ISBN: 0-87243-080-4

Published by
Templegate Publishers
302 East Adams St.
Springfield, IL 62701

Dedication

This book is dedicated with much love to the members of the Lothlorien Community, past, present and future, individually and collectively, because they are very much a part of the Catholic thing; and also to all those, both communities and individuals, whose sharing of prayer, work and gifts has made possible this small part of the great enterprise.

Acknowledgements

The author is grateful to the publishers of the following books from which quotations have been used in the text . . .

Twelfth Century Renaissance by Christopher Brooke (Harcourt, Brace, Jovanovich) for the Theophilus quotation on page 68.

Catholic Art and Culture by E. I. Watkin (Sheed & Ward) for the quotation on pages 76 & 77.

Steinbeck: a Life in Letters edited by Elaine Steinbeck and Robert Wallsten (Viking Penguin Inc.) for the quotations used in Chapter 3.

Camelot and the Vision of Albion by Geoffrey Ashe (Panther Books) for the quotations used on pages 99 &100.

TABLE OF CONTENTS

INTRODUCTION

The theme of this book is something called "Catholic". To call it the "Catholic Church" is not good enough, because this "thing" I want to explore is wider than the boundaries of the vast community so described; and also, many times, parts of that Catholic Church have not been "Catholic" in the sense I want to discuss. Yet, the historic entity called the Catholic Church is essential to this wider concept. In practice, it seems possible to explain what I mean by "Catholic" only by exploring the concept in its manifestations, from various angles, and hoping, in the end, to be able to sum up what has been discovered and to interpret it so that it makes sense to people now — people called "Catholics", certainly, but also to a great many other people who are variously attracted, infuriated, enthralled and repelled (but always intrigued) by the Catholic thing.

A not unfamiliar example of reactions to the Catholic thing occurred in my own family. In middle age, my mother was received into the Roman Catholic Church. When she talked about the reasons for her decision, one of the things she said was "I feel at home there." She felt welcome, and comfortable, and supported, in a life that had been full of difficulty and stress. But not many years later she slipped away from that allegiance and afterwards was sometimes bitter about what she called the "stuffiness" of the Church, the preoccupation with the rules, the intolerance and narrowness.

These are very familiar attitudes and experiences. Many still turn to the Catholic Church because they are looking for security, for firm guidance and sure hope in a bewildering world. Others (or the same people, as in this case) leave it because they discover that the other face of that security and support is rigidity and authoritarianism. (This is less so now, but among the reasons for writing a book of this kind is the need to discern the

7

development in ideas about what on earth the word "Catholic" symbolizes now, in minds that entertain it.)

It is true that everyone, at some stage, needs support and security in order to grow, spiritually as well as in other ways. So it really is right and good to look to a place where these things may be found, and to find comfort and relief in them. But most people, unless something has gone wrong with their development, don't want to be dependent for good. Like children growing up, once they have found a sure foundation, they need freedom to discover their own way and meaning, and if their parents try to restrict them they rebel. Many Catholics do rebel, as I said; however, not only do millions of them "stay put" (and they cannot all be feeble or inadequate people) but enormous numbers of people who are not Roman Catholics or even Christians continue to be fascinated by the presence and life of that Church, and to draw from it ideas and inspiration. And among those who have remained Catholics there have always been a large number who are, unquestionably, not only not sheep-like but in fact of transparent integrity. They are not people who require to be cushioned and supported, nor are they people who will stifle doubt and criticism for the sake of a quiet life.

So even at this very personal and immediate level of experience, there is clearly "something else" going on here, something which is not to be explained, as people often explain it, by the human desire to feel safe and supported by a great and rich religious tradition, which envelops people in magnificent ritual, and provides for them a clearly-marked highway to heaven.

This book is about the "something else" going on. It is necessary to write such a book at this particular time, because Western culture has reached a point at which precisely that "something else" is vital for its sanity, let alone its salvation. It must be clear already that by this "something else" I do not mean something that necessarily happens in the context of the Catholic Church as a recognizable body with an ascertainable membership. I do indeed mean that it is present in the visible Catholic Church, but the "something else" is not going on only there. What may be the relationship of the "something else" to the visible Cathoic Church is one of the questions to which answers will, I hope, emerge, but here I want to suggest an answer by sketching two allegorical figures.

One of them is a very familiar personage. Her name is "Mother Church." She is, in many ways, an admirable and dedicated person, deeply concerned about her children, endlessly and tirelessly careful for every detail of their welfare. Her long experience has taught her to understand her family very well. She knows their capabilities and she knows their weakness even better. She is patient and imperturbable, quite unshockable (she has witnessed all of the considerable range of human wickedness in her time) and there are no lengths to which she will not go to help those who turn to her in their need. She is also well able to educate her family. She has a huge fund of stories, maxims and advice, all of them time-tested, and usually interesting as well. She is very talented, skilled in creating a beautiful home for her children; she can show them how to enrich their lives with the glory of music and art. And there is no doubt that she loves God, and wishes to guide her children according to his will.

On the other hand, she is extremely inclined to feel that her will and God's are identical. In her eyes there can be no better, no other, way than hers. If she is unshockable, she is frequently cynical. She is shrewd, with a thoroughly earthy and often humorous shrewdness. She knows her children's limitations so well that she will not allow them to outgrow them. She will lie and cheat if she feels it is necessary to keep her charges safe; she uses her authority "for their own good" but if it seems to be questioned she is ruthless in suppressing revolt. She is hugely self-satisfied, and her judgement, while experienced, is often insensitive and therefore cruel. She is suspicious of eccentricity and new ideas, since her own are so clearly effective, and non-conformists get a rough time, though after they are dead she often feels differently about them.

This is Mother Church, a crude, domineering, violent, loving, deceitful, compassionate old lady, a person to whom one cannot be indifferent, whom one may love much and yet fight against, whom one may hate and yet respect.

But when Mother Church was born it appears that she was

not alone. A twin sister was also born, and her name is Sophia — the Greek word for wisdom; but in fact this name is seldom used because she is one of those people who show a markedly different side of themselves in different relationships, and her many friends, as well as her enemies, tend to call her by pet names, or (in the latter case) by uncomplimentary nicknames. Among her many names are Romantic Love, Mysticism, Superstition, Inspiration, Adventure, Imprudence, Sanctity, Folly. Another reason why few people know her real name is that as they grew up together her twin sister found her so difficult to deal with and so embarrassing that although she was both too good-hearted and too conscientious to turn Sophia out she did do her best to minimize her part in the business of caring for their common charges. Mother Church, in fact, did not much like it to be known that she divided the responsibility with her twin, though sometimes her better nature prevailed and she admitted, in bursts of generous homage, that she couldn't possibly manage without Sophia.

It was, in fact, easy for Mother Church to allow the impression to prevail that she alone had the care of all these children, because Sophia was often not in evidence. You never knew where she would be or what she would be doing. At one time she would be telling marvellous tales or singing strange songs to the babies. At another she would be found inexplicably and bitterly weeping, and the next moment swapping outrageous jokes with somebody. Sometimes she was inaccessible at the top of a turret, wrapped in prayer, after which she returned to the family with reports of marvellous visions seen from her window, which upset everybody and sent them off on quests and adventures. When her sister asked sensible questions about her methods and aims, she gave ridiculous answers or refused to answer at all. Frequently she did not come in to meals, didn't hear quite clear requests for help, or came to greet rich visitors in clothes fit for the barnyard. She also wrote and illustrated books which the children read instead of learning their lessons, and played the piano to them when they were supposed to be doing the dishes. She grew roses in the places where her sister wanted to plant potatoes, and when the roses bloomed she cut them all to make wreaths for the children's heads, instead of decorating the house when visitors were expected. (But the wreath that she wore on her own head, when nobody was looking, was a wreath of brambles.)

Nearly everybody loved Sophia, because one couldn't help it, yet even those who loved her admitted that it was just as well Mother Church was there also, to sort out the muddles Sophia made, sweep up after her riotous games with the children, apologise to the neighbors for her odd behavior, provide answers to questions she raised, and generally keep the place going. Otherwise, how could anyone grow up properly?

But the strange thing is that the two sisters, in spite of everything, have always been devoted to each other. They still are, though their respective admirers, alas, do not always copy them in this.

This book is very largely concerned with the antics of Sophia, yet, all the time, I am conscious that she is not, and cannot be, the only one. The relationship between the two is strange, yet essential, and we shall see what I called "the Catholic thing" acquiring its special character precisely from the interplay of that relationship.

No better example can be found of what I mean in practice than another kind of symbol which will serve to introduce, and illustrate, my theme.

In the mid-1960's it became apparent that the vast medieval church of York Minster was about to fall down unless immediate and radical measures were taken to repair and reinforce it. There were severe and rapidly widening cracks in the walls of the fourteenth century central tower, and at the west end. On investigation it became apparent that the foundations were failing because the builders had enlarged the structure without having much idea of what lay beneath the ground. Add to this changes in the water table, the vibration of the traffic in a modern city, several centuries of failure to notice warning signs, and you have a recipe for disaster on a grand scale.

It hardly needs to be spelled out that this impending disaster, and the reasons for it, accurately parallel what seems to be happening to the old Christian churches and to the Roman Catholic

11

church in particular.

At York, no disaster occurred. A plan was formed which, for boldness and vision, made architectural history. The whole huge structure was, first of all, put onto what amounted to temporary supports while the foundations were completely dug away and replaced with wider and stronger ones. This digging unearthed the earlier foundations of the Minster, as well as the remains of the Roman military headquarters for the northern province of Britain, and the local street plan of the Roman city of Eboracum. In the process of rescuing the Minster for the future, its earlier history and pre-history were uncovered, recorded, and to some extent preserved. At the same time, the whole fabric was renewed where necessary.

The extraordinary enterprise drew on the most sophisticated skills of modern engineering technology, hand in hand with the expertise of archaeologists and historians, glass workers and carvers. It seemed, at first sight, a combination of talents unlikely to be harmonious; yet the team effort succeeded, with each worker enlightening the other. The technicians, accustomed to planning in detail, found that this job required leaps of imagination and the resolving of problems which could not even be predicted until they arose, for nobody knew what might be uncovered as the work progressed. And here the archaeologists could help, knowing about ancient methods of building and experienced in excavation and the behavior of soil layers. The temporary support systems gave an opportunity for craftsmen to restore time-damaged carving, and to learn in doing so still more of the genius of the men who carved before them. The combination was an experience which proved unforgettable for those who took part, and even for those who observed.

A feat of this kind costs a great deal, and the approximately two million pounds had to be raised by public appeal. Gifts poured in from all over the world, but one of the most remarkable facts in this remarkable enterprise is that two thirds of the money was raised within one county of Yorkshire — one county, though admittedly the biggest county, of the small country of England. A great part of it consisted of the gifts of ordinary people.

12

This happened, not in some "superstitious" Latin country but in one which prides itself on being an "advanced" industrialized nation. Yorkshire itself was one of the earliest homes of the industrial revolution, and its industrial cities were centers of wealth as well as dirt early in the last century. Yorkshire means wool mills, and coal. Yorkshire means thrift, an independence that values "brass", and the man who makes it. It has still raw memories of unemployment and hunger marches. Yorkshire people have known want, and are traditionally careful, and the younger ones value possessions and prosperity accordingly.

Yet Yorkshire produced the means to repair its Minster. The great stone thing that had stood through the centuries (for so long partially concealed by scaffolding for repairs) was part of the background of life, scarcely noticed. When, suddenly, it seemed it might disappear, the reaction was a kind of panic. A new awareness stirred, a sense that this thing must not die. It was beautiful, yet Yorkshire is, on the whole, unimpressed by beauty which has no cash value. There was more to it than that.

The great structure which was threatened with collapse was not merely a beautiful relic but the symbol of the entire life of the country. It made little difference whether the symbol had a clear religious significance or not; stretching back into the past, it was embedded not only in the remains of the Roman garrison, but in the thinking and feeling of a whole culture. To lose that would be like being exiled, and only force, or near-despair, drives a person into exile from his or her own place and people.

There is even more than this: this place of prayer is a prayer, the inarticulate prayer of people who cannot pray, don't want to pray, think it ridiculous to pray, but find a strange reassurance in the fact that someone does. All through the five years of the great rescue enterprise, the daily services of the Minster continued. When a bell rang, the noise of power drills, the clanging of hammers and girders, the chugging of concrete mixers, the shouts of foremen, suddenly ceased. Winding sedately among the scaffolding came the procession of choir-boys and clergy, in clean white surplices, filing into their places to sing and pray and preach. And when the service was over and the last indifferent little boy had gone, the building work began again. This,

13

said that daily routine, is not merely an expensive bit of historical conservation; it is an expression of proper human priorities. This place matters, not only because it is humanly beautiful and beautifully human, but because its beauty testifies to the true nature of human kind, beyond its need for money and security, beyond even its reverence for the past, its hope for the future, and its love of beauty which created this great thing. In 1972, exactly 500 years after its completion (the central tower was the last part to be finished), the restoration was complete, and was celebrated in a great service of thanksgiving.

What has been done at York could probably not have been done even fifty years ago. The technology was not available. It was not just a question, then, of preserving the past, but of the present using of all its skills and zeal to give to the future a glorious possession, which is yet the possession of no time or people or place, but of the human spirit. One of the things, for instance, that most profoundly affected the people working on the rescue was the realisation that, by all normal calculations they could make, the structure should not have been standing at all. The foundations were simply inadequate to hold it up. Yet they did.

This book is about an enterprise, spanning many centuries, yet it is also a new enterprise, and in both ways it is fittingly symbolized by the old and new enterprise which is York Minster. In bringing together many people, many talents, and many points of view, it not only uses them but changes them as they interact. To allow one type of view to dominate would be to unbalance and finally destroy the enterprise, yet there can never be a stasis, a perfect balance, except momentarily. As one of the people who worked on the Minster said, we have to have "humility and an appreciation that some of the factors we are dealing with are unknown and may be unknowable." There is always a need to watch for cracks, to accept the need for even radical measures of repair, yet the repair is not a replacement, though it may involve — as at York — the rebuilding of the entire foundation, using temporary and ugly supports meanwhile. This is, in a way, what the Catholic Church has been doing to itself in the last fifteen years. The sheer ugliness and patchiness of interim supports have made many wonder whether all the trouble is worthwhile. There are, after all, many smaller, beautiful and more accessible structures which can be used. Wouldn't it be better to admit that this huge thing, lovely and loaded with history as it is, has had its day, that all things have a natural life-span and that it is unnatural and even ungrateful to go to such lengths to prolong it? Wouldn't it be kinder to pull it reverently down and use the bits for other and more up-to-date buildings?

The answer of Yorkshire, and others, to this question was, "No — we need the Minster." And so the great enterprise began, or rather began again, for it first began in A.D. 627 when Edwin, King of Northumbria, built a chapel in which to receive baptism at the hands of Bishop Paulinus. No trace of that chapel remains, but the later buildings and re-buildings grew on the spot.

The need for it has something, indeed, to do with its size. It soars above surrounding houses, yet it is on a human scale. It does not dwarf human beings, as sky-scrapers do, nor does it come down to their level like little brick chapels. It draws them upwards, it gives them wings — but their own wings.

My theme, taking this as a framework and "parable", is the Catholic enterprise, its makers and re-makers, its shifts of balance, its failures and its astonishing persistence and recoveries. It is huge, it is human, it is old, it needs repair. What is the special nature of this thing, that makes it worth the struggle? Is there some quality that makes it valuable to humanity, a thing worth preserving, re-making, handing on? Or is its natural life-span over? I think we need it, and that it is worth all the labor of reconstruction. Those who made it, and those who labor at it now, don't merely bring to it their own qualities and abilities; they find those changed, developed and challenged, in disconcerting ways, by the enterprise itself. It makes them, as they make it. (And not all those involved are Catholics, as we shall see.)

There is a special quality in Catholicism which is not exclusive to it but which is nevertheless its essential characteristic. It is the quality of catholicity. The Catholic enterprise has been the attempt to integrate the whole of human life in the search for the kingdom of God. It is an enterprise which is doomed to failure, historically, yet also destined to succeed if the New Testament promises are to be taken seriously.

The failures are obvious enough. Sometimes the search to emphasize man's spiritual nature leads to an over-emphasis on the "spiritual", denigrating natural beauty and pleasure, so that "the Church" appears as an elite of almost disembodied mystics; the reaction to this is indifference and cynicism among those who can't take this kind of thing. Sometimes, more commonly, the attempt to include the social and political aspect of life in the divine plan leads to treating the structures designed to assist this as if they were themselves the divine plan; the result is corruption and rigorism, side by side. The reaction is a renewed search for the direct spiritual experience of God, apart from "structures". Sometimes the attempt to bring all human skill and talent into God's service leads to an over-valuing of beauty and skill for its own sake, and there is a violent reaction in favor of austerity and simplicity. Sometimes cultivation of the intellect seems the way of saving the people from superstition, but then a barren and over-rational theology drives people into extravagant "private" devotion. Then, perhaps, a distrust of elitism puts the emphasis on "simple piety" and obedience, and gives much scope for the exploitation of credulity. Or the discovery of the revolutionary social implications of the Gospel goes so far that it seems to cut out the love of God, and people drift away, looking for consolation in versions of Eastern mysticism.

So there is never a completeness, never a time when the work is done, though sometimes the unrealised wholeness may be glimpsed in a person, or a moment of history. Yet, however gross the failures, there is an inner vitality that will not admit defeat. It will not give up trying to bring all aspects of human life into the kingdom of God. The historic Catholic enterprise, with all its faults, stands as an assertion of hope in human beings, their capabilities, their destiny, their inner and indestructible sanctity.

So it has to go on, and if it is to go on, it has to undertake this huge work of repair and restoration, which sometimes looks much more like a demolition. But this work can never be purely a restoration. The very drastic quality of the work involved dem-

16

onstrates that much more is involved than re-creating past glories. That re-creation *is* part of the work, and it forms part of the exploration in this book; but if that were all it would not be worth doing.

We are creating for the future, not just preserving the past. We are, in fact, trying to make the structure better. We can't go back to the past, but to pretend we have learned nothing useful through the centuries is wrong. Neither can we ignore the present. Modern technology can be destructive, but it can also be creative, and that applies to new skills in linguistics, psychology, anthropology, philosophy and historical research, as well as in engineering and archaeology. The present searches the past for the sake of the future. When we understand better what we have inherited, we shall know ourselves better and make better use of ourselves. The Catholic thing belongs to all of Western mankind, and to the rest of the world insofar as Western culture has touched it. It is necessary to make it fully available once more, and that means a huge enterprise, one undertaken with "humility and an appreciation that some of the factors we are dealing with are unknown, and perhaps unknowable." Yet, we should not be falsely humble about it, feeling that our age has nothing to contribute except reverence for the past.

I take as my text another sentence of Bernard Feilden, who guided the York project:

"One can argue that the building has stood 500 years in spite of the calculations, and by conserving the existing fabric and augmenting it one must be able to make it a bit better."

For "500", say "2000", and you have the Catholic enterprise, past, present, and future. But we need to remember both the twin sisters who are the Catholic thing, and return to them, later, to help sum up.

Chapter 1
THE TEAM

Let's begin with a series of portraits. Some are saintly, some unsaintly, some scholarly and some unscholarly, clerics and lay people, "born leaders" and those who never wanted to lead at all. But they have two things in common: they had a very great effect on the work in which they were engaged, and that was (and is) the Catholic enterprise. I have called them "the Team" in the sense that the Catholic enterprise is, at any one time, kept going, or even pushed along very fast, by a comparatively small number of people who happen to have the qualities required. They may not know each other, or even know that the others exist. They may have no wish or intention of being important in the work. But they are important, whether they like it or not.

My collection is picked out over the centuries and my choice has been made to help me in my purpose of uncovering the quality of the Catholic thing. If there is such a thing, it is here that I must look for it first of all. This enterprise somehow evokes the enthusiasm of people who have little in common, and yet their common involvement challenges their attitudes and views, confronts them, undermines their assumptions, shows them new ways. And they, as they respond to this challenge, create (sometimes without knowing it) the enterprise in which they are involved. They modify, enlighten, prod, define, check, comfort or stabilise it, as they have the talent and as the needs of the case demand.

When Bernard Shaw wrote the famous Preface to his play "St. Joan" he quoted a letter he had received about the play "from a Catholic priest". The letter from Shaw's correspondent expressed what seems to me the thing about Catholicism, from one point of view. "In your play", the letter said, "I see the dramatic presentation of the conflict of Regal, Sacerdotal and Prophetical powers in which Joan was crushed. To me it is not the victory of any one of them over the others that will bring peace and the Reign of the Saints in the Kingdom of God, *but their fruitful interaction in a costly but noble state of tension.*"

Whether this was a fair comment on the play or not, it is certainly a magnificent statement of what my study is about, though nowadays we may more easily appreciate the statement if the three catagories are expressed as the political, the religious and the charismatic powers.

But the unnamed writer of that letter was almost certainly not a priest at all, but Friedrich von Hugel, who often signed himself "Fr. von Hugel".

And Shaw's is not the only mind in which the name of Friedrich von Hugel raises no echoes. There must be few now living who have heard of him, though he died in 1925, and was arguably the greatest Catholic of his time, not excepting Newman, who was his friend.

To begin with a man most Catholics (not to mention others) have never heard of may seem perverse, but that quotation shows reason enough. Baron Friedrich von Hugel is an excellent beginning because he was greatly and delightedly a Catholic, yet also catholic with a small "c", truly "a man for all seasons" in an even wider sense than Thomas More himself.

He achieved, as far as a person can, the integration of all aspects of life in the search for God's kingdom, which seems to me to be one of the specific marks we are seeking. Other persons show the way extremes can help to balance the whole; von Hugel shows the brilliancy of that moderation and balance which is usually held to be dull, compared to extremism. At a time (the later half of the 19th century and the first quarter of the 20th) when Catholics were usually both defensive and intolerant, von Hugel was open, inclusive, humble and yet confident. Probably his best loved work is his "Letters to a Niece", later published by that niece, Gwendolen Greene. She was an Anglican, and was encouraged by him to be a *good* Anglican. His profound respect for people, his sensitivity to truth and goodness wherever he met it, made him revere the presence of God in every faith, awed and thrilled to discover yet more of the divine bounty and wisdom. To discover God in people made him rejoice like St. Francis at the sheer exuberance of divine love. "Now that's fine!" he would shout, delighted. Once, when he was giving religious instruction to some children, one of his daughters heard all of them shouting with laughter. "Religion must be the most amusing thing in the world," she remarked. To von Hugel it certainly was a delight and a glory. He was self-disciplined and even ascetic, yet he had a huge capacity for enjoyment, and a power to evoke it in others. "I always try to get the child to come up in people," he said, and he usually succeeded.

He laughed a great deal himself. He would, I think, have laughed comfortably at the idea that it mattered whether or not his name was remembered. But even if his name is forgotten the results of his influence on others were very great, and have shaped Catholic thinking since then in many ways. It seems the right time, and a good place, to remember him once more.

Friedrich von Hugel was born in 1852 and died in 1925, thereby spanning one of the periods of deepest demoralisation and spiritual pusillanimity in the history of the Catholic Church. Yet he epitomised not only what is greatest and most enduring in Catholicism, but also the best hope of unity with other churches, at a time when such a hope seemed not only remote but impossible. He was the true prophet of the "new" Catholic enterprise.

How great a prophet he was is only slowly coming to be appreciated. His beautifully balanced holiness, his humanity and humility, made him less startling than his more extreme contemporaries. G. K. Chesterton's loud humor and wild paradoxes, Hilaire Belloc's witty and outrageous Catholic chauvinism, are more obviously attention-catching; but neither approached him in learning, insight, or goodness. The Modernist controversy which caused wounds whose scars still make the Catholic Church wince, and alienated so many other Christians, caused him profound grief, and made him suspect in Rome. The remembered names of that crisis are those of men who broke with the Church in bitterness and despair, like the fiery Tyrrell, whom von Hugel loved. Yet von Hugel himself was more profoundly and painfully aware of what was wrong with the Church than those who broke with her. Like Erasmus before him, he could fight what was wrong and yet cling to the essential mission, and do both without bitterness. He endured the official distrust of his beloved Church without resentment, and in his work became a point of growth for unity among Christians which he could never have been if he had rejected his Catholic allegiance.

The actual arguments involved in the Modernist controversy now seem unreal, but the point at issue was whether the discoveries of science, and the findings of modern scholarship in history, linguistics and archaeology, could be applied to the interpretation and understanding of Scriptures, and of Christian belief in general. The whole argument was falsified from the start, because each side held to a crude and undeveloped version of its own views, a scientific fundamentalism opposed to a Catholic one. Those few who attempted to use scientific and newly available scholarly sources and methods (such as the new psychology) to arrive at a deeper understanding of their faith were immediately lumped by Rome with those Christians who were publicly (from pulpits sometimes) denying the divinity of Christ, the possibility of miracles or the existence of life after death.

The panicky theological reaction was unpleasant but probably inevitable, given the mediocre education of most of the clergy, the underdeveloped and extremely doctrinaire forms of the new "scientific" discoveries, and the atmosphere of European politics where "liberal" meant "anti-Catholic". Much worse was the sheer nastiness of the methods used to silence opposition. The blanket condemnations, the cruel stupidity that would not distinguish between honest and anguished doubt and open rejection of authority, the "vendetta" that could ruin a career and a life in the name of Christ, and stamp out all intellectual search in the name of orthodoxy — these were the things that did the permanent harm. Catholic scholarship suffered a blow that took half a century to heal, and the promising beginnings of rapprochement between the Anglican and Roman churches were crushed. Above all, faith and hope were killed in many hearts. This episode of Catholic history does not have the horror of the Spanish Inquisition or the medieval persecution of the Jews, but for ruthlessness and psychological brutality, for sheer inhumanity and lack of basic decency, it is hard to forgive. And this was the Catholic world in which Friedrich von Hugel lived, undauntedly struggling to explain the truth he perceived, refusing to be frightened by Rome or flattered by those who hailed him as their champion against her. He represented the real and perennial Catholic enterprise.

Von Hugel saw the Modernist exaggerations as the inevitable result of "the intellectual inertia under which, for so many years, professors of ecclesiastical exegesis have allowed Catholicism to be buried". He was profoundly saddened that what seemed to him the God-given opportunities to discover new depths in the traditional faith, through the new worlds of discovery in science and scholarship, should become merely a war between equally pig-headed orthodoxies. He longed for a synthesis, a renewal of the old by the new, such as Thomas Aquinas had achieved in his time. And, in his own work, he achieved this, but he suffered the traditional fate of the true prophet: "O Jerusalem, Jerusalem, thou that killest the prophets—." He himself died at a good old age, but the great movement he had hoped for was killed by the passionate intransigence of one side and the timid brutality of the other. It took the volcanic consequences of the second Vatican Council to make possible what von Hugel had worked for, but by then the circumstances were far less favorable. The atmosphere of breadth and leisure, and above all the close interrelation of spirituality and Christian scholarship which was von Hugel's ideal, had by then become almost impossible. He was acutely aware and indeed almost tortured by the failures and sins of his Church, but he remained always capable of exultation, awe, and sheer delight at the riches of it, the Catholic variety and strength and beauty and vitality.

Rather than follow his career, which was both eventful and, from another point of view, quite humdrum, let him be the introducer, let him set out the theme of this book, and celebrate it a little, for the personality of the celebrant can make up in intensity and glory what I refuse him in page space. I think, for instance, that von Hugel brings out very clearly the peculiar polarity within the Catholic thing which I referred to under the allegorical form of the two sisters, of shape and spirit, structure and inspiration, that search for wholeness which is the impossible but essential Catholic quest:

"Official organisation and authority are part, a normally necessary part, of the fuller and more fruitful religious life; but they are ever only a part, and a part in what is a dynamic whole — one movement in what is a life, in the deepest sense of the word. The lonely, new and daring (if but faithful, reverent and loving) outgoing of the discoverer and investigator are as truly acts of, are as necessary parts of, the Church and her life as his coming back to the Christian love and community, which later will then test his contribution by tentative application to its own life, and will in part assimilate, in part simply tolerate, in part finally reject it. And such a lonely, venturesome outgoing appears in all kinds of degrees and forms, in every sort of life. The inventive, often most daring, even at first opposed, philanthropy of the Saints belongs entirely to this exploratory, pioneer class of action in the rhythmic "inspiration-expiration" life, in the breathing of the living Church. The Church is thus, ever and everywhere, both progressive and conservative; both reverently free-lance and official; both as it were male and female, creative and reproductive, both daring to the verge of presumption, and prudent to the verge of despair. And Church officials are no more the whole Church, or a complete specimen of the average of the Church, than Scotland Yard or the House of Lords (though admittedly necessary parts of the national life) are the whole, or average samples, of the life and fruitfulness of the English nation."

This may seem to be obvious enough, yet it is still the case that to most people who are not Catholics, and indeed to many Catholics, it is the official, the prudent, the conservative, that "*is*" the Church, and "the lonely, new and daring" are seen as revolts *against* the Church, even when undertaken by those who (inexplicably, and — it is supposed — probably from cowardice or ignorance) remain Catholics. Von Hugel said it was not so, and he was right, as we shall see. He said this at a time when the "official" was bearing down intolerably on the Church, when the "inventive" people were, often enough, being forced out because neither they nor the "officials" could see that *both* are needed, because without each other neither can survive as a living Church.

Von Hugel discovered the balance, the richness and what he called the "noble tension" of the Catholic thing most fully displayed in the flowering of the early middle ages, and indeed this is where I shall be looking for it, though not only there. He found it in Italy, first of all.

> "Born as I was in Italy, certain early impressions have never left me; a vivid consciousness has been with me, almost from the first, of the massively virile personalities, the spacious trustful times of the early, as yet truly Christian, renaissance there, from Dante on to the Florentine Platonists. And when, on growing up, I acquired strong and definite religious convictions, it was that ampler pre-Protestant, as yet neither Protestant nor anti-Protestant, but deeply positive and Catholic, world, with its already characteristically modern outlook and its hopeful and spontaneous application of religion to the pressing problems of life and thought which helped to strengthen and sustain me, when repressed and hemmed in by the types of devotion prevalent since then in Western Christendom . . . I had to continue the seeking and finding elsewhere [than in these 'types of devotion'] yet ever well within the great Roman Church, things more intrinsically lovable."

This passage is from his enormous work, *The Mystical Element of Religion* based on the life of St. Catherine of Genoa (so, incidentally, his "massively virile personalities" were of both sexes). In his battle to discover, live and celebrate the true Catholicism, von Hugel suffered intensely; he knew that in a sense he had to "make history" as he did so. "What a costing process that is!" he wrote. He spoke of "having to strike for all

24

one is worth, and yet be cautious; of having one's poor inner world to keep in order, whilst fighting a larger and different world outside; and doing so necessarily, in much isolation, with, say, a dozen or so of dearest friends, scattered over Europe and America" (and, I should add, several denominations) "to inspire and help one . . . Certainly the effect upon myself is being considerable. I have become a good bit more of a person, please God, of the right, the spiritual humble sort, by battling and toiling with and in and over these great realities and problems."

One might think, from all this, that von Hugel saw the Catholic thing as an affair of great battles and "massively virile personalities." In reality, he had an intense appreciation of the importance of ordinary people and ordinary affairs. He insisted over and over again that a proper Christian life must include other interests besides religious ones, and his own passionate interest in geology is only one example of this. In all of his interests he found God, yet not by looking for "edification", but simply because God is there in the sheer reality of "the particular tone of my brother's voice, the leaping of my dog in the grass, the scent of apricot on the old red-brick sun-baked wall, the iridesence of this opal, the sound of the grinding of the pebbles on yonder sea-shore." He wrote to someone who was setting out on a series of visits and destined to pack and unpack for some weeks:

"Not even a soul in heaven . . . can take your place, for what God wants, what God will love to accept, in those rooms, in those packing days, and from your packing hands, will be just this little packing performed by you in those little rooms."

In one great vision, one life, one Catholic experience, he placed the soaring of the mystic, the struggles of the interior life and of the exterior battle for truth, or the details of packing a suitcase efficiently. "You understand?" he went on. "At one moment, packing; at another, silent adoration in Church; at another, dreariness and unwilling drift; at another, keen, keen suffering of soul, of mind, in apparent utter loneliness; at another, external acts of religion; at another, death itself." Another time, he quoted the remark of the well known hymn writer, Father Faber, who, in his final illness, had received the last Sacraments, and later asked for them again. He was told it was the same illness, so he couldn't have them again, and he remarked: "Well, if I can't have the sacraments, give me Pickwick." And he settled down with Charles Dickens' comic masterpiece.

Not only common things but common people, the "blessed common" of Julian of Norwich, were von Hugel's beloved. One of the "saints" he knew was a washerwoman he met in church, "whose feet I wish I could become worthy to kiss." Children in the park knew and welcomed him, out for a walk in his cloak and wide-brimmed hat, with his small dog and his deaf-aid, or carrying a collection of little paper bags when he had been shopping. He was popular in local shops, because he enjoyed both the people and the shopping. The author of the introduction to a selection of his work refers to his care for "little, insignificant people," but has to add immediately that "he did not regard them as insignificant." To him, nothing was insignificant, because truth was not abstract but incarnate. Because nothing is trivial, nothing is of final importance except God, least of all one man's work. His work was interrupted by periodic nervous breakdowns, but he did not pity himself. They only made him more sympathetic to the darkness that others suffered. In his last illness, when he knew he might not live to finish his book "The Reality of God," he wrote to his niece: "I would like to finish my book — but if not I shall live it out in the beyond." In the same letter he expressed his sense of the generosity of God, which must be matched by the generosity of the Christians:

"Let us try to be generous and accept . . . Plant yourself on foundations that are secure — God — Christ — Suffering — the Cross. They are secure. How I love the Sacraments! I am as certain of the real presence of Christ in the Eucharist as of anything there is. Our great hope is in Christianity, our only hope. Christ re-creates. Christianity has taught us to care. Caring is the greatest thing — caring matters most. My faith is not enough, it comes and goes. I have it about some things and not about others. So we "make up and supplement each other."

That, of course, is why there is a Church, not just converted people. But it can also be applied to divided churches, as von Hugel knew, and he wanted each person to find what he or she needed, in what he had to offer and what the Church has to offer. He was once praised as "the greatest living apologist for the Roman Church," on which he remarked ruefully that having hoped to do well in the dog class he was much discouraged at being given first prize among cats. This exploration of the Catholic enterprise is not intended, either, as polemic. It is an offering presented with much love. As von Hugel wrote to his niece: "Take only what you can and what helps."

Augustine of Hippo, probably the most famous of converts, is the second character in my Catholic gallery. All his life he was the complete despot, though one full of compassion for those he ruled and a fierce fighter on their behalf. A greater contrast with von Hugel can hardly be imagined. Augustine had little or no sense of humor, no interest whatever in natural things, a vast and comprehensive intolerance and little talent for human relationships except those of teacher and disciple.

Some people hate Augustine as virulently as the Irish hate Oliver Cromwell, which is some measure of the man's personal dynamism and symbolic importance, in both cases. Augustine's greatness is almost overpowering, and it is a one-sided greatness, of a kind that could (and sometimes nearly did) over-balance the whole structure. He needs perspective. Contact with von Hugel gives one perspective. That perspective allows us to see that Augustine was not a colossal "normative" force but an eccentric, a genius, a one-sided giant whose influence still must not prevent us peering past his vast but twisted shadow to perceive other kinds of greatness and quite different traditions and emphases, all within this Catholic thing. If the greatness of Catholicism consists in its attempt to keep what von Hugel called the Regal, the Sacerdotal and the Prophetical in a "noble state of tension," then Augustine's pull was in the direction of the Sacerdotal, in which he tended to merge the other two. To maintain a proper tension we shall need to call on others.

All the same, Augustine's intellectual style penetrated European thought for centuries and marked the whole course of Western philosophy with an indelible dye. It gets fainter with much washing but the colour is still noticeable. Colour, incidentally, is worth noticing about Augustine. He was African, possibly a black African, but almost certainly dark skinned. The interesting thing is that we don't know for certain because in spite of his fame the point wasn't considered important by his contemporaries. It says something about the culture of the time that nobody thought it worthwhile to record the skin colour of the most illustrious and controversial bishop, theologian and polemicist of the age.

Augustine is labeled "saint", and the latter part of his life justifies it, but holiness is not the thing that strikes one first about him. His most obvious characteristic is his passionately analytical egoism, which led him to study minutely the processes of his own thought. This gives his "Confessions" an extraordinary perceptive intensity, but it also made him a very bad observer of other people, because he saw them solely in relation to himself, and one has to piece together the evidence almost against his intention. (There is evidence, for instance, that he had a brother and a sister, but one would never know it from his narrative.)

His family were comfortable, prosperous, middle-class people, anxious for a good career for their son. He hated school, with good reason, since it was the kind of bad expensive school that arises to meet the demands of newly rich parents wanting a "good" education but having little idea of what that means. Its aim was to instil the required basics of a "gentleman's" education, by rote and the rod. But Augustine was the sort of boy who mops up knowledge wherever it is lying around. His parents were dazzled, and they spoiled him and praised him. His mother was a Christian, and a good if conventional one, but she didn't have the boy baptised because infant baptism was not yet the norm and she evidently felt he was unlikely to stick to the promises during his wild early years. She was probably right, though

Augustine blamed her for it later.

He went to Carthage to pursue his studies, and did all the things that a clever, spoiled, undisciplined young man with plenty of curiosity and no moral standards might be expected to do. He despised his parents' ideas, both his father's genial and conventional worldliness and his mother's anxious and equally conventional piety (he saw no more in it than that, at the time). After a time, in natural reaction to both his home and his own excesses, he took up with the sect of Manichees, who taught that the body and all material things were the creation of the dark evil principle, while the spiritual reality, created by God, could be released from its material prison by the secret wisdom, the enlightenment of the elect. It was an elaborate and persuasive theology, of a kind which is often popular in cultures in decline, when sensitive people feel stifled by the sheer weight and crassness of "establishment" ideas and structures. Augustine, like his modern equivalents, probably found in it a satisfying way of rejecting his background and being as "different" from the stupid, conventional mass as he felt himself to be.

Unlike many spoilt young men, Augustine managed to combine parties, sexual experiment, and odd spiritual explorations with a great deal of study. He almost couldn't help it — he had the kind of mind that seizes on intellectual problems and wrestles with them, even against his every inclination. So, at a very early age, he moved to Italy and eventually got himself a professorship in Milan. Before that he went home for a while and upset his mother by taking his mistress with him. But he couldn't stand his father's naivete or his mother's emotional outbursts about his way of life. His mother, Monica, also ended up as a saint, but at this stage she was that terrifying thing — a frustrated, hysterical, pious woman. Her brilliant son was the object for feelings never satisfied in an "arranged" marriage with a jolly, bad-tempered, insensitive and casually unfaithful husband. After her husband's death she concentrated on her son. She was a really good person, but unself-critical, and the strict physical self-control that had been drilled into her as a child did not help her to understand or control her feelings about her son. She made scenes with a religious flavour, pur-

29

sued Augustine back to Carthage in her attempts to control his life, and for all his rejection of his home he hadn't the nerve to stand up to her directly. Instead, he took a ship for Italy without telling her, a fact which reveals a good deal about their relationship.

Left behind in Africa, Monica was forced to come to terms with the realities of her life. She followed him later, but by then she had changed. Meanwhile Augustine was rising in his career, admired, sought after, surrounded by hero-worshipping students, for his second outstanding characteristic was his immense charm. He attracted people, and had the gift of friendship, though his friends were to be either his disciples or his masters, not his equals. But his egoism was neither stupid nor uncritical, and his very success, far too easy as he saw it, made him question the meaning of his life, and with it the dualist theology of the Manicheans. Having begun to question, his mind refused to let go. It wrestled with God, sex, politics, came up with a decision to become a Catholic Christian, and in the process worked out some theological principles which shaped all his future work. Through him, they shaped the flow of Catholic theology from then on until the even more powerful flood originating from Thomas Aquinas became the main stream. But the Augustinian waters were still flowing, and recently their importance has been re-assessed, with a certain awed surprise at the clarity and abundance of this intellectual spring.

Augustine's struggles with his sexual desires, before accepting baptism, are famous. For him, sexual feeling was so intimately bound up with all that he most disliked in his past life that he was never able to disentangle it. His own distrust of sexuality influenced his theology of marriage and of grace, and through him it affected Christian attitudes to sex and to the body for many centuries. But he thought the thing out clearly and fully, trying to make allowance for his own bias; that is the measure of the man.

His mistress, faithful to him for fifteen years and the mother of his only son, was sent away by Monica, who was now established in Milan and wanted Augustine to make a respectable marriage. This unnamed woman's devotion, and her sacrifice (she left her son in Italy with his father) Augustine admired but took for granted. Converted, he was still the supreme egoist. He didn't marry, for he realised finally that for him it had to be celibacy. The moment came, through a snatch of a child's song half-heard, telling him, he thought, to open the Bible and read, and so finding the text that bade him "make no provision for the flesh" and its passions, but to accept Christ in purity. His subconscious mind had done what he had been asking it to do for some time. From that moment he was a Catholic Christian, and he took with him the group of friends who had been waiting for his lead.

His egoism and his charm went with him into his new life, but both were converted. His passion for self-analysis had led him to the font, and thereafter he applied what he had learned on the long journey to the understanding of the whole human predicament and God's dealing with it. Having disentangled himself from Manicheism, he set out to expose its errors and defend and expound the Catholic enterprise.

He wanted to devote his life to solitary prayer and study, and went back to Africa determined to do so. But his new faith interfered. It forced on him the necessity of attending to others' needs and his enduring charm brought him plenty of people in need. Gradually he found himself with a large pastoral responsibility. The long battle with Donatist heretics demanded all his strong will and debating ability. That struggle shows us a side of him, a ruthless sternness and intolerance, which twentieth century Christians find hard to accept. He ended up as bishop of the important diocese of Hippo, at the time when barbarians were rapidly crumbling the edges of the Roman Empire, in the process over-running the then fertile and highly civilized North African provinces. The brilliant scholar's pride and individualism, the fierce fighter's sense of strategy, became the bishop's indomitable courage and resourcefulness in coping with enemies within and without. His charm was transformed into the attractiveness of intellect fused with compassion. The egoism was also transmuted, and became the power of decisive and supportive leadership. He continued to refer all things to himself, but that self was dedicated with all the single-mindedness of his ambitious nature to the service of God and of his people. He served his people *his* way, and made others do the same, and as far as he was concerned, what was good for all of them was what he said was good.

For all his faults, his intense love of the God who finally claimed him had taken over his whole life. This was no philosopher's God, no Manichean principle of light, but God-in-Man, personal, eternal, lover, ruler and intimate friend. His passionate regret for the wasted years, his perception of the presence in all those years and those experiences of the hidden beloved, come through to us with almost frightening vividness, in a passage that repetition has failed to stale or weaken:

"Late have I loved Thee, O Beauty ever old and ever new! Late have I loved Thee! For behold Thou wert within me, and I outside; and I sought Thee outside and in my lovelessness fell upon those lovely things that Thou has made. Thou wert with me and I was not with Thee. I was kept from Thee by those things, yet had they not been in Thee, they would not have been at all. Thou didst cry to me and break open my deafness; and Thou didst send forth Thy beams and shine upon me and chase away my blindness. Thou didst breathe fragrance upon me, and I drew in my breath and do now pant for Thee; I tasted Thee and now hunger and thirst for Thee; Thou didst touch me, and I have burned for Thy peace."

Augustine gave a huge push to the Catholic enterprise even if it was a push rather to one side of the road. His emphasis on man's powerlessness for good, his total dependence on God, was the result of personal experience, and in his own life it balanced his natural egoism and ambition. Historically it reached its most extreme form in sects and churches which broke away from Catholicism when the Catholic church had gone too far in the opposite direction. In isolation the doctrines of predestination and natural depravity became tyrannical, as in the case of the strict Puritans, and in the Evangelical attitude to children. The very inhumanity of such unbalanced theology gradually weakened its hold. And within the Catholic experience there were already counterbalances in operation.

But Augustine was a Roman, and on the positive side what he gave to the Catholic experience was, among other things, the impress of Roman culture as it came to him in the great classical authors, much as he despised their subject matter. It formed his mind and his style while he rejected its teaching. There was much of the traditional Roman paterfamilias about him — grave, severe, studious, energetic, and just even in his despotism.

As he lay dying, the barbarians were at the gates of his city. The Roman world was dying, too. One of his last acts was to bully the rich to give up their treasures to feed the poor of the besieged city, and he himself lay in a room stripped of all saleable articles, but hung about with copies of the penitential psalms, so that he could read them as he died.

Augustine was a man of Rome, classical Latin was his language and he could imagine no other world; he used its ideas to express his own, even though he saw it dying and corrupt around him.

The third of my "team", Heloise, grew up in a world quite the contrary of Augustine's, one so full of newness and a sense of discovery that to it, far more than to the French Revolution, might be applied Wordsworth's words:
"Bliss was it in that dawn to be alive,
And to be young was very heaven."
Heloise was very young indeed when she met the middle-aged scholar, Abelard. Abelard and Heloise are arguably the most famous pair of lovers in history. Abelard's highly original, incisive and ruthless intellect re-directed the theological development of the great twelfth century renaissance, but my interest is chiefly in Heloise, who was by far the greater person of the two.

Without Heloise, Abelard's thought could never have been as rich or as human. She tried to submerge herself in him, but the result was to change him fundamentally. Through their strange and tragic experience of love the whole Christian feeling about the nature of human love was enhanced, made more strange, more sensitive, more problematic.

If Peter Abelard's brilliant mind produced something more valuable for posterity than a conventionally outstanding addition to the theology of his time, it was because of his experience of love — Heloise's love. He was already a renowned scholar at the budding university of Paris, clearly making himself a great career (and many enemies) as a teacher, and, like Augustine, surrounded by a circle of admiring young men lapping up his thought like a lot of famished kittens round a bowl of milk. But one of the kittens was female, the gifted and ardent young ward and niece of a Canon of Paris, Fulbert. Her thirst for learning could not be satisfied along with the rest, since she was a girl and could not study with the young men. Her uncle and guardian doted on her and was intensely proud of her scholarship and he was flattered when the famous Abelard, who had seen her, asked to take her as a private pupil. Abelard was already in his thirties, Heloise still in her 'teens, very beautiful and with a subtle and ruthless intelligence which, unlike his, was wholly at one with her feelings. In her mind, there was no contradiction between her passion for Abelard as a source of learning and her quickly developing passion for Peter Abelard the man. Whether the love affair that followed was mainly on his initiative or hers it is impossible to say. It began, he says, with mere lust on his part, and it seems likely that she foresaw the consequences most fully and was consciously prepared to accept them, for she had a single-mindedness in love that Abelard never possessed. But she could not foresee the full tragedy.

At that time it was illegal but not unusual for a cleric to marry. The marriage would be valid, but although the exact circumstances are not at all clear it seems that for a cleric as well known and respected as Abelard, set on a brilliant academic and ecclesiastical career, it probably meant the end of promotion. Abelard, by that time passionately in love, was willing to marry Heloise, hoping by this means to placate her uncle who was plunged into angry shame by their liaison, and it was Heloise who tried to dissuade him. She would rather be the whore of the great Abelard than drag him with her into obscurity and shackle his freedom with domesticity. In the end she consented to marry him but the marriage was to be kept secret. She knew, however, that this would not appease the rage of her guardian.

They had one period of idyllic happiness, when they travelled to Abelard's old home in Brittany. Their only child was born there, and remained there later on to be cared for by Abelard's sister. The little boy was saddled with the name "Astrolabe", which is just the sort of thing one might expect from a couple of intensely intellectual romantics. They rationalised everything they did according to their own ideals, and were typically insensitive to the normal priorities of life or the probable feelings of other, less highly-wrought, people. They did not consider the possible reaction either of their son to his outlandish name, or of Heloise's uncle to their secret marriage and public scandal.

For the end came when Fulbert, driven to near madness by jealous misery over this adored, once untouched, paragon of a niece, hired some ruffians to break into Abelard's lodging and castrate him. We owe to this gothic horror a unique development in the humanist strand of Catholic culture.

Both of the stricken lovers entered religious life, which was the only way available to them to dissolve the marriage. Abelard gradually re-established himself as a teacher, after long struggles, and much later he wrote an account (one which is obsessively analytical and self-centered yet sensitive and trenchant) of his various trials and his persecutions by incompetent rival theologians and scholars, his tragic love and marriage and its outcome. This account was shown to Heloise, and she reacted with the first of the letters between them which are among the most famous letters in all literature.

So it came about that this strange, illicit, and disastrous love, in its destruction produced acute and courageous reflections on the nature of human love, of marriage, of the relation between divine and human love. The exchanges between the anguished minds of the parted lovers refined and hammered out new insights.

Heloise's whole devotion was to Abelard. She consented to enter religion because he wished it, and for no other reason. When she was Abbess of her community, loved and respected and consulted, she still suffered intensely from longing for her husband, and for their intercourse, both physical and intellectual. She felt profoundly guilty because she had taken upon herself the vows and life of one dedicated to love God alone, yet her sole love, it seemed to her, was for Abelard, her entire life an act of obedience to him, a gesture of heroic pagan despair, not of Christian love; but she could not do otherwise.

Out of their attempts to make sense of this contradiction, and of their whole human and religious predicament, grew Abelard's later theology, one which emphasised the God of love present in the human Jesus who suffered and cared with and for mankind. It is the intention that counts, said Abelard, God looks at the heart. It seems obvious enough to us, and in fact this subjective moral standpoint can be as one-sided and destructive as the legalistic one, as we are now discovering. But it was an insight that was stirring in the minds of men and women of that time, and it was Abelard who gave it the precision and power to affect the development of Christian thought down to our own day. It was also something he had learned from Heloise.

Her contribution to the Catholic enterprise was to pin down remorselessly certain moral paradoxes displayed in her own life. She would not evade them, and could not (with the theological material available) resolve them. Or rather, she could not resolve them intellectually; but her life did so, for it forced later generations to realise the fundamental oneness of love, human and divine. Heloise's tragic marriage unlocked an understanding of the spiritual nature of the marriage bond itself, and showed why it can properly be linked to the love of Christ for his Church. She thought herself unfaithful to God in her faithfulness to Abelard. It remains for us to recognise that her honesty and refusal to compromise were in fact the fulfilment of the vocation to love God. Thus do men and women involve themselves in the great enterprise, and serve it without being aware of the greatness of their service. It has the power to transform such service, and in so doing to transform the servant.

At first view the only things in common between Heloise and my next representative of this extraordinary team are that they were both women and both French. Yet it would be hard to say which had the greater influence on the quality of the Catholic thing from her time onwards. Heloise's influence was expressed through Abelard and thence affected the whole moral sensitivity of Catholicism — not alone, of course, but as a powerful ingredient. The influence of Bernadette Soubirous is of an even odder kind, for she was in no way an original thinker, and never intended to have any influence at all. All the clever and pious people who arranged her life for her were determined that she should conform to a pattern arranged by them, and she *tried* to conform, but in spite of it all she re-modelled Catholic piety. Her heroic, stubborn obedience to her Vision, which nothing could make her deny, not only created the largest centre of pilgrimage the Christian world has known, apart from Jerusalem itself, but altered the "feel" of Catholic spirituality from an ascetic, defensive and elitist cult of perfection to a warm, popular, penitential, but practical religious sense — aesthetically crude, liturgically unsophisticated, but realistic, hopeful and immensely resilient. It was the "Lourdes type" of Catholicism which carried the Catholic people through the intellectual and psychological demoralization of Christianity which followed the scientific ascendancy and the rise of the technological culture. Catholic religious conviction came through, not by confronting the challenges of science and the new humanism but by ignoring them. (When the Church tried to confront them, as in its dealings with the Modernist movement, it only further destroyed its own credibility.) The Catholic religious sense could afford to ignore them because it was, if narrow, basically satisfying, and realistic about life as experienced by the poor and uneducated and exploited.

Bernadette was all those things. She was also asthmatic, and her family were not only poor; they were despised, since her father was an easy-going inefficient miller who finally lost his mill and his job and had to rely on odd scraps of work to keep his family from starvation — often only barely. He had to house them in a cell once used to confine drunks and vagrants, but abandoned as unfit even for them. The story of Bernadette's visions of a "beautiful young lady" is very familiar, but all too easily fitted into a conventional pious frame, a story of a sweet, pliable, ignorant peasant girl favoured with visions of the

37

Mother of God, a mere passive recipient of divine instruction.

Bernadette, in fact, was neither passive nor pliable; she was an extraordinary young woman. In a world in which mild venality was the accepted means of survival she had a fierce integrity, and boxed her little brother's ears when she found he had accepted a tip from one of the many miracle-hunters. Every kind of pressure, from threats of prison to pious blackmail and bribery, were tried in order to get her to deny her extraordinary and shocking story, or at least take back some of it. Nothing moved her. Frightened, ill, under-fed, and entirely alone, she refused to be bullied or wheedled into saying what was required by others. She reported faithfully the appearance and words of the "beautiful lady" who had appeared to her in a hole in the rocky cliffs outside the town, and had entranced her and claimed her whole devotion.

Bernadette, like Heloise, was a woman wholly dedicated to love. Nothing else mattered. Because the Lady told her to, she carried messages to the formidable parish priest of Lourdes, asking for a chapel and processions. If he chased her out and mocked her, that was just something that had to be faced. What mattered was to obey. Because the Lady told her to do so she scratched in the mud at the back of the grotto where she saw her vision, to find water which *must* be there, because the Lady had told her to wash in it, and drink it. There was mud mixed with the trickle of water she found, and the mud smeared her face and, when she tried to drink, made her vomit before thousands of miracle-hungry people; but that was of no importance, compared with doing the Lady's will. When, later, a baby was healed in the water newly flowing from the place where she had scratched, Bernadette was not interested. When hundreds and thousands and later millions of pilgrims flocked to Lourdes, Bernadette hid from them, first in her home, then in the convent school of Lourdes, later in the Mother House of the same Order, at Nevers, as a nun herself.

She was questioned and cross-questioned by officials of Church and State, hostile, suspicious questioners who wanted to trip her up and prove her mad, or a cheat, or out for profit. To the government she was a political embarrassment as proof of the superstitious backwardness of the provinces. To the Church she was a probable source of ridicule from hostile rationalists, a stumbling block which refused to fit into the neat highway of Catholic life. They all wanted to get rid of her. They all failed. She was questioned by neighbors and friends, and by an unending stream of visitors, who pursued her into her hiding places. Ten times a day she might be called to the convent parlour to face yet more questions — curious, adoring, credulous or sceptical. She hated it, and had to stop outside the room a moment to wipe away tears of fatigue and misery, before she could go in with a quiet smile and curtsy, prepared to give these people the answers they asked for, because that was the work the Lady had given her to do.

The Lady had left her by then. The visions had lasted only a few months, and Bernadette knew she would never see her Lady again this side of the grave. The rest of her life was devoted to the memory and service of her love, in total obedience to what that love demanded of her. (In this, she was very like Heloise.) In her convent she was misunderstood and suffered from moral bullying, but at least she had some respite from the crowds, and loneliness was what she expected, for the Lady had, after all, finished with her. It was the Lady's glory and her wishes that must advance. The only time she lost her calm, apart from that flare-up of anger at her little brother's venality, was when people hailed her as "saint", and "blessed one". In this she was not so much repudiating an undeserved honour as she was outraged that anyone could be so stupid as to attribute to her what clearly belonged to the heavenly Lady. "How silly you are!" she cried. Vanity never touched her, was not even a temptation to her, because her love filled her whole heart and left no room for self-regard. Others assumed that she *must* be tempted to vanity, and deliberately slighted her to keep her humble. Bernadette minded, and was hurt, not in her pride but in her sensitive, loving soul — but her sensitivity was never recognized, people didn't expect a peasant girl to have delicate feelings.

So Bernadette disappeared from sight, and had apparently no influence on the development of the extraordinary phenomenon of Lourdes, that centre of prayer and hope and occasional extraordinary healings which today attracts more pilgrims than ever before, and has to build more and more hostels for them. Yet it was on her word alone that the enterprise was built. The character of the Lady, her appearance, her gestures, her wishes, her promises, the healing powers of the spring, were known through Bernadette and through Bernadette alone. So it was to Bernadette that the Catholic world owed a new kind of religious awareness.

The rigorous, dignified, rational religion of the eighteenth and early nineteenth century, a religion for aristocrats and nuns and priests in which the common people could participate at their own low level, was swept away by a homely, understandable, *accessible* piety. The Mother of God, who in any case seemed more approachable than her Kingly Son, appeared suddenly in Bernadette's description as a young, informal, friendly presence, coming with gestures of love and concern for the poor and sick and weak, calling to penitence, but in no way frightening or remote. And, through her, the Christ was also nearer, a friend, not a judge.

The artists and pious writers tried to turn "Our Lady of Lourdes" into a remote and dignified figure. They hadn't a chance. The genuine message was ahead of them, guaranteed by the solid, stubborn integrity of Bernadette. All over Europe and America the banal little plaster statues, the bottles of Lourdes water, the hymns and the replica Grottoes proliferated, spreading the message that God had hidden certain things from the wise and learned and aesthetically sensitive, and revealed them to little ones. The Catholic enterprise had taken a new direction, under the unwitting guidance of a "stupid little peasant."

Nineteenth century France, in which Bernadette lived and died was rent by the battle between the Church, identified with royalty and the ancien regime, and the forces of republicanism allied with Science and Atheism. (We shall see another aspect of this battle in a later section.) Bernadette, unaware of the battle, was at the heart of it, but her integrity and grasp of essentials made the artificiality of the labels attached to the two armies very apparent. The two sides in an essentially political struggle tried to fortify their adherents by making the issue a religious matter (as, later and tragically, in Northern Ireland). In France the struggle was seen as a crusade by enlightenment against ignorance and superstition, or of faith against unbelief, according to one's point of view. Thus, if she had ever heard of them, Bernadette would have felt an instinctive comradeship with Edmund Campion and the other English Catholics under Queen Elizabeth I, a group which fought to maintain the principle that the old religion, and that only, was what they desired to preserve, while maintaining loyalty to their country and its Queen. But the struggle was identified by others along the inevitable political lines. Catholics were allies of Spain and traitors to the Queen, whatever they might pretend, or so popular opinion, fostered by careful propaganda, maintained. And chief among the Popish terrors were the Jesuits. Catholics themselves have a kind of love-hate relationship with the Society of Jesus. Jesuits are supposed to be cleverer than normal human beings should properly be. And if Catholics feel a slightly nervous admiration for the formidable discipline and rigorous intellectual training of the Society, it is not surprising if other churches have often regarded it with suspicion bordering on obsession. The persuasiveness and elusiveness of Jesuits have a firm place in the mythology of English-speaking non-Catholic Christianity.

My own upbringing was vaguely Anglican, and although there was not much religion in it I absorbed a strong suspicion of Catholicism, which was connected in my mind with the Inquisition and Jesuits lurking up chimneys. (This last I got from Thackeray's "Esmond".) So when, at the age of sixteen, I began to ask questions about Catholicism, I brought with me on my search some curious mental luggage, and when I learned that there had been *Catholic* martyrs, who died for their faith under Good Queen Bess, I was at first incredulous. I had thought that in the Protestant/Catholic conflict it had always been the Catholics who did the persecuting, and all martyrs were Protestants, under Bloody Mary. (This notion is still enshrined in English history books for children.) Then I came across the story of Edmund Campion, most famous of the English martyrs, who has become a symbol of them all. And he was a Jesuit.

Little as he wanted to take sides in the struggle between Protestant Elizabeth of England and Catholic Philip of Spain, much as he loved his country and disliked the political manoeuvering of his Church, Campion could not escape the partisan label. As Bernadette and Lourdes became in time a Catholic weapon against the atheists, Campion became, after his death, a banner to wave against the Protestants, but in his lifetime he was to the Protestant party a sinister symbol of Catholic trickery, and to the Catholics a symbol of hope and courage in an increasingly hopeless situation. (Bernadette, too, at the time of her visions, was a symbol of God's immediacy and real concern to the poor and helpless.)

Edmund Campion was unique, yet also typical of a whole group, the peculiarly English brand of resistance movement. An Elizabethan gentleman, learned, courtly, witty and gifted, he typifies thus far the heady Elizabethan atmosphere. He came from a good but not aristocratic family, won a scholarship to Oxford University at fifteen, and earned a brilliant reputation there. When the Queen visited the University he delivered an address before her which delighted her, and the Earl of Leicester showed him special favour. He could have been one of the many young men who rose to fame at her Court, or in the Church under her leadership, for Elizabeth and her minister, Cecil, were well aware that their new Church lacked distinction either of scholarship or sanctity. They were on the lookout for good honest churchmen, and prepared to favour them. But Edmund was more and more doubtful of that Church, and eventually took the step of being reconciled with the old and forbidden faith, which cut him off from all possibility of a successful career in England. Like other young Catholic men, he went abroad, first to Ireland and then, when that grew dangerous, to Douai in Belgium. After a time he was admitted into the Society of Jesus.

Other men in similar circumstances were pursuing useful and distinguished careers abroad, and for a time Edmund Campion, his training completed, taught and preached in Prague. But the situation of Catholics in England was worsening, and the pressure on them to conform was gradually increasing.

42

Isolated, pestered, heavily fined for not attending the new services, deprived of career opportunities, Catholic families were falling away out of sheer discouragement. At first they had thought that the new religious settlement was bound to be temporary, but they were realising that restoration of the old faith was a more and more remote possibility. A deep gloom had fallen on them, and a kind of bewilderment. They did not know where to turn or what to do for the best. It was imperative that priests should be available to celebrate Mass for them, comfort and encourage them, make them realise that they were still, in their loneliness, part of a great enterprise, and one, moreover, which was engaged in a searching process of reform and rethinking, and was no longer the stagnant and worldly organization which had made the Protestant Reformation inevitable.

So little groups of disguised priests began to trickle into England. Most were secular priests, some were Jesuits. A very few felt that work for the restoration of a Catholic monarchy by means of a foreign invasion was an essential ingredient in being a faithful Catholic, and they combined priestly ministration with political plotting. Elizabeth's government, glad to be provided with a popular reason for suppressing the old faith, naturally tarred the whole Catholic community with the same brush of treachery. But in fact most of the men who travelled the country, preaching and encouraging and taking the sacraments to little groups of Catholics, were only interested in sustaining their wavering faith. The priests were Englishmen, and were as revolted as any other Englishmen at the thought of Spanish rule. Some, perhaps, would not have been sorry to see Elizabeth go but, whether by natural inclination or by the careful training they received before being sent on the English mission, they separated themselves from political arguments, and condemned those who joined in plots against the Queen.

The stories of those decades of hidden ministry are as strange and heroic as any in history and I shall come back to them later on in a different context. It is enough to remember here that priestly ministry was subject to the death penalty, and torture was a likely preliminary. On her side, Elizabeth did not want to kill, but she did want to discourage "popery" as a political reality, by every means available, while keeping, if possible, the loyalty of the whole nation. So the persecution was patchy and curiously capricious, yet the law was clear, and magistrates who chose to enforce it had the legal power to do so. A priest had to go disguised from one household to another, with a fair certainty of ending a brief life under the knife of the executioner. The penalty for treason, which was intended to recall the fate of Judas Iscariot, was not just hanging; it involved being cut down while still alive and disembowelled, before the body was cut into quarters and thus displayed, the better to discourage potential traitors.

It was this kind of life that Campion led, after his return to England. But he brought to it a special Elizabethan bravura. He seemed to take delight in daring the "establishment" to find him. He wrote, and had printed at the secret press in the woods at Stonor, his "Ten Reasons," a statement of reasons for holding to the old faith. One day copies were to be found on the benches of St. Mary's, the University Church of Oxford. The statement was witty as well as well-reasoned, and the news spread and the stories were passed on. He would turn up in London, then disappear and be heard of next in some remote country area. Stories spread of his exploits, his narrow escapes, the gay effrontery with which he would show himself openly, maintaining that public places were the best disguise. His neat, well dressed figure and pale face with pointed beard might well have been the subject of one of Nicholas Hilliard's lovely miniatures. He was soon a legend — a bogey to Elizabeth's police system, a symbol of courage and hope to her Catholic subjects. From confusion, despondency and defeatism, he brought the remaining Catholics to a condition of steady, unambitious endurance. There were some who, harassed and impoverished, did look to the King of Spain, but others learned that they had to choose between their faith and any kind of worldly prosperity or even peace of mind. They settled in to sit out the persecution for as long as might be necessary, and to do so with a cheerful heart. Men like Campion made it possible for them to face the dark future with patience and not too much bitterness.

The system by which priests were passed from one friendly

44

house to the next was not spy-proof. Although many were sympathetic to the recusants, or didn't want to get involved, there were enough who would betray them, either out of genuine religious or political conviction, or out of fear, or for money. Walsingham's secret police infiltrated the groups of Catholics, as spies have always infiltrated such groups. Sooner or later, most of the priests on the English mission were caught, sometimes in the very hiding-holes designed to save them.

Campion was finally caught at Lyford. He was taken to London and paraded through the streets with his feet tied beneath his horse, a gesture of triumph by the captors of the "seditious Jesuit", as an inscription pinned to his hat labelled him. He was then imprisoned in the Tower and tortured in the usual way to obtain incriminating evidence against himself and others, but he was also repeatedly offered his life and the Queen's personal favour if he would be sensible and recant. The government did not want a martyr. Campion yielded nothing either to bribes or the rack. When he finally came to trial he could not walk without help because the racking had broken the tendons of ankles and wrists, and those who saw him said he seemed an old man. He protested loyalty to the Queen, and challenged any Protestant divines to debate with him, but his formidable intelligence and biting wit had made his adversaries wary. No one responded. "In condemning me you condemn your ancestors," he told the judges. His sentence, in the atmosphere of anger against Catholic Spain, was a foregone conclusion. To be a priest was, in the popular mind, to be "seditious" and a traitor. According to custom, he was roped to a hurdle behind horses' heels, dragged to Tyburn, the site of the public gallows, and there hanged, cut down alive and disembowelled, as the sentence demanded.

Cecil, the Queen's astute adviser, once called Campion "a diamond of England." He was no doubt much relieved to think that the diamond's sparkle was dimmed forever. But in fact it never did stop dazzling, and the gallantry of Edmund Campion was recorded and repeated even by the historians most hostile to his beliefs. His particular kind of cheerful, understated courage, his wit, his learning and his warmth and friendliness, made up a special, compelling influence which no one who comes into contact with his story can resist. The brilliance of the great age of Elizabeth is both embellished and challenged by the greater and different glory of this diamond. He, and those who shared his work, added a special and lasting quality to the core of the Catholic experience, for unknowingly they laid the foundations of a Catholicism of a conscious minority, a thing never before considered.

Half a century before Edmund Campion lived Erasmus of Rotterdam, also a man of the Renaissance and a man of vast learning, wit, and piety. He was no kind of saint. Whether he would have died for his faith if required we cannot know, and he was never faced with such a challenge, but he had integrity and courage of no mean order. He saw very well the evils in the Church which were provoking its rejection by the Reformers, and he also saw the flaws in the reforming ideas, which were to ally the Protestant cause with the new economics and the rise of capitalism. If he was not a martyr, he was prepared to suffer a great deal rather than compromise with either of these alternatives.

Erasmus was a typical "poor scholar," the illegitimate son of a priest; in fact Charles Reade's famous novel, "The Cloister and the Hearth" is based on the story of his parents. Both parents died of the plague when he was still at school, and the struggle to get an education was severe. Eventually, at twenty-nine, he was sent to Paris.

Three men who studied at the same College Montaigne of the University of Paris were Erasmus, John Calvin and Ignatius Loyola, each in his own way seeing the need for reformation. Paris at that time was not the lively-minded University of Abelard's day, and Erasmus's typical comment on his theology teachers was to compare them with Epimenides of the Greek tale, who slept for forty-seven years — the only difference, said Erasmus, was that Epimenides did eventually wake up. It was this kind of remark that made Erasmus enemies wherever he went, but although he often exaggerated, his savage jokes were the reaction of a genuinely sensitive Christian mind, outraged at the state of the Church and its teachers. (His temper was at least partly due to his health — he was allergic to salt fish, a staple diet of the poor, and altogether had a bad digestion besides being subject to recurrent attacks of malaria.)

Erasmus may be remembered most easily as satirist, but his main impulse was as a reformer and he thought of reform in terms of educating, changing by reforming the mind. His method of argument, at all times, broke through the crust of a decadent Scholasticism, "arguing infinitely about infinity, and pressing a vacuum until all is vacuous", as another scholar said. Indeed his test of the worthwhileness of all studies was that they must serve for "edification and example, to piety and morality." In other words he was suspicious of the split between learning and behaviour, already developing in his time, and in our time firmly entrenched in the "scientific mentality" as the absolute value of "pure science", which is to be pursued regardless of the uses people make of it.

But the hydrogen bomb and the Nazi experiments were far ahead. Erasmus had learned his attitude to theology and scholarship from his earlier school-masters, one of whom had also been head of the College Montaigne. These were the "Brethren of the Common Life", known to Christians ever since mainly because one of them was Thomas a Kempis, author of the "Imitation of Christ". The "Imitation" was the product the "modern piety", the "devotio moderna", which emphasised the following of Jesus in holiness of life, rather than a more abstruse mysticism, or scholarship for its own sake. It was an attempt to recover the catholicity, the wholeness, of religion, endangered by too much specialization, either in learning or in "special" mystical ways. That was Erasmus's background, and it is important to remember this, because he figures in history as a scholar first and foremost. He was a scholar, but he knew that scholarship for its own sake is at best a waste of time, at worst a dangerous evasion of responsibility. When theologians argued about whether or not the fires of purgatory were "material fire", Erasmus commented acidly that it would be more sensible to try to live in such a way as to avoid finding out.

Erasmus was always a man of independent mind, one who

refused to be forced into partnership when reason and common sense did not lead him there, and he had a prophetic hatred of warfare, a thing which almost everyone else assumed to be an inevitable and necessary political instrument. These acceptable traits have to be set against his obscurantism and credulity. He thought the investigation of "Nature's secrets" impious and stupid, he was so ignorant of the realities of the labour and money markets that he was sure any able-bodied person could earn enough to keep himself. He couldn't be bothered to discover how trade operated, even while the operations of the new merchant classes were visibly changing the face of Europe. He swallowed whole the most extraordinary fables, provided they were vouched for by a classical author. (Readers of C.S. Lewis's "Narnia" books will recognize their old friends the engaging "Monopods" in Erasmus's suggestion that there may exist creatures called "Skiopodes" who protect themselves from the glare of the sun by the shade of their single broad foot.)

He was not interested in what was going on in the art world either — this at the height of the Renaissance, the very name of which means to us Michelangelo, Titian, Palladio and Bernini. Nor did Erasmus take more than a fleeting interest in the discoveries which were changing the map of the world. He knew they were going on, but they had no significance for him, unless they happened to link up with something that he thought important. When he dedicated a book (an edition of St. John Chrysostom!) to the King of Portugal he praised the Portuguese ruler for making the voyage to "the Indies" secure, but added that he had heard that sugar prices were climbing, in spite of this easier transport, and hoped the King would do something to curb the monopolies that brought this about. This is a good example of his tendency to over-simplify issues, whether mercantile or political, yet to do so always with an eye to morality and justice.

But this apparently naive simplification was also his great strength. He concentrated on what seemed to him of ultimate importance and he measured importance in moral terms. He wanted others to make just moral judgements and act on them — the King of Portugal, for instance. He could not see why rulers would not agree when so much was at stake. To him, it was very simple. "It would, in my opinion," he wrote to the Duke of Saxony in 1517, "be of particular service to the general well-being of the Christian world if by means of special conventions the boundaries of the dominions of every ruler were to be regulated for the general weal, which boundaries, once established, could not be restricted or enlarged either by bonds of marriage or by treaties, while simultaneously the old legal titles should be abolished, which each ruler is wont to produce according to circumstances whenever he desires war." In our time, the League of Nations failed to convince rulers of the need for such "special conventions", and the United Nations has done no better. So the world is still "endlessly shaken by outrageous feats of arms" as Erasmus put it. Were Erasmus, and the few other faint voices who have cried the same cry, foolish Utopians? The fact is that even the reiteration of such an ideal, even the endless and boring and practically fruitless discussion of possible ways and means is better — incomparably better — than the acceptance of war as the proper and only means to settle political differences. This Erasmus knew. He knew it because of his special combination of solid, unmystical, moralistic piety and his intense enthusiasm for the "new" classical learning.

His passion for the classical masters gave the breadth and precision that made an otherwise possibly narrow and naive religious sense into an accurate instrument of understanding and criticism. The excitement which scholars felt at recovering the works of the great Greek and Latin thinkers is hard for us to recapture, after four hundred years during which Latin and Greek studies were daily drudgery for schoolboys, and are now almost entirely discarded. But Erasmus, with some other humanists, was trying to do two things. One was to make available the wisdom of the ancients, which he considered to be infinitely superior to any modern learning. For him and for others, the influence of Greek and Latin thinkers was a means of spring-cleaning a culture cluttered and clogged by habits of thought too long unexamined, and preserved rather than really used. The second thing he was trying to do was to keep Latin as a living language. Erasmus wanted Latin to be a means of communication between intelligent peoples, and he saw no contradiction between this idea and his demand for a vernacular liturgy. Erasmus's best recent biographer, Roland Bainton, remarks that he should be the patron of liturgical reform, and this is very much to the point, for at every turn Erasmus wanted people to *understand.* He distrusted polyphony and disliked the organ because he thought that both of them obscured the words of the liturgy. Feelings are useful, but what matters, Erasmus felt, is the word — clear, edifying teaching, and whole-hearted praise.

As in liturgy, so in morality and belief. Erasmus remained a Catholic all his life, but the latter part of it was made wretched by constant attacks from both Lutherans and Catholics, each of whom accused him of adhering to the other side. The Lutherans said he was becoming a reactionary, that he was abandoning his earlier demands for reform, watering down his virulent criticism of abuses in the cult of saints, indulgences, and monastic life, no longer insisting on the religion of the heart rather than of out-ward form and symbol. They said he was giving in to the Papal party to save his skin. From the other side, Catholics exhorted him to rise up and condemn the monster, Luther, and accused him of heresy because he would not join in sweeping condemna-tion of all that the reformers did and said.

Erasmus replied and explained, to no avail. During those years when Europe was being remorselessly split into two camps, few people were prepared to think. Slogans and battle cries were the mode, and Erasmus would not use them. He knew that most of what Luther said and demanded was right, but he would not go all the way with him. On the other hand, he could not see that because there were abuses in the Catholic Church he had to abandon the Church. Towards the end of his life, con-stantly in great pain from kidney stones and other ailments, harassed and accused on all sides, he tended more and more to qualify earlier statements, to distinguish and particularise. This maddened his critics, who saw it as evidence of cowardice. But Erasmus was no coward. "Would that with my little body I could allay this dissension," he wrote. "How gladly would I lay down my life." But not for causes thrust on him by others: "I would be happy to be a martyr for Christ," he said, "but not for

Luther." Part of his tendency to qualify and explain was the natural and proper result of age and experience. Earlier judgements needed to be re-thought. Part of it was anxiety produced by the accusations and harassments. He examined and re-examined his teaching, but far from being proof of timidity this is proof of his tremendous integrity. If he had been willing to compromise, to be adopted as champion by one side or the other, he could have had praise, money and safety in either camp. He would not compromise. He continued to the end his striving to see clearly and judge justly, in all that turmoil and bitterness.

He did not like controversy. His greatest achievement in his own eyes was his Greek New Testament, which, with its translations and commentaries, was to make a reliable version of Scripture available to all. He was in such a hurry to get it printed that he overlooked several inaccuracies, but that is typical — he cared more for what the Book could do in service of God and men than for his scholarly reputation. He cared about education — for all, including the poor, and women. He held, like his friend Thomas More, that women should be educated. The minds of adolescent girls should be filled with study, he said, and even when married and with children a woman should never cease to learn.

Respect for Erasmus has increased enormously in our time, not without reason. His stringent honesty shows the only true way to Christian unity, and indeed to any kind of enduring peace between groups of people. His common sense dared him to say openly what others mumble in corners. "The sum of our religion is peace and unanimity, but these can scarcely stand unless we define as little as possible," he wrote in a preface, "and in many things leave each one free to follow his own judgement, because there is great obscurity in many matters, and man suffers from this almost congenital disease, that he will not give in when once a controversy is started, and after he is warmed up he regards as absolutely true that which he began to sponsor quite casually." Not that Erasmus thought it didn't matter what people believed — he was too acute an observer to think that — but he knew, again from observation, that violent controversy does not serve the cause of truth, and even the wildest heretics are best treated with tolerant realism. He said (and it sounds startlingly modern to those who think liberal theology was invented in the last ten years) that the Church is "the hidden society of those predestined to eternal life, of whom the greater part is now with Christ. No individual can be identified as a member, but we are to believe that there is such a society on earth which Christ united by his spirit, whether among Indians or Africans or in any other part of the world not yet explored."

Evidence from other writings indicates that by "predestined" in the above passage he simply meant people who respond to God's grace. He did not believe in "predestination" in the Lutheran sense; in fact this was the point at which he firmly parted company with Luther, calling the doctrine "monstrous." Indeed, in the whole debate with Luther on free will, Erasmus showed a heart-warming refusal to be tied to logical consequences when logic went against common-sense and justice. "God is a tyrant if He condemns a man for what he cannot help" — that is, being predestined to hell because God did not choose to give grace. "It is as if a master should kill a servant for having a long nose." (Erasmus himself had a long nose!) Luther was logical, saying that if God were omnipotent, predestination followed, though "common sense and natural reason are highly offended." Erasmus could not accept that logic, and in refusing he anticipated much later theological wrestling.

Erasmus, in his time, was regarded with suspicion by the Papal party, and appreciated, later, chiefly by Episcopalians. But he was firmly a Catholic, not out of timidity but because he knew that a totally "purified" Church is not possible, and the attempt to enforce one leads to spiritual pride, persecution, censoriousness and loss of Christian peace and love.

However grave the abuses that Erasmus denounced (and newer versions of them must still and always will be denounced), the Church needs to be inclusive, not exclusive. Inclusiveness is not laxity, it is simply a realistic view of the human nature which God loves and works to redeem.

An incident in Erasmus's life raises one of those historical "ifs" which are so futile and yet so fascinating. In May 1516 Erasmus returned to the Netherlands from Basel, in Switzerland, where he had been living while he worked on his New Testament and other books. At that time he was fifty years old, the acknowledged leader of liberal and reforming thought in the Church. He went back in order to be near the court of the Emperor Charles, whose councillor he had just agreed to become. When he reached the Netherlands, he found a letter from Pope Leo waiting for him, inviting him to Rome, to be adviser to his Holiness. But it was too late. Erasmus felt obligated to Charles. "If only the letter had reached me at Basel!" he wrote, regretfully refusing. It was the next year, 1517, that Luther posted his Theses on the door of the Castle church at Wittenberg.

We can only wonder what might have been the course of European history if Erasmus had received those letters in time. Leo's first impression of Luther's now famous Theses was that here was yet another quarrel between religious orders, this time the Augustinian Luther against the Dominican Tetzel. When he came to realise the wider implications of the debate, his views were formed by those nearest to him, men determined for reasons of their own to exalt papal prerogatives at the expense of any modifying influences. Basically, they feared the power of the German princes. They fanned the flames of distrust until the fire became so hot that no one could get near enough to pour water on it. Erasmus tried, but he was far off; sixteenth century postal services were erratic, and Erasmus did not get the letter inviting him to Rome until it was too late.

The careers of Erasmus of Rotterdam and Dorothy Day of New York could scarcely have been more different, but both were concerned for the integrity of the Catholic experience. Erasmus spent his life trying to modify extremism in order to restore the vision of the essential gospel. Dorothy Day has spent her long career in trying to recover that same vision, for the sake of the whole enterprise, and in order to do this she has been driven to what many regard as an extreme. Yet, in her extreme of gospel truthfulness, she has refused — as Erasmus did — to join the chorus of fashionable condemnations, either against the "institutional" church or against communism. Intellectual as well as spiritual integrity is what these two members of the Catholic "team" have in common. There the resemblance ends. Erasmus was a unique genius in talent but not in kind, for the Christian scholar is a venerable and familiar figure. Dorothy Day is a new kind of member for the Catholic team, one who could not have appeared except in our own time. She has recognizable "ancestors" in some aspects, women like Angela Merici or Mary Ward or Margaret of Scotland who saw a job that needed doing and got on with it regardless of precedent or public opinion. But only the special ideological stresses of our own period could call up Dorothy Day's particular combination of traditional "charitable" labour and political witness, united in one consistent, uncompromising, and well argued Christian commitment, causing acute embarrassment to both Church and State.

Dorothy Day's background was Newspapers. Her father was a journalist, and she became a journalist herself after leaving college. By then her family had moved back from Chicago to New York, where she had been born in 1897. Dorothy was not brought up within the framework of Catholic ideas. She found them. Her early associates and ideas were those of the "left wingers" of the twenties in New York, and she worked for papers with a Marxist platform, for her earlier Christian contacts seemed to have nothing to say about the appalling poverty she saw around her. Like so many others, she rejected Christianity as hypocritical and devoted her considerable talents to socialism. But she hadn't the temperament that is satisfied with denouncing social evils, or even working to change things politically. She discovered in herself the need to identify with the poor, and she moved out of her parents' home and into a New York tenement. The impulse was partly a need to overcome her own revulsion from the repulsive aspects of poverty, just as Francis Bernardone had exchanged clothes with a beggar and embraced a leper. The only way to love was to share, and that meant smashing the barriers of fastidiousness and fear. She had an attitude to poverty and the poor which is a familiar part of the Catholic enterprise, and as such she is a good representative member of the ever-renewed team of its leaders. When, after a long hesitancy, she was received into the Catholic Church in 1927 she was affirming by outward action the necessity she already recognized inwardly. She had no illusions about the attitude of Catholics in general, and the hierarchy in particular, towards social problems. But she has a strong vein of earthy common sense which is not more shocked by the worldly timidity of some bishops than by the violence or petty dishonesty of drunks. The Church she joined consists of a very usual collection of human beings, with all the possibilities of weakness and self-deception that implies, but one with a doctrine which continues uncompromisingly to state truths about the dignity of human beings, the duty to love them, and the fact of their eternal destiny which nothing can destroy except their own free choice. Becoming a Catholic meant that a whole body of articulate thought about social issues, poverty and want, love, death and resurrection was available to her, to give the force of centuries to the power of her own inward conviction and personal experience. She had become part of a great enterprise, to which she was to contribute a new clarity and a new direction, just because she was part of a whole — not a whole which was a uniform lump, but a living and varied and uneven thing, growing and irrepressible and unpredictable. Only such an enterprise could have satisfied Dorothy Day, or been able to include her without distorting or suppressing her.

Manifestly, it did neither. An utterly faithful, observant, theologically acute and "Thomist" Catholic, she founded a movement which is among the most significant in America, and not only for Catholics. In 1932 she met Peter Maurin, a professor of French turned itinerant workman, one of that peculiarly French breed of peasant philosophers, tough, egoistic, ascetic, absent-minded, almost unaware of physical surroundings, and profoundly and articulately Catholic. He supplied Dorothy with a much-needed intellectual and cultural leaven for the rather stodgy American Catholicism which she was valiantly trying to combine with her communist idealism and her passion for the cause of the workers. Peter Maurin's mind was in touch with the radical tradition of French Catholicism. He had ideas about Christian communes, about working on the land, about sharing of property. He had ideas about hospices for the homeless, like the medieval ones. He gave her books and articles to read; in fact, he supplied her with an education in certain vital aspects of basic Catholicism. The new knowledge combined with the old experience was the beginning of a quiet but effective revolution.

For if Peter Maurin supplied ideas, Dorothy did something about them. Without her, he would probably have gone on talking and hoping, for his idea of a perfect audience was people who did nothing but listen. Peter believed that the Lord would provide what was needed; and he was justified, because the Lord provided Dorothy who did a great deal more than listen. With his ideas she launched the Catholic Worker, both the newspaper and the movement. In her own account of its origins, in her book "Loaves and Fishes," she tells how it began. "Among his ideas," she wrote, "was one of publishing a paper. But how can it be done without money? I wanted to know." At the time she and her small daughter (child of a marriage which had ended in divorce some years before), along with her brother and sister-in-law, were living in a small, poor apartment. She had, as she said, "a typewriter and a kitchen table and plenty of paper" since she worked as a free-lance journalist. That was plenty, because Peter Maurin said, "In the Catholic Church one never needs any money to start a good work." Certainly that was the principle on which the Catholic Worker was founded.

The statement was not quite accurate, in fact, for it cost fifty-seven dollars to get the first edition printed. Dorothy had slowly and painfully saved up the money through the winter. The first issue of the Catholic Worker appeared on May Day 1933, costing one cent a copy. (This is still the price charged, a symbol of the apparently lunatic but absolutely practical methods of the whole movement.)

It will be many years before Dorothy Day's contribution to the Catholic enterprise can be properly assessed, but during her long life she has established a style and an ideal which are in the direct line of those who have chosen voluntary poverty as the necessary way of bearing witness to the presence of Christ in the poorest and most neglected. But she combined this witness very effectively with others. The paper continued to come out several times a year, to publicise Catholic teaching on social justice and to analyse with passion and realism current problems of labour, race relations, and all the things that happen to poor people which the better off prefer to forget. It suggested what could be done and reported what was being done. The paper was only the begining. Another of Peter's ideas was hospices, the now famous "houses of hospitality". The first one virtually happened without planning, as such things do, for the paper attracted the attention of the unemployed and homeless (in itself a tribute to its mixture of realism and warmth) and some of them drifted along to the office set up in an old barber shop below the apartment. These people had to be fed, and so began the tradition of free meals which still continues.

Giving food and clothing and — when possible — shelter to people in need is neither new nor unusual. The special quality of the Catholic Worker movement lay in the attitude of the workers to their guests, the genuine fellow-feeling, the total acceptance of each one as a person to be respected and served. There were no qualifications, no demands, just a practical, unsentimental love.

I find it difficult to write about this movement, because it is in some ways the perfection of response to the Gospel — "Sell what thou hast, and come, follow me." Its uncompromising adherence to the strictest Gospel poverty and openness, sharing the cast-off clothes which are collected for the poor, living as they live, never turning away even the lazy and dishonest, is the kind of splendour that the Catholic enterprise is always capable of revealing, at the very moment when it seems to have sunk out of sight in a fog of pietistic worldliness. The intransigent pacifism of the Catholic Worker, as well as its emphasis on the need to work the land for food and people, not profit, antedated the wave of post-nuclear pacifism and post-pollution rural communes of the sixties and seventies. The Catholic Worker was pacifist, agrarian, egalitarian, not because these things suddenly seemed necessary (though they did) but because these are obvious Christian principles developed and spelled out over centuries in the radical Catholic tradition, in very precise terms. Dorothy Day, and the movement which she began, inherited a social gospel evolved by the Catholic Church from its experience, including the experience of its own disastrous mistakes. She emphasised the oldest teachings, those of evangelical poverty, of the mystical identification of the Christian with the poor man or woman, who is in turn the poor Christ, emptied of glory for love of human kind, sharing the suffering and despair of the lowest and most abused.

The Catholic Worker is very one-sided. As Erasmus was one-sided, ignoring social questions almost entirely and oblivious to anything that did not directly teach; as Campion was one-sided, serving only Catholics in a situation of religious confusion and hatred; as Bernadette was one-sided, intellectually deprived and isolated; as Heloise cared only for what related to her beloved; as Augustine's theology saw mostly and absorbingly the incomparable power of grace catching up the helpless human in its loving embrace; so also Dorothy Day's teaching and life emphasise just one aspect of the whole. It leaves out (though she herself loves and appreciates them) concerns for beauty, for the stability of local culture, for the thankless but necessary tasks of the lawyer and politician or the "remote" yet vital work of the philosopher and theologian. Perhaps the part of the whole enterprise in which she labours and which she symbolises is the one which has to endure whatever else may be destroyed, and it is an element without which the rest is useless and rapidly corrupted.

Looking back over my selection for the Catholic "team", it seems to me that von Hugel is the most nearly catholic of the group, one of those rare Christians who are not necessarily holier (singlemindedness and one-sidedness go easily together and singlemindedness is essential to sanctity) but embody more perfectly the ideal of wholeness and balance. But von Hugel knew, as they all did, that the aspect of the Catholic enterprise which Dorothy Day and the Catholic Worker movement represents is ultimately the essential and specifically Christian undertaking. It is, in his language, the *costingness* of faith. He, who loved intelligent company and the pleasures of friendship and of the mind, was convinced that Catholicism in practice must cost everything a person has to give, and that any fastidiousness, of the kind which makes good people turn their eyes away from horrible things, is wrong and un-Christian. Beauty and intelligence, law, government and all service of human kind are, must be, part of the enterprise, but the cultivation of any of these, even "for God's sake" is not enough if it cannot embrace the repulsive face of humanity. "The touching, entrancing beauty of Christianity," von Hugel wrote in a letter "depends upon a subtle something which all this fastidiousness ignores. . . . A soul that is . . . dominated . . . by such fastidiousness, . . . is as yet only hovering round the precincts of Christianity, it has not yet entered the sanctuary, where heroism is always homely, where the best always acts as stimulus towards helping, towards being (in a true sense) but one of the semi-articulate, bovine, childish, repulsively second-third-fourth-rate crowd. So it was with Jesus himself; so it was with St. Francis, the Poverello; so it is with every soul that has fully realised the genius of the Christian paradox . . . The heathen philosophies, one and all, failed to get beyond your fastidiousness; only Christianity got beyond it; only Christianity — but I mean, a deeply *costingly* realised Christianity — got beyond it. It is really a very hideous thing; the full, truly free, beauty of Christ completely liberates us from this miserable bondage."

That is a good note on which to end this chapter, because it provides the essential qualification. Catholicism has to be catholic, open not only to the highest but to the lowest, the repulsive, the self-hating; it can never be a cult of the beautiful, which is why it is not for the religious connoisseurs or the seekers after fulfilment. In Eliot's phrase, the cost of belonging to this team, in even the humblest capacity, is "not less than everything."

Chapter 2
THE MODEL

Much of this book is concerned with the exciting and un-predictable behaviour of that aspect of the Catholic thing which I have evoked in the introduction under the symbol of the twin sister called Sophia. Yet, as we shall see, she never works alone. Her more sober sister always has a greater or lesser share in her work, and in this chapter it is, in fact, that other sister, Mother Church, who takes the leading part — yet the work is not hers alone, clearly. This chapter is about one time and place at which it seemed that the Catholic enterprise was about to achieve its aim of creating the kingdom of heaven on earth, drawing all aspects of human life into one great and holy Catholic thing. This time was the twelfth century in Europe and it was Mother Church's great moment, but also a moment at which the co-operation between the two sisters was closest and happiest.

In my introduction I also used the story of the restoration of York Minster as a kind of allegory of the Catholic enterprise as a whole. Of course the thing itself, that vast stone structure, is the product of the enterprise it symbolises, and in particular of the medieval part of it. But that part is, itself, a kind of "model" for the enterprise I want to explore.

In trying to plan, or explain, any large complex structure it is a help to have a small model to look at, for although the model cannot begin to do justice to the thing itself it does enable the viewer to carry essential proportions and shapes in his or her head, and so interpret more easily the huge reality. It seems to me that history provides us with something of this nature, which is a help in trying to discover a perspective on the vastness and complexity of the Catholic thing. This "model" is that of the high point of the medieval achievement.

I shall concentrate on the twelfth century (as a rough cultural reference rather than as an exact time span) partly because to sketch the whole medieval period would be so superficial as to be valueless, but mainly because the twelfth century is a unique and marvellous cultural phenomenon. Of course in discussing the twelfth century I shall be referring also to other periods, but my choice of this particular period is not arbitrary. The medieval enterprise sought to build the City of God in the city of man, and to do so in detail and at every level. People believed, then, that it could be done, that the perfect human commonwealth, in which Church and State lived in harmonious marriage, and labour, art, learning and business all served each other as loyal and loving children of one family, could be realized if only everyone tried hard enough and with sufficient devotion. Medieval Christians sought to make every aspect of human experience an expression of Christ's kingdom, and since that is the task of the Catholic enterprise it is clear that their efforts are significant. But the twelfth century was the high point, the peak of hope and enthusiasm and real achievement, before the inevitable disillusion and corruption — slow, uneven, but thorough — began to show itself unmistakably.

For of course the medieval enterprise failed, and its failure was so large that it shattered Western culture into fragments. Not only did it split into separate religious camps (as it were dividing Europe vertically) but it was also divided horizontally at many levels. Not only heaven and earth were separated, but politics were split from scholarship, reason from feeling, the market from the Church, science from morality, and ultimately home from work and love from everything except family and sex relationships. It didn't all happen at once, of course; nor did all the divisions show themselves clearly. But in time this compartmentalising of life did occur, and we, now, suffer the consequences of it.

This is the reason why the twelfth century enterprise, both the achievement and the failure, are important to us now. We know now, to some extent, what the mistakes were, and we are not likely to repeat them. We need, much more importantly, to realise the vision that underlay the achievement, however flawed: that sense of the oneness, the interdependence, of all created things. It is the lack of this vision which has made advances in science and technology a source of both actual and potential destruction, not only in war but in times of "peace", instead of what they should have been — a means to a true peace and a better life for all humankind. Now, painfully, many people (including younger scientists) are trying to discover some sense of that interdependence, so much more mysterious and crucial than we had supposed. Yet it is not a discovery, but a recovery. Only it is now being made with much more information, hard-won, to assist it and make it more accurate and more realistic. There was too much still unknown to our forefathers; but they saw the vision, and their "seeing" is one we need. In this brief evocation perhaps we can manage to see through their eyes for a while and, so enlightened, refer with more confidence to our own task. Perhaps we, like the restorers of York Minster, can "make it a little better."

The medieval enterprise was bound to fail; it is easy to say this from our historical vantage point. We can even say that it was folly to try, the thing was so patently impossible. Yet it was tried, and from the other side it did not look an impossible venture. On the contrary, it seemed the obvious and necessary enterprise in which the Church must engage, as it emerged from the wreck of the Roman Empire and its long-drawn-out struggles to Christianise (more or less) the new barbarian kingdoms.

The Church, through those centuries we lump together as "the dark ages," had discovered a cultural as well as a religious identity. It had had the experience of being the *only* guardian of scholarship and civilized standards, the influence that directed pagan creativity and craftsmanship into new and original channels and produced an explosion of beauty in Romanesque churches, metal and enamel work, sculpture and illumination. This experience fused culture and religion; it also fused politics and religion, since monks and other church-men were usually the only educated men, and were therefore (all over Europe) the advisers of kings, the makers of law, the architects of government and the negotiators of peace, when peace could be made.

Out of those centuries grew the assumption, born of that experience, that it was proper and inevitable for the Church to shape the whole pattern of human life into as godly a mould as might be. For all the mistakes it involved, the flaws it ignored, the arrogance it easily bred, this was a great enterprise, and it was one consciously and enthusiastically pursued. There was this one moment in history, a "moment" lasting about two hundred years, when the Catholic Church had (or thought it had) the means and opportunity to create the ideal human commonwealth. The political power, the moral prestige, the tested tradition, the manpower, were all there and, most important of all, there was the right atmosphere. The sense of newness, of limitless possibility, of optimism and sheer exuberance which comes through in writing of the twelfth century makes what we have learned to call the "Renaissance" seem brilliant but burdened, gorgeous yet neurotically self-absorbed and afraid. We can call the earlier "re-birth" naive, and with justice. But it was a naivete of simple lack of experience. It was neither insensitive nor unintelligent.

By the middle of the thirteenth century the impulse was already weakened and fragmented. The structures stood, and continued to stand, for centuries; indeed some remnants of them still endure, within later ones, in law, education, and public morality, as well as in buildings. But the thrust of sublime confidence had gone. The cultural achievement was at its height and continued to blossom and fruit, but the burst of exuberant growth was over, and the signs of disease were clear to see.

It was a Titanic enterprise, not only in its great giant scale but in the sense that the Titans were the rulers of the Time Before — the age of peace before the Old Gods, the Golden Age, which was to be recovered and made perfect in Christ. The medieval enterprise was the truly Titanic attempt to create an integrity of body and soul, time and eternity, the particular and the universal. And the understanding of this is not just an interesting historical divertissement; it is vital to the psychic health of the Western world. It is a measure of our cultural disorientation that such a statement should seem idiosyncratic, an exaggeration for effect. It is simply true. That does not mean, of course, that in order to recover communal sanity the Western world has to subject each citizen to a course in medieval history. It does mean that we need, as a culture, to realise what our origins are, what are the attitudes and aspirations that shaped our inheritance, and so to realise where the growth went wrong, and where in our time we have been even more wrong. Then we can learn from both.

"Everything we think is the fruit of the Middle Ages," said Jung in 1934, "and indeed of the Christian Middle Ages . . . It lives in us and has left its stamp upon us for all time and will always form a vital layer of our psyche, just like the phylogenetic traces in our body. The whole character of our mentality, the way we look at things, is also the result of the Christian Middle Ages; whether we know it or not is quite immaterial." This is a judgement we cannot avoid accepting, and if it is true it is also important. If, in the last hundred years, it has become apparent to our culture that, as Jung says, "everything we think is the fruit of the Middle Ages" then this parentage is nothing to be ashamed of. Indeed we are discovering that the Middle Ages had some ideas and attitudes whose loss has caused, and is still causing, terrible damage. Some (such as E.F. Schumacher) would go so far as to say that it is only by trying to rediscover, in our own terms, the universal vision of medieval thought that there is hope for our time.

If we are to make such an imaginative recovery, we can easily begin with two words which are strongly evocative even now. One is "monk" and the other is "gothic". For the medieval enterprise was to a great extent a monastic one in its beginnings, though at a certain point in the growth of complexity and gorgeousness in church building, lay professionals of all kinds began to be the makers of beauty. (Though monastic patrons remained vital, and influential, the great cathedrals were not built by monastic craftsmen. Kings and great merchants paid for the building, as well as rich abbots, and the final, fantastic flowering of gothic had very little at all to do with monks, except as princely patrons.) Yet there is no break, but a confusing continuity, in which historians still quarrel about the extent of actual monastic craftsmanship. At one time it was fashionable to dismiss the monk-craftsman as a nineteenth century romantic fantasy. Better knowledge has reinstated him, but he is set beside the growth of lay craft guilds.

When they think of the middle ages, "Gothic" is where people mostly start. At the watershed stands the first great Gothic building, and it was created by a monk, working mainly with non-monks. That man was Abbot Suger of St. Denis. He stands at this high point of the monastic achievement, when much that the monks had initiated was already becoming the province of lay craftsmen, clerical scholars and teachers who were not monks; but the great monasteries were and remained patrons whose vision and initiative made possible great work in art, government and education. For there was not one morality for the world of piety and another for commerce and government.

Abbot Suger was a government minister, a most energetic and imaginative patron of the arts, a talented biographer, and also an excellent (if not very saintly) Abbot. Perhaps not many people could combine all those roles, but Suger did, and nobody thought it strange or complained that he mixed religion and politics. Mixing religion with politics and indeed with any other human concern was what Suger and his many distinguished monastic contemporaries were interested in doing, and they did it very well. In Suger we are challenged by a conception of human life as a vast variety, yet all drawn together in the service of God, and that service, in turn, expressed in visible, tangible forms, forms explicity intended to catch the heart and harness the wayward spirit in an experience of awe and longing.

The great Abbey of St. Denis needed drastic repairs during Suger's rule. Besides, the crowds of pilgrims which came to visit the shrine and relics of France's patron saint were becoming too great to handle. When a monk had the duty of displaying the relics of St. Denis he was liable to have to jump through the nearest window to avoid being crushed by the seething mass of the pious. So, at least, said the energetic Abbot, explaining why it was decided not merely to repair but to enlarge, making room for a more splendid and more accessible shrine.

Abbot Suger wrote a detailed account of the process of re-building. He was a man of considerable vanity, like many great entrepreneurs, and he omitted to mention in his account of the re-building the names of the craftsmen and artists who worked on the project. But his own energy, ingenuity and irrepressible confidence come through very clearly, as well as his genuinely religious enthusiasm and the intensity of thought with which he brooded over every aspect of the vast undertaking.

The variety of concerns was great. First, money had to be raised. Much of it came as gifts from pilgrims and others, but the work needed also some basic, regular sum to count on. Suger set aside a certain part of the great Abbey estates and concentrated on boosting its productivity, so that the increased income from this should provide the flow of cash, and keep the work going all the year round. (I make no apology for stressing the manifold practicality of this project, because it is typical of the period and its particular Catholic ethos.)

Suger was much concerned to harmonise the new buildings with the older parts. For this, columns were needed to match the original marble ones, and no suitable marble was obtainable, it seemed, nearer than Rome, which would have meant sending the marble by sea via the Straits of Gibraltar, the English channel and the River Seine. Even Suger felt this was an exaggeration of zeal, and for years he and the masons and architects brooded and worried, but in the end the solution was found, not by the Abbot's ingenuity, but, as he affirmed, by "the generous munificence of the Almighty . . . to the astonishment of all and through the merit of the Holy Martyrs." In fact, it was discovered that a local quarry, from which millstones were cut, had a lower bed of high quality stone, suitable for "very fine and excellent" columns. Thus, every detail of the work engaged his anxious thought, from timbers large enough for the great roof, to the workmanship of reliquaries and the colour of windows.

In commissioning the decoration of the new Abbey, Suger was concerned about symbolism as well as beauty. It was not merely intended to impress but to uplift and instruct. Just as he saw no oddity in solving one building problem by his own wits and another by divine intervention, there was no dividing line between aesthetics and spirituality, nor between these and the details of fund-raising.

A passion for display was certainly present in all this building and decorating, (though this became more pronounced later on), but the attitude that called on skilled craftsmen in glass and in metals, and set them to providing the objects used in worship, was deeply and matter-of-factly religious. It was not pious, in the sense we give that word. In that sense, Suger was probably not a very pious man. He was a medieval man, and never stopped to wonder whether the lavish use of precious and beautiful things was or was not a good thing in a church. He just knew it was, and he knew it in a very clear and explicit way. Not only did carvings on capitals and corbels and the glass of windows evoke scenes from the Bible and lives of saints; decorations of a more abstract kind also had meaning. The glint of jewels and gold symbolised the glory of God as it is refracted and multiplied in the small lights of earthly holiness. Colours, in glass and gems, had each a special symbolism, to convey messages to the worshipper. Suger loved precious stones. His own chalice, which still exists (though St. Denis is gone) was carved from a sardonyx, set with gold, where pearls and darker gems glisten within delicate curled decoration, and the handles curve like vine tendrils.

St. Denis was "the cradle of Gothic", and Suger laboured to bring forth the baby for that cradle, laboured mentally and spiritually, and even physically as he sweated over the sweating masons, endlessly working to push plans ahead, overcome obstacles, persuading, exhorting, and bullying. The re-building of St. Denis took place in the 1130s and '40s. Some years earlier, a German monk who wrote under the name of "Theophilus", wrote a remarkable book called "The Various Arts", in which many processes of church decoration are described, from religious themes to be embodied, the relations of patron and craftsmen, to the smallest details of each craft involved — glass-making, book-making, metal work, and so on. His own speciality was metal work, and it is probable that he was (under his own name) the maker of some very beautiful portable altars and reliquaries which still exist. His approach to his work shows the framework of thought within which Suger and other church builders of the time operated. He refers to David and Solomon as examples of the will to worship God, by his direct command, in the beauty of "works in gold and silver, bronze, gems, and wood, and in art of every kind". He exhorts the craftsman to pray for the gifts of the Spirit to assist his work, warns against having too much of an eye to the fee (though the reward is, he feels, a perfectly proper concern) and reminds him that nothing worth while is done without God's help. In one passage he describes the feeling of the good craftsman as he looks at his work and that of others adorning the house of God. His words express perfectly the vision of a man like Suger, of human workmanship empowered by the Spirit and leading back to Him. (No doubt much less exalted forms of satisfaction also formed part of the Abbot's state of mind when he surveyed the results of so much effort, but the passage is a fair expression of what he was honestly and wholeheartedly trying to do, and not only he, but a whole age which produced such an explosion of inventiveness and beauty in the service of God.) Thus, "Theophilus" addresses the artist and craftsman:

"Animated, dearest son, by these supporting virtues, you have approached the House of God with confidence, and have adorned it with so much beauty; you have embellished the ceilings and walls with varied work in different colours and have, in some measure, shown to beholders the paradise of God, glowing with varied flowers, verdant with herbs and foliage, and cherishing with crowns of varying merit the souls of the saints. You have given them cause to praise the Creator in the creature and proclaim Him wonderful in His works. For the human eye is not able to consider on what work first to fix its gaze; if it beholds the ceilings they glow like brocades; if it considers the walls they are a kind of paradise; if it regards the profusion of light from the windows, it marvels at the inestimable beauty of the glass and the infinitely rich and various workmanship. But if, perchance, the faithful soul observes the representation of the Lord's Passion expressed in art, it is stung with compassion. If it sees how many torments the saints endured in their bodies and what rewards of eternal life they have received, it eagerly embraces the observance of a better life."

This inspiring view of work done encourages the craftsman to further efforts, and to adding fine work in covers for Gospel books, in reliquaries, censers, candlesticks and many other things. All the skill and devotion of many men is lavished on this great work which joins heaven and earth.

But there was a danger in this exuberance of gorgeousness. It was the danger of pride and distraction, of valuing beauty for its own sake, not God's or man's, of the vanity of having better craftsmen, more gaping pilgrims, more royal endowments in the form of yet more splendid chalices and tombs, than some other Abbey. The Catholic enterprise, was, by the very enthusiasm of the manifestation, in danger of narrowing its scope, becoming no longer Catholic. The Cistercian reform, in culture as in monastic observance, fled from that danger. When the perfect balance which was sought, and occasionally achieved, by the pursuit of beauty toppled too far on the side of worldliness the monastic tradition produced an emphatic counterpoise. Catholicism was re-thought and renewed, freshly motivated and infused with a rather stern vigour. Cistercian Abbeys were to be plain to the point of starkness, and Bernard of Clairvaux was the man who ensured this. Mystic, poet, ascetic, preacher of the crusades, Abelard's implacable enemy, a man capable of tender friendship and blinkered bigotry, Bernard excited both hatred and intense admiration and love, in his own time and ever since. He was not the founder of the reform; the reform had started at Citeaux, in Burgundy, with a group from a Benedictine Abbey who sought a more secluded and stricter life. Their second Abbot, the Englishman Stephen Harding, gave the reform its constitution, but it was Bernard, joining it in 1112 with several brothers and a number of other young men, who gave it the driving force which led to its rapid expansion throughout Europe.

The reform was an attempt to recover the original Benedictine simplicity. But because it was in violent reaction against what Bernard felt were the aberrations of the great monasteries, the puritan emphasis was very strong.

The huge Cluniac Order was his especial target, yet it had been itself a great reform, at a time when Norse invasions and political chaos had so demoralised the older monasteries — alternately bullied, patronised or plundered as they were by local rulers — that monastic life had become almost impossible. The

Cluniac reform was undertaken by men of noble birth and enormous courage (both of these being essential under the circumstances) and it re-established monasticism on the grand scale in every sense. European art and architecture owes more to the Cluniacs than to any other single group. It was an aristocratic movement, emphasising scholarship and the splendour of liturgical worship, while lay-brothers (who were not really monks but monastic servants) did the manual work. This gave it great power in a feudal society, and the Romanesque style of building spread with the Order. All over Europe grandiose churches rose in weighty splendour, and their village-size monasteries, with their workshops, farms, guest houses and schools, were centres of culture over great areas. In newly converted lands of Eastern Europe they stamped the crude and bewildered religion of passively baptised populations with the beginnings of culture as well as doctrine.

But the dangers were clear. Bernard denounced these princely, elegant, cultured gentlemen in monks' robes, and demanded a return to the simplicity and purity of the Gospel, to a Golden Age of monastic perfection that never was.

Every detail of life had to fit this passion for undistracted service of God. Square, plain churches, no coloured glass, no carvings, un-illuminated office books (though Stephen Harding had allowed and encouraged illumination), manual labour for all, and plenty of it. The first Cistercians built their own churches, and nobles and rich men might not be buried in them (such tombs had been a frequent occasion for lavishness in other monasteries). The ideal was lofty, the life produced many saints, and also a tremendous leap forward in agriculture, for the Cistercians built their monasteries in remote places to keep clear of the concerns of the world and its cities. Since they depended on the land for a living and emphasised frugality and hard work, they concentrated on making the land productive, and succeeded. They were responsible for establishing sheep farming, for instance, in the North of England (and from this, at least in part, the later phenomenal prosperity of England developed, through trade in wool and woollen cloth).

Yet, for most human beings, the work of hands and voice

and mind needs to express and encourage the half-conscious search for God. The fact that the Cistercians gradually allowed a little more decoration, added round apses to those stark eastern walls, and re-introduced the beauty of precious metal and glass, is not all due to loss of fervour. It is impossible to draw the line, but some of it was a right feeling that to propose and embody a high ideal is one thing, but ordinary human beings need a little boost in order to sustain their striving for it. (In the same way, much later, the High Church revival in the Episcopalian tradition recognized the validity of the medieval passion for richness and beauty in worship and in the place of worship.)

The monastic enterprise, then, was unbalanced repeatedly in two different directions: towards comfortable worldliness and power-seeking, and towards a puritanical ideal which in practice could not be sustained without damage. And each time the tendency to accomodate human weakness got out of hand, the slogans called for a return to the Golden Age, the perfect simplicity of early Benedictine monasticism. What, then, was the especial excellence of the earlier life, that it should be a model for the ages?

Its excellence was, arguably, one of those rare moments of balance, a way truly human yet leading onwards to something greater. It began with one young man's desire to break free from the decadent culture of Rome.

Early in the sixth century a man named Benedict went into the remote countryside to find solitude and a hermit's life, and, as so often happens, found that others wanted the same thing and wanted him to direct the affair. (We shall see the same thing happening to the very different Celtic monks.) The growth of the earliest small, scattered, communities he established was rapid but stormy. In the years during which he survived attempts on his life by un-reformed monks he had plenty of opportunity to decide what did, and did not, make for a stable Christian life.

He was a Roman. In him the traditional Roman respect for order, moral rectitude and self-help found a continuation in a different setting. He drew not only on his own experience but on older kinds of monasticism, and learned from their weaknesses

71

as well as their strengths. His monks were not to be holy eccentrics, like some of the more outrageous Desert Fathers, nor wandering ascetics; he disapproved strongly of monks who went gadding about the countryside. (The disapproval is so emphatic that one feels it must proceed from personal and unpleasant experience of these sixth century footloose "weirdies".) He drew on older rules but adapted them to the conditions he saw around him. What he saw was a widespread anarchy of competing barbarian kingdoms encroaching on dwindling pockets of remaining Roman power and "classical" culture. It was an unstable political situation favourable to demagogues and dictators. It was inevitably accompanied by economic stagnation. The peasant population lived in misery, had no security, and was exploited by war-happy princes. Trade and regular communications were constantly disrupted.

If men — ordinary, un-saintly men, peasants or scholars or noblemen's sons — were to seek salvation in such a situation, they had to take the situation into account. They had to create their own stability and order; they had to feed themselves, and indeed supply all their normal wants and have enough to dispense hospitality. Yet they must not be rich enough to attract the roving eye of some impoverished war-lord.

But the practical needs of survival were also the needs of the spirit seeking God, the spirit working in un-virtuous, muddled people, who still long obscurely for goodness, for the "something else". The Benedictine life is centred on the Work of God, the sung office in choir, and that prayer is intended to spread through the day. Yet the rest of the day is not merely to be a necessary attention to mundane tasks, but everything in it is also a prayer. The craftsman's skill (to be exercised "without boastfulness") the drudgery of digging and weeding, the work of kitchen and brewhouse, are all made one. Every stage of spiritual development, from that of the beginner still liable to fits of violent temper or laziness, to the mystic absorbed in God and needing extra solitude, must be catered for. The scholar and the peasant work side by side as brothers, and both are valued. Good food is important, but not too much. Decent cleanliness and order (beds, not straw on the ground) are not luxuries but requirements for a godly life.

To keep the record straight it has to be admitted that there was also a strong streak of gloom in the Benedictine ethos (not very surprising, considering the times) and the balance is spoiled by an emphasis on world-rejection, fear of damnation and what seems to us an altogether unhealthy demand for constant awareness of personal sinfulness. In spite of this, in such a setting a person could search for the Kingdom of God and have some chance of finding it within. What is more, this way of life was ideally suited to survive, because each monastery was self-contained not only in necessaries of life but in government. This meant that however many were over-run and wiped out (and many were, in the following centuries) if only one remained it could be the seed from which others could grow again. This is, indeed, what happened, so that the history of the mainland of Europe until the twelfth century is, in a sense, the history of Benedictine monasticism. The education of kings, the preservation of learning, work of arbitration and diplomacy, the handing on of crafts easily forgotten in a war-torn country — these were among the monastic tasks. And besides whatever specific civilizing work they undertook, as need arose, there was the basic fact that the monasteries existed and continued. If, in time, there came to be an over-emphasis on the monastic as the only certain way to heaven, it is not surprising that it seemed so to many people.

When it worked, which it did surprisingly often and well, it was a way of life that provided for nearly all aspects of human personality. It combined stability and a sense of corporate identity with opportunity for the development of personal talent, yet with reduced risk of doing work for show or for profit. In this the monastic ideal strongly recalls the achievement of the Shaker communities in the United States. This sect, which was indeed more like a religious order than a denomination, emphasised simplicity and usefulness in everything made, and taught that each thing should be made as perfectly as possible, but also it must be made for a good and sufficient purpose. The doctrine that beauty of form results from beauty of moral direction and spiritual harmony produced domestic articles, buildings and

73

even farm machinery of a strong, serviceable yet elegant beauty which has seldom been surpassed. Even to see photographs of these things is to feel a response of sheer delight and inner satisfaction at such perfect proportion and harmony. The Shakers, like the monks and nuns at the high point of the monastic achievement (which is not the same as the high point of aesthetic glory inspired by monasticism) produced beautiful things because they had managed to bring the whole of life into a balance — precarious, as history shows, but real and splendid. Their artifacts were beautiful, and so also was their life.

The Shakers were celibate and so, of course, were the monastic orders. This means that they achieved their living harmony of life — bringing into order and balance the social and the private, the material and spiritual, the intellectual and the emotional — by excluding that area which constitutes the biggest concern for most people: sex and the resulting children and family patterns. This is why many people reject the monastic enterprise as a dead end, a "luxury life" which bypasses the real problems. Certainly it sets them aside, and one of the most dangerous imbalances of the monastic enterprise has arisen from the tendency to see the monastic way as the only proper way, and all other Christians as very secondary indeed. Dietrich Bonhoeffer praised the Catholic Church for recognizing the monastic movement as a way to recover a sense of the "costliness" of the Christian life, after it had been weakened by custom and rapid growth in numbers; but he also blamed it for allowing monasticism to become a Christianity within Christianity, the "perfect way" for the few, leaving to the rest a chance of salvation by minimal and mostly negative standards.

However, what people intend consciously to do and what they actually achieve are often two different things. Monasteries may not have intended to compensate for their withdrawal from family responsibilities by breeding a wider culture around them; but that is what they did. I am not merely talking of the work of hospitality, teaching, nursing and poor-relief which the monks gradually took on, but of the effect that their existence had on other people, in practical and in symbolic ways.

The early middle ages had a far less starry-eyed notion of life

74

inside monasteries than the nineteenth and early twentieth centuries. Nobody thought monks and nuns were all good, but everyone could see that, as a way of life governed by a system of values, it worked. When monks were criticized (and as time went on they were criticized more and more) they were viewed with anger, resentment, or cynicism not because the monastic ideal was being questioned, but because the monks were not being what their habit and rule proclaimed. But when the system was working fairly well, even with frequent lapses, it provided a framework of thought about life, its purpose and its priorities, which was available to everyone. So the monstic ideal provided a kind of touchstone by which to test the validity of domestic and economic life, and indeed monks were among those who tried to work out in detail the application of Christian ideals to the most practical details of life in the market place, the workshop, the home, or the palace.

The aspect of the medieval undertaking which seems strangest to us now is the enthusiasm for law. The making of just laws for Church and State was an exciting and vital part of the attempt to establish the reign of God. True, the attempts of the great medieval jurists to create a perfect commonwealth could not finally succeed; the conditions were too varied, the traditions in different places sometimes incompatible, human nature too greedy and timid, and kings too jealous, for this enormous venture in law-making to succeed. But the enterprise itself was a magnificent one. Surpassing even the logic and good sense of Roman law, the monastic jurists (and the clerks and nobles who learned their trade from them) tried to order human life in ways intended to be both efficient from the point of view of keeping the social system in working order, and also — much more difficult — truly *just* to each human being. Each person was considered not merely as a political unit but as someone with a spiritual dimension, having inherent rights and duties and an eternal destiny.

When we consider the barbarities of medieval punishment and the inequity of social organisation, this may seem a strange claim. There was, nevertheless, an extraordinary measure of success even in this failure; it rested on the outstanding fact that, when it came to the point of argument, the *principles* of justice were laid on the basis I described. While brute power could always override them, it was quite clear that this overriding was unjust. The difference this makes is easy to see when we consider that, in our world, governments seldom accept any external norms of justice except what the public will accept — or can be made to accept. Justice becomes simply the administration of law, and law is what is made by the State, to suit itself, and itself is simply the will of the most powerful citizens, whether they hold official posts or not. In democratic countries the electorate has to be placated, but this is a tactical necessity with little moral basis. And there are (as recent American history has shown) ways of executing policy without the knowledge or consent of the electorate. The medieval idea of justice referred to God as its source, not just in pious asides but in painstaking argument over Roman law, "natural" law, and the texts of Scripture. While this left plenty of room for hypocrisy, or for such distortions as judicial torture, it did have to refer itself explicitly to something greater than any human power. The strange dialectic of medieval judicial theory and practice shows the struggle to disentangle justice from custom, might from right, social or political status from inherent human value.

One of the most common, and most justified, accusations against the Catholicism that re-formed itself after the cataclysm of the Reformation was its legalism, its reliance on regulation of every aspect of life. This was an abuse, and the reaction against it has been understandably intense and, as always, unbalanced. If the balance is to be redressed it is necessary to realise that the task of law-making was, so it seemed to churchmen, laid on the Church as an unavoidable, God-sent work. It was accepted with a confidence that the application of truly Christian ethical standards to the creation of an orderly state might indeed be the way to make the Kingdom come "on earth as it is in heaven". I cannot do better than quote the great historian of Catholic culture, E.I. Watkin:

"In face of these successive floods of barbarian invasion the first and supreme need throughout the Dark Ages was government, the establishment of law and order. The Herculean task was begun again and again and yet again as each new attempt at Christian civilization was made on the ruins of a former. The indomitable courage to undertake it was drawn from faith in a Divine Ruler and from the support of the sole society and the only Government which had survived the collapse of the older order, the Church He had founded, and ruled through His earthly representative. The organisers and rulers during these centuries were predominantly ecclesiastics or laymen such as Charlemagne and Alfred working in close collaboration with them. . . . . The Christian leaders of Europe were men of profound religion, men who sought the glory of God and wished to make human society serve His glory. . . .in face of odds seemingly overwhelming and undismayed by constant defeats they strove against barbarian anarchy and violence and laboured for the Kingdom of God. . . . It was the contemplation and praise of the cloister that trained men who evangelised and civilised heathen hordes and brought waste places under cultivation. It is true that these centuries of heroic struggle against human and natural disorder imbued Latin Christianity with the legal spirit that has often degenerated into legalism and with which the Orientals reproach it. And it produced a powerful hierarchical government, which inevitably fostered an ecclesiastical bureaucracy. But the germ and principle of both these developments and therefore the occasion of their corresponding abuses lay in the Divine Constitution of a visible Church. And the foundations of Christian Europe could not have been laid otherwise."

The Victorians still felt able to make strong and unashamed ethical judgements, and a book by the very Victorian novelist Charlotte Yonge epitomises the clash of incompatible moralities in those centuries of struggle. The book — a particular favorite of mine — is called "The Little Duke" and the title refers to Richard of Normandy, grandfather of William, Duke of Normandy and conqueror of England. The barely Christianized Norsemen were in conflict with the more civilized but hardly more honourable King of France, and Richard's father, William

Longsword, was assassinated at a meeting called by his enemies under pledges of truce, to arrange a peace. It was treachery and oath-breaking of the worst kind, for the Duke had come unarmed to the conference. His son, the boy Duke, only eight years old, was taken to Rouen to attend his father's funeral and to receive the homage of his vassals, but before that he must honour his father's body, lying in state in the church. In Charlotte Yonge's evocation of the scene the boy — still shocked by his father's horrible death, bewildered by his new and barely understood responsibilities, exhausted by a long ride among preoccupied adults — finally confronts the wounded body, and is overcome with grief and rage. His father's vassals seize on this childish rage, and call on him to undertake the sacred duty of vengeance. He puts out his hand to swear the oath on his father's sword; he recalls in a confused way all the hero-tales of his fierce people, the stories of war, revenge and conquest that he has heard since he was a baby. But at that moment, his hand is seized by Abbot Martin of the great monastery of Jumieges, his father's friend and guide. He bids the child remember where he stands, his father's own desire for peace — the peace for which he gave his life — and the absolute Christian demand for forgiveness of injury.

Here is the confrontation of the Old Gods and the new Christ, but also of a system based on principles of warrior honour and power alone, with one of law based on impersonal — or rather Divine — justice which treats all alike and demands obedience from both ruler and ruled. The scene is vivid and truthful: the conflict in the little boy, the outraged pagan honour of the older knights whose Christianity is only skin deep, the intransigent sternness of the monk who represents the law-giving, peace-making mission of the Church and knows that he cannot give way.

Richard withdrew from the oath, and thus chose his allegiance for life, but the struggle was by no means over, for him or for the Church. It was another two centuries before the ethical principles embodied by Abbot Martin could be regarded as the self-evident basis for the ordering of daily life and indeed in some places it never held sway. In the fifteenth century, for instance, King James of Scotland returned from long exile in England where, in privileged custody, he had grown up with the King's sons and learned the customs of civilized Christian Europe. When he finally assumed his throne he was determined to bring the rule of law to his own country, and to make it clear that all alike came under one justice. In the years of his exile Scotland had been left to the power of feuding local chiefs, and even those who ruled in his name did so only for their own enrichment, killing and stealing where they liked. The only principle was the "honour" of the nobility and the only sanction the power to revenge. When James arrested, tried, and executed three generations of the noble family that had worked against him and oppressed the powerless, killing and robbing at will, he did so in order to demonstrate that even the highest came under one equal law. But the other nobles saw his act as simply one of private revenge for failure to support his cause, and regarded it as a monstrous betrayal of the "caste" honour of the nobility. Law, to them, was a matter of penalties inflicted on peasants and merchants; it could not touch the nobility. They never forgave him, and James himself was later assassinated as a result. Before we throw out the law with the legalism we should consider what the lack of it can mean.

The basis of order was conscience, to the mind of the medieval jurist, and human law could not override divine justice. The great twelfth century French jurist, Beaumanoir, wrote that if a "bailli" (seneschal) is ordered by his lord to do something against his conscience he is bound to disobey, "for the obedience he owes is to be understood as doing right and maintaining loyal justice. Nor will a *bailli* be excused before God if he wrongs his own conscience following the command of his lord, and it is better for such an officer to leave the service than that, because of a command or anything else, he wrongs his conscience." This was written by a *jurist*, not a spiritual guide, and it shows the inseparability of private conscience and public duty in the medieval ideal, even if practice often fell far short of it. The point is, there *was* an ideal. The falls were many, but they were recognised as such, and often redressed by the available courts.

It is interesting, in the light of twentieth century debates about the morality of revolution, wars of liberation, and violence in defence of freedom, that the twelfth century John of Salisbury held that it is right to kill a tyrant. Thomas Aquinas taught that the removal of a tyrant is not a sin, or "seditious", because "a tyrant who nourishes discords and seditions among the people subject to him, that he may more safely rule, is really more seditious."

Less drastic ways of controlling rulers were naturally better, and the truly absolute monarch was, in fact, a product of Renaissance political pragmatism rather than of medieval respect for royalty, which distinguished the man from the office and held that the man should be made to perform his office rightly. In Hungary, for instance, a law of 1222 laid down that the lesser nobles should meet annually to review the actions of the king and his chief executives, with a view to correcting mistakes. When kings grew restive under such treatment, they were liable to be faced with angry archbishops or revolting barons — or both, as in the case of King John of England who was forced to sign the "Magna Carta". This was not, as legend has made it, a "People's Charter", but it was certainly a severe restriction on royal power. Many jurists and theologians were of the opinion that a republic was a more suitable form of government for a Christian state than a monarchy, and the independent urban republics of Italy were there to prove that this was a perfectly good alternative.

It was not only the fully independent republics that prided themselves on their local rights, and their laws and "customs" governing markets, roads, property, and so on. The variety in legal and political structure was enormous, which is not surprising when we realise that communications were slow, and that the various parts of Europe had for so long been cut off by the chaos of war as well as separated by the different surviving "tribal" traditions in many places. In Roman law, on which medieval canon and civil law was based, any "whole" or unit ("universitas") could make its own laws. In practice this right was limited by the rule of overlords, or of large and rich communities to which smaller ones voluntarily subordinated themselves in return for protection. But the degree of self-government achieved even by villages comes as a surprise to those who think of the Middle Ages as exclusively feudal, and of feudalism as a system of rigid subordination of ruled to ruler at every level. Many towns and villages elected "consuls", for instance, and in a few the electorate consisted of the whole population. These men were "town councillors", who had judicial and executive powers. Sometimes local princes encouraged this broadly based democracy, because it undermined the tendency for power to be gradually concentrated in the hands of a wealthy nobility or a group of rich merchants, as happened in Bruges, for instance. There, in 1240, only the members of the Hanse, the rich merchants' association, could hold public office. This tendency was against the medieval ideal which stressed the rights and dignity of all citizens; but it shows why, in spite of the popularity of republican ideas in the theories of scholars and jurists, a monarchy often seemed more likely in practice to preserve the real liberty of the subject. A King, properly kept in his place by the Church, had a better chance of controlling families grown too powerful, whether by nobility or wealth, than an elected body. But the republican ideal died only slowly. Even if the practice became more cynical about the equality of citizens, the ideal remained enshrined in public statement.

The last and strongest manifestation of the power of the "people" was found in the corporate power of the trade guilds. For instance, in Bologna in 1288 a law was passed which excluded from representing the people or sitting on the general council anyone "who has not worked in a craft with his own hands", a notion which makes many modern left-wing revolutionaries seem incurably bourgeois. It didn't last, of course; by the time of the Renaissance the great merchant families were firmly in power, and virtually absolute in their own territory. But the ideal was still cherished, and it was revived later.

There was social conflict, violence and corruption; there was brutal harshness in punishment. These things were, however, recognised as evils and denounced; and the denunciation was not regarded as "disloyal" to State or party, as can happen when the only criterion is the law itself and the power to enforce it. Only brief examples can be quoted, but the attitudes and atmosphere are demonstrated by, for instance, the fact that in the "customal" of Clermont-en-Beauvais it was laid down that debtors might not be imprisoned for more than forty days, because a longer period of imprisonment was "a thing contrary to humanity". Also, although the practical inequality of the sexes was obvious, the *ideal* of the time upheld their equality, and the law protected women vigorously. In the case of bankruptcy, for instance, a man's wife had precedence over all his other creditors, to get back her dowry and marriage gift. In some places there existed wholly female craft-guilds (as well as male and mixed ones). Women could be "Masters" in these guilds, and where the guilds were the basis of political life they could hold public office. In fourteenth century Provins, twelve percent of the voters in a public plebiscite were women — either widows who had taken over their husbands' craft and guild offices, or married crafts-women. This may not sound very remarkable in our age of universal suffrage, but compared to the status of women even fifty years ago it is worth pondering.

When towns were being planned and extended (and medieval towns were usually *planned*; they didn't just happen, as romantic tourists seem to imagine) their charters would normally include provision for sanitation, including the building of bath houses and the paving of streets. The plans also included hospitals and almshouses for the old, in both of which, as one charter lays down, "the poor of Christ shall be received"; these institutions were to be "free of all tax". (The hospitals, incidentally, took in not only the sick but poor travellers, poor women in labour, and orphan children as well as other local poor.) The care of the poor was regarded not as an optional extra but as an essential, and the responsibility for it was put squarely not only on the local government but individually on all those who were not poor themselves. Hence large gifts and bequests were made to found hospitals, or endow beds; these always included a request for the prayers of those who used the facilities. Such gifts may have been prompted more by fear for one's eternal condition than by pure compassion, but at least it was taken for granted that such relief of suffering was a plain, unavoidable duty, from which there were no exceptions.

In popular history, there are two indelibly black marks on the medieval period. One is judicial torture and the other (associated with it) is the Inquisition. Without excusing the horrors of either — nobody could — it is worth noticing that harsh and horrible physical punishment was an inheritance from the Roman system, and the use of torture not as punishment but as a means of obtaining evidence was brought in originally to replace the earlier custom of trial by ordeal, which could be used to secure the conviction of the innocent. In addition, the use of torture in the medieval period (unlike the Renaissance) was hedged with all kinds of limitations and warnings against causing serious or lasting harm, and required the presence of impartial witnesses to secure this. Later, when absolute rulers acquired greater control, there were fewer religious scruples and torture became more severe. In the end the limitations evaporated, so that by the sixteenth century judicial torture was a fathomless horror. Parallel with this, non-Catholic historians have noticed that the Church courts of inquisitions were set up partly because the panic over heresy (which was akin to witchcraft in the popular mind) had led to the lynching of heretics without a vestige of a trial when local feuds found a convenient means of private revenge in carefully worked up mob hysteria over "heresy". The greater ruthlessness that rapidly crept in was severely criticised by some of the inquisitors themselves; one of the fiercest inquisitors, "Robert the Bulgar", who is said to have burned nearly two hundred people in one day in a village called Montwimer, was arrested soon after and sentenced by the Church to life imprisonment.

There is no doubt that the Inquisition became a monstrous thing which the Catholic Church had to repent painfully. But it was not an invention of the Church. It was, in fact, modelled on the methods of the Italian secular courts at the time. Ironically, it was the great surge of Utopian enthusiasm, the longing for a "perfect" and democratic State in which the welfare of the whole community should be guaranteed, which made everyone ultra-sensitive to any possible threat to the social, political, or religious order. Crimes — religious or secular — were a threat to the community, an attempt to undermine the creation of the ideal commonwealth. It seemed less important to obtain valid evidence and administer impartial justice than to secure a confession of guilt and so get rid of the menace.

It was from the Church itself that an attempt to redress the balance eventually came. In the thirteenth century the bishops' councils acquired greater power, and used it to denounce — among other abuses — the methods of the Inquisition. The result of this was a series of reforms promulgated by Pope Boniface VIII, among them the provisions of legal aid, the publication of witnesses' names (to prevent anonymous accusations) and a general down-grading of the inquisitional system to a local affair run by local bishops. (Notoriously, Philip II of Spain used this localisation to develop his own special and infamous "Spanish Inquisition". By that time the doctrine of divine right of monarchs, and the generally ruthless character of political and dynastic, as well as "religious", conflict had changed the whole scene. Licence was given to cruelties that the "brutal" Middle Ages would have rejected as obscene and "a thing contrary to humanity".)

If I have dwelt at length on the legal and political theories and practices of the "High Middle Ages" it is partly because most people never do, but also because "law and order" have become, on the one hand, slogans of oppression, and on the other hand, indecencies to be rejected. For the twelfth century Catholic enterprise, law was an area of discovery and invention. The chaotic contradictions, the Utopian theory and the varied practice, were the results of a genuine creative effort, part of the attempt to make a whole, "universal" human life-style governed by Christian principles. The materials available were wildly heterogeneous — surviving Roman law, tribal customs, Christian apocalyptic idealism, the influence of Moslem and Jewish philosophy and tradition, as well as the realities of local power struggles, the increasing influence of merchants and cities generally, the restless intransigence of the craft guilds. Areas of law that to us seem clearly mapped and obvious were to them pioneering territory.

There was, for instance, great confusion of theory and practice in marriage cases. Through this briar-patch of conflicting custom and opinion the great canon lawyers attempted to cut a clear path, their only tools being respect for the free human decision involved (which forbade forced marriage, or taxes on marriage) and the rights of the defenceless to protection and support. The principle that a valid marriage required both free consent (with witnesses to guarantee it) and consummation, was only hammered out with difficulty at a time when overlords claimed the right to marry off (or refuse marriage to) their serfs, and noble families regarded marriageable daughters as a useful form of currency for buying lands and influence.

These same daughters were sometimes less than passive in the matter. One reason why women in the West did indeed enjoy a high status and were not always successfully handed around to please their fathers was that they could be, and often were, extremely well educated. Although some authorities on "manners" disapproved of educating women for fear of making them unmanageable, there was strong propaganda in favour of a good education for women, because women were free human beings, and human beings have a need for and right to whatever wisdom is available. The great women's monasteries were centres of learning and art; laywomen also (Heloise is only one example) were often educated, and in some cases became outstanding scholars and teachers. The canonist John Andreas, who died in 1348, educated his daughter so thoroughly that when on one occasion he became ill she was able to deliver the necessary lectures to his students. (He said, however, that she had better wear a veil, presumably because otherwise the students might find the experience too exciting!) Highly educated women were not common; neither were they rarities.

Indeed, this was a time when education was sought after. The intellectual ferment of the time was bubbling in every city and monastery, and the inclusion of women in this search for wisdom was a part of the irrepressible idealism and hope which thought of the perfection of the Kingdom of God not as a metaphor or an interior experience, but as a concrete possibility. In the kingdom, all are equal and all are wise, and learning embraces every aspect of reality, since God made it all.

The gloomy view of human nature which understandably resulted from the centuries-long agony of a continent at the mercy of rapacious, often murderous rival rulers (and their no less repulsive supporters) took a long time to die. The early medieval period still officially held that most people (even monks) were probably damned. Even the Saviour could not wholly break the devil's hold on fallen mankind. But with Abelard and other teachers of the twelfth century a new mood of hope, a new emphasis on God's conquering love and compassion, began to displace this. Men and women looked with new eyes at the world and saw that it was good, because God has made it good. Later, the Black Death cast an even darker pall of pessimism over Europe, but in the twelfth century that time was far off.

In that earlier time, hope and enthusiasm and a vast and holy curiosity prevailed. Creation was God's gift, and consequently all that God had made might be profitably studied. The tools for study were few by our standards, and natural science relied on ancient authors and everyday observation. The aim, however, was "catholic". The desire was to discover a unifying design in all of life, to discern God's plan for the perfection of human and all created existence, from the nature and uses of herbs to the theology of angels.

Medieval education was anything but narrow in its scope, even if its reach was limited. Formal education consisted of the famous Trivium and Quadrivium; first, Grammar, Dialectic and Rhetoric, which only sound dull because the disciplines they indicate have narrowed so much since then. Grammar meant Latin literature, the whole classical inheritance of philosophy, poetry, and story; dialectic taught people to think accurately, critically, sifting ideas and evaluating them, and rhetoric trained in the art of communication. The medieval "Quadrivium" — Arithmetic, Music, Geometry and Astrology — ensured a breadth of study unequalled until quite recently. It is not so long since mathematics and any kind of science were rare ingredients in education (except for useful people like accountants and surveyors); music was an "extra" to be cultivated by young ladies with nothing better to do with their time. But the emphasis on the science of measuring and number (for music, to the medieval mind, came into that category) shows also the sense that order was of supreme importance. "How things are arranged" mattered, in every aspect of life. Metaphysics and theology therefore crowned the educational syllabus, for they were concerned with "how things are arranged" in the world of intangibles which underlies and knits together all that is tangible, binding the temporal to the eternal in a perfect design.

But education is more than what is learned in schools. Medieval education was shot through with a variety of cultural influences, woven together by poets, singers and artists into strange and beautiful patterns. The Teutonic and pagan tradition brought with it the "Nibelungenlied", tales of the old gods and heroes mixed with barely christianised stories. The Norse Sagas, folk tales from France and Britain and pagan Celtic myths melted into Christian legends and met Moorish poetry and stories drifting in with returning Crusaders. Above all the Romance movement provided a whole new cultural tradition; but the Romance literature belongs, with the Grail legends, in a later chapter.

Many fairy tales and legends, as well as the main myths that shape the thinking of our world, come to us from the Middle Ages. Shakespeare drew themes and plots from the medieval world, used its metaphysics, echoed its enduring anxieties and obsessions, and so handed them on to us.

The "moment" of the Catholic enterprise when it seemed possible to men and women that Christianity, properly organised, could create heaven on earth, could not last. It produced fearful results in the end. The desire for wholeness and unity led to a fear of anything that broke the whole. This obsession with heresy led to heresy itself. People broke away in desperation from an orthodox theology grown obsessively suspicious. The panic reactions of the increasingly bureaucratised Church drove many into division, when a more open attitude might have allowed fruitful development. For the air was alive with speculation in the twelfth century, and paradoxically, it was this very eager, thrusting confidence in thinking that created both the vision to be striven for and the fear of anything that threatened the vision.

The conviction that human life must be whole meant that the Church assumed a duty to direct temporal — including political — affairs, even though the areas of responsibility of Church and State eventually became clearly defined. Jurists and theologians were aware of the dangers of confounding the two, yet the State had, in the medieval scheme, to be subordinate to the Church since all must obey God's law and the Church was the interpreter of that law. The Church inevitably became not only more concerned with political issues, but more political in its own structure, with all the weaknesses of a political machine. Its statesmen and diplomats worked side by side with those of nations whose own officials were, more often than not, themselves churchmen. This fact at first helped to make both laws and administration more aware of true justice, and it also kept a check on greedy exploitation of the people, whether by kings and barons or by the great merchants. It restricted warfare, not only by laying down narrow limits for the waging of a "just war" but also by banning warfare on Sundays and holy days (at one point war was limited to a three-day week!) and by imposing duties towards the wounded and prisoners.

But these, and other achievements, did not prevent the evil that crept in, and turned the structure of the Church into a bureaucracy more concerned with its own wealth and prestige than with the Kingdom of God. The result was the falling apart of Christendom, and a sickness in the Catholic Church itself which took many centuries to cure.

Yet perhaps the enterprise was worth while all the same. For a while, men's and women's lives unfolded not only through the natural seasons but in each season were also caught up into the succession of the liturgical year. Medieval popular songs link spring and resurrection, the darkness of winter and the light of the new-born Saviour at Christmas. St. John's day was midsummer day; pagan and Christian symbols became indistinguishable. Harvest thanksgiving blended with the old fertility rites, and the Mother of Jesus presided over the gathering of the Earth Mother's plenty. Wild flowers acquired names of saints as well as of the ailment they helped to cure — St. John's Wort, Lady's Bed-straw, Star of Bethlehem, as well as Lungwort, Eye-bright and Pile-wort. The bells that called the monks to prayer called the labourers to the fields, and in the fields men bowed their heads, perhaps perfunctorily, at the sacring bell of the Mass, when God was made Bread again, heaven and earth joined inextricably. In the churches the judgement paintings warned horribly of likely damnation; yet the carvings of corbel, hammer beams and misericord were delicate, observant of man and beast, funny and sad, robust, awed, and sometimes extremely secular. The "doom" on the walls might proclaim a God of wrath, but the newer, gentle Mother and Child proclaimed a different message; and the taut crucified figure, bowed with grief for man's pain, was a God of compassion, and of hope for burdened people.

The music of the monks had sounded through centuries of war and misery. Side by side with the marvellous Gregorian chant came a newer music of harmonies and delicate decorations, echoed in the market place by the songs and dances (we call them "carols") which celebrated seasons, feasts, fairs, marriages and births and ghostly adventures.

Life was not all work, hard as it was, for there were saints days and feast days, markets and fairs, with dancing and feasting for all, and often a great deal of drinking. People went on pilgrimage, too, from every walk of life, leaving everydayness for strange places and adventures. The urge to wander which is now disapprovingly allowed to "irresponsible" young men (in the hope that they will "get it out of their system") was regarded as a laudable enterprise for medieval men and women of all ages. A surprising number left their homes and jobs to go on pilgrimage, sometimes for years.

Indeed, there was altogether more scope for eccentricity than we allow in our own time. Without becoming a social outcast one could be, for instance, a hermit and live alone in a remote hut, or belong to the guild of Beggars and never lift a finger and yet have "Union Benefits". One could travel ceaselessly all over Europe and never "settle down", and yet have a respected role as a "beadsman", collecting souvenirs from every major and minor shrine from Compostella to Walsingham. Those who preferred not to marry had plenty of scope, for not only was the celibate vocation respected, but a clerical status whose celibacy was purely nominal was common, and "scandal" was minimal. Indeed, sexual ethics were, in all classes, surprisingly uncertain and irregular from our point of view; when life was almost entirely public, except for the richest, little was hidden, and there was little room for squeamishness or prudery.

The medieval enterprise, exemplified especially in its twelfth century peak of hope and vitality, would be a misleading model if we saw only the aims and ideals, the glorious plan for a just, devout and intelligent society. We know many other things, some good, some bad, some tragic, some funny, in which the designers did not interest themselves. Yet the model gives us a frame of reference, a thing small enough, even in its exuberant richness, for us to see, quite easily, from our historical vantage point.

The very limitations of scientific and technical knowledge of the time make it easier for us to take hold of the central vision which inspired the developments which were made. The time-scale of twelfth century people was tiny compared to that of an age accustomed to concepts of geological time, and even to the "light years" of astronomy, which stretch our imagination beyond anything conceivable to the middle ages. Their "world" was manageable, imaginable, although strange, mysterious and dangerous. They lived easily with mystery, because so much was mysterious, whereas we are suspicious of the unknown and inclined to equate it with the non-existent. All this, which limited them in one way, liberated them in another, giving them the confidence to attempt to realise the great vision, unconfused. It is this "smallness" which is yet never parochial or narrow-minded, which makes it so helpful to us as a model. We can get an imaginative hold on the vision that inspired them, precisely because it had not, then, to grapple with the huge and sometimes monstrous growth of knowledge, sprouting uncontrollably in many unconnected areas of human experience. It is, therefore, a human situation in which the Catholic enterprise can be seen in operation, in a setting of nations with a strong cultural identity embracing all the diversity. Here are all the elements we shall be tracing later in this book, together, at this point, in an interaction which was soon to become impossible.

Here are the leaders and heroes on whom all depends. And here, as I shall explore in the next chapter, are the odd phenomena, the miracles and legends and obsessions. Here are the revolutionaries and political radicals seeking freedom and justice for the poor, here are the craftsmen and labourers who raised the great cathedrals, the pilgrims who thronged to look at them, the scholars and educators who made the universities places of such splendour. There have been many as great or as holy since, but never since have we been able to see the Catholic premise so clearly spelled out in a pattern of living. Even the "heretics" shared it; they merely thought they knew better ways to build on it. Even the scoundrels shared it; they acknowledged the demands they refused to accept. It seems to us, for instance, cynical or hypocritical to plan to devote ones' declining years to repentance and amendment after a life of violence in the pursuit of wealth, which was quite a common intention of medieval bad lots! It does at least show that dishonest businessmen or ruthless careerists were aware of having refused a real human option. It is, of course, much easier to take the modern way — to dismiss the option of righteousness as unreal.

Chapter 3
UNKNOWN FACTORS

When York Minster was being restored, the knowledgeable and experienced team had to admit that there were "unknown and perhaps unknowable" factors which vitally affected the structure and its restoration. If that is true of a Cathedral it is even more true of the subject of this book. This chapter is concerned with a few of these "unknown factors", and gathers together some strange and fascinating material which may appear, at first sight, to have little to connect one part with another. All of it may, indeed, be dismissed by some as not worth serious consideration as aspects of Catholicity. But then I expect the eminent archeologists and architects who were asked to work at York did not, when they began, consider seriously the factors which actual experience of the project forced them to recognize. It was certainly the influence of the unpredictable Sophia to which they were subjected. She obliged them to think some new and outrageous thoughts and this is certainly her chapter, but again it will be clear that she does not work alone, even here.

The "unknown factors" gathered here (and they are a tiny sample of a vast field) live on the frontiers of experience. They are not fully describable except in symbol and myth. Yet they are so thoroughly mixed with the facts of history and of everyday life that they cannot be disentangled. These factors play an immeasurably important part in human life, as can be shown in the experience of at least one modern man, who came up against a particular "area" (in several senses) of the operation of unknown factors, and who was, on the face of it, as unlikely a traveller in fairyland as any building technologist. This man was one of the many people who go through a large part of their lives quite contented with the satisfaction of family, career and friends but when they approach middle-life become inexplicably discontented. They may put it down to boredom with their marriage or their job, but changing this seldom removes the discontent for long. There is "something else" they need, some "unknown factor", which is essential to full human life, yet for which our culture makes no provision. Of course this sense of nameless need can come at any time and some people have it all their lives, or may have it in childhood and lose it later (for a time at least) but "midway this way of life we're bound upon" is the point at which many people first experience it urgently and painfully, as Dante did. He found himself, at that point in life, setting out on his exploration of hell, purgatory and heaven, the whole "inner world of human life" which opens upon eternity. And it was "midway this way of life" that the novelist John Steinbeck experienced it, too.

His experience is the starting point for this part of my book, because of the way in which he set out to find the thing he needed. An author noted for the realism of his novels, he was a son of the pragmatic U.S.A. He had long lost any awareness of "something else" in life besides material preoccupations, until the so-called "realities of life" became increasingly unsatisfying and even repulsive, and he was forced to look for an "unknown factor". He looked for it, although he did not realise this, in a thoroughly "Catholic" context — the myth, the ideals, even the place, are all Catholic.

Steinbeck reached this point at the height of his powers and success, or so it seemed to others, though not to himself. He wrote to a friend:

"Why this terror of being through, since everyone will inevitably be, one day? Is it a race against remaining time, and if so, is it well to race in an inferior machine? Is it an unadmitted passion for immortality? . . . Or is it the fumbling motions of a conditioned animal, the dunghill beetle, robbed of his egg, which ploddingly pushes a ball of fluff about simply because that is what dunghill beetles do?"

If he was "through", he wanted to know. But he thought he wasn't; he wanted a new direction, a new "Quest". He had been for some time becoming more and more absorbed in a project for re-presenting Malory's fourteenth century poems of the Arthurian legends, the "Morte d'Arthur", for modern readers, and his conviction that this myth was needed, by the public but primarily by himself, became a kind of faith, a single "lamp of hope" he could follow in the "dark wood" which he like Dante had entered. It led him to take a cottage in Somerset for ten months, ostensibly to do research on Malory in "Arthurian" country and in reach of the British Museum, but also because he needed to get away and "see" his life, and begin the new journey.

This intense need, hard to articulate and deeply disturbing, is a pointer to one of the "unknown factors" in human development which the Catholic thing has always known as something to be reckoned with, though often "Mother Church" has treated it with a certain wary distrust as an off-beat and "peculiar" manifestation. "Unknown factors" are disturbing to the orderly mind and dangerous at the best of times, and those forces in the Catholic enterprise which, especially since the seventeenth century, favour the well-lit, the rational, the comforting and explainable and tidy, have not been happy with the vast twilit realm of mysticism and miracle which borders so obviously on magic, superstition, fantasy and even madness. But not all non-heavenly experience is hellish, after all. There is a third road, as the Queen of Elfland told True Thomas:

"And see you not that bonny road which winds about the fernie brae?

That is the road to fair Elfland

Where you and I this night maun gae."

True Thomas came safely home, after seven years, as do many others.

Fortunately, even the most tidy-minded Catholic is prevented by the very doctrines of the Church from outlawing spiritual imponderables altogether. There are the New Testament miracles, which Catholic doctrine refuses to explain away entirely, and visions and revelations and dreams in Scripture, which make it hard to dismiss similar phenomena at other times and places without extreme illogicàlity and special pleading. Nobody *has* to believe in any visions or miracles outside of Scripture, as Catholic apologists were never tired of pointing out, but equally it would be "rash" to deny the possibility of them. And while the apologists apologise to the ghosts of rationalism, real people continue to experience "unknown factors" and to want to make sense of them, as John Steinbeck did.

It is no coincidence (unless coincidence is a word for one of the unknown factors) that Steinbeck's chosen place for "making his soul" was the geographical heart of the Arthurian myth. Before he left New York he wrote:

"I know that what I am looking for in Somerset I can find right here. . . But in the haunted fields of Cornwall, in the dunes and the living ghosts of things, I do wish to find a path or a symbol or an approach. . . My looking is not for a dead Arthur, but for one sleeping. If this does seem to be taking a trip to southernmost England very seriously it is so because it is much more than that to me. . . ."

And so he and his wife Elaine (one in name with Elaine, the Arthurian heroine) rented a cottage at Bruton in Somerset, and no doubt discovered that Cornwall and Somerset are not the same place, even if both are Arthurian regions.

"We have a cottage that was occupied at the time of Edward the Confessor and was old when it was listed in Doomsday Book",

he wrote to a friend, and to another:

"It is probable that it was the hut of a religious hermit. It's something to live in a house that has sheltered sixty generations. There is nothing in sight that hasn't been here since the sixth century. If ever there was a place to write the "Morte", this is it. Ten miles away is the Roman fort which is the traditional Camelot. We are right smack in the middle of Arthurian country."

To Elia Kazan he wrote most revealingly of all, in words that lead into the heart of the "factors which are unknown and may be unknowable", at least in the sense of not being fully explainable by reason alone.

"Two years ago I discovered that writing had become a habit with me. . . . My life had become dusty in my mouth. . . . And you remember that I stopped writing. . . . it was some of the hardest work I ever did, sitting still in a busy

95

world, aching for nothingness or the meaning that could only come out of non-participation. . . . I must go into figures of speech to try to explain. Externality is a mirror that reflects back to our mind the world our mind has created of the new materials. But a mirror is a piece of silvered glass. There is a back to it. If you scratch off the silvering, you can see through the mirror to the other worlds on the other side. I know that some people do not want to break through. I do, passionately, hungrily.

"And so I came here, to the hills near Glastonbury which has been a holy place since people first came to it maybe forty thousand years ago. . ."

Glastonbury is one of the holy places, and since in a book such as this I have to choose, I chose Glastonbury. I chose it not because it is "typical", since holy places are as idiosyncratic as holiness itself, but because, besides being a "classic" holy place, it is also linked to the legends of Arthur and the Grail, and this is important.

It is possible to discuss reasons for the existence of holy places, but when all the explanations are over there remains the fact. Some places have seemed, and still seem, to be meeting points between the worlds. Sometimes, perhaps, they become so by long association, like Compostella or Jerusalem or Mecca, though even then it may be that the obvious historical reasons for the location of a centre of pilgrimage have overlaid an earlier and different association. And sometimes, like Lourdes, a great spiritual experience transforms not only the person who first undergoes it but in their measure all those who follow, and in some way the place itself. But sometimes the origins of the sense of "specialness" go so far back that nobody knows how it all began, whether it was an event, or an experience, or something in the place itself that people came to recognise. All we do know is that, as Steinbeck said, "it has been a holy place since people first came to it", or at least as far back as any record takes us. Glastonbury is not just a medieval holy place, but one gradually and increasingly associated with the great Arthurian myth, which is the only complete and original myth to emerge from Western Christendom.

It is a Catholic myth, catholic also in that it contains elements of pagan mythology, not haphazard but completely integrated, and it is one whose appeal is universal, at least wherever western cultural experience is present. Glastonbury and Arthur have both undergone a re-discovery in this generation, providing a mythology for seekers of "alternative" ways of life. So it spans long centuries, not exactly as history, but as something "behind" history.

Glastonbury is in one sense not at all "unknown". You can visit it any time, and buy souvenirs, and visit the ruins of the Abbey which Henry VIII's men (notably the notorious Layton, an experienced dissolver of monasteries) visited about ten o'clock in the morning of September 19th, 1539. The last Abbot of Glastonbury was Richard Whiting, known until then as a generous and prudent rather than an heroic man. He was arrested and taken to London but he refused to surrender his Abbey to the King, as demanded. Meanwhile, the Abbey was searched and found to be full of splendid loot. The monks were evicted, but given a pension of five pounds a year, and the commissioners carried off portable valuables for the king. But the old Abbot was obstinate, so he had to be "removed", in a fashion very familiar to us in our own times. Thomas Cromwell, Henry's Lord Chancellor, noted with quite unconscious cynicism: "Item, the Abbot of Glastonbury to be tried at Glaston and also executed there with his complices". Whiting was "a very weak man and sickly" and in his eighties. He was taken back to Somerset, and tried in the Bishop's palace. Various local complaints were produced to back up vague charges of treason (unspecified) and of robbery — this one based on the fact that some of the Abbey treasures had been hidden from the commissioners! The old man was condemned as ordered, dragged on a hurdle through the town of Glastonbury, past his empty Abbey and up the steep slope of the strange smooth hill called Glastonbury Tor. There he and two other monks were hanged, cut down, and hacked into four pieces, as the law required.

This was not yet a usual fate for people who resisted the religious changes, and there were odd things about it. To put up a gallows on the steep, stony Tor was difficult and unnecessary. The town would have been the obvious place, and more people would have seen and been frightened by it.

But the Tor was symbolic, the Tor was a place of magic, the place of the old gods, the place of legend and vision. To execute the obstinate old man on the Tor was to punish, symbolically, the defiance of an intransigent spirit, the spirit of a place that would not surrender. And the spirit was the spirit of Arthur, who in time had come to symbolise the best of Catholic Christendom, but also a certain unclassifiable spirituality, as we shall see.

As far as anyone can tell or guess, Arthur was a British war leader, of a Romanised family, who successfully resisted the encroachment of the Saxons for some time, probably by the use of cavalry, which the Saxons did not have and which made Arthur and his men extremely mobile. A final victory at a place (not certainly identified) called Mount Badon, procured a long truce before the barbarians finally moved in and banished the British-Christian culture to Wales and legends. (By then, anyway, they were less barbarous and beginning to be Christianised).

The story of how Arthur, the war leader, gradually became "King Arthur" and acquired a round table and its famous knights is centuries long and involves historians, poets, a tomb in Glastonbury Abbey, and a whole crop of legends linking him with the old gods and with Celtic Christianity, and above all with the Grail. Although Arthur is a northern legend he was adopted all over Europe. There is a carving of Arthur in the Cathedral of Modena in Italy, and another at Otranto. Arthur belongs to the whole of the West.

There are two aspects of the Arthurian myth which are especially important in understanding the unknown factors which actually hold together the Catholic Christian experience, though they are hard to identify or quantify. One is the persistence of the myth in the subconscious mind of the West, and the other is the Grail, which links the myth and the world in which it grew to wider experience of what C.S. Lewis called "the deep magic from beyond the dawn of time". This is the realm of the great mystics, but also of their humbler kin, the people who have "second sight", gifts of healing or prophecy, or an awareness of the things that make plants and animals grow, and a sense of kinship with them. And there are also the visionaries, who are not necessarily mystics, and not necessarily saints, but who are part of the evidence for the factors which are, indeed, unknown in the sense that we can't fully understand or explain them, but which are very well known indeed in the sense that this dimension of life exists and is of major importance. The Catholic enterprise has been informed and accused through the centuries by this type of experience, which is essential to it, but which must never be allowed to usurp the place of faith or of reason.

In the summer of 1966, seven years after Steinbeck's stay in the neighborhood, a series of careful excavations began at Cadbury, twelve miles from Glastonbury. This was the hill which might be "Camelot" in the sense that it could have been the headquarters of Arthur, or at least of an "Arthur-type" war leader of the required date (late fifth and early sixth centuries). Five seasons of digging established that Cadbury had been such a headquarters, and that there were layers showing occupation from neolithic times onwards. The "Arthurian" finds were not the most numerous, nor were they spectacular. The claims of the organizers were modest and careful. But the surge of visitors and enquirers continued in unabated enthusiasm.

Geoffrey Ashe, whose long absorption in the whole Arthurian business did more than any other single influence to collate evidence about Glastonbury, was one of those concerned with the dig, and he gave his impression of these visitors and the questions raised by their presence, in a book called "Camelot and the Vision of Albion":

"South Cadbury Castle, to give the place its full name, is a hill fort of the iron age before the Roman conquest . . . .
Camelot, strictly so called, the Camelot of romance, has lost touch with history and geography. It is a symbol . . . but Cadbury Castle could have been the original Camelot in another sense, as the real Arthur's headquarters . . . Every public allusion to the Cadbury project brought in inquiries, contributions, orders for literature, offers to help —

dozens, hundreds of them from both sides of the Atlantic. Cadbury Castle is far from easy to climb, yet during each six-week season of excavation, over five thousand visitors climbed it . . . Thousands of excavation reports were sold to them, and also sent by mail . . . Why is there a ready-made public, young and old, for the cycle of legend which the middle ages called "the Matter of Britain", for Arthurian fiction, non-fiction, for Broadway musicals? Why do authors of Arthurian books receive so many readers' letters? Why is Glastonbury so disturbingly magical that most of those who touch it seem to go mad? Why the persistent feeling that the Arthurian shrine will be the scene of some vivid re-birth — a feeling which . . . today attracts the junior mystics of post-hippiedom? Why the persistent feeling that the return of Arthur himself — his awakening in the cave (under Cadbury hill) or his homecoming from Avalon — has a valid, if uncertain, meaning? . . . The spell is a fact. It has proved itself in terms of hard cash, hard work, and immense consequent benefits to the archeology of Britain. To call it a load of rubbish, a waste of time, is not to exorcise it but to make it a more intriguing riddle."

As we have seen, Steinbeck came under the spell, and so, earlier, did Bernard Shaw, and Laurence Housman. One of the greatest of modern poets, Charles Williams, spent a large part of his life studying the "Matter of Britain", and his Arthurian cycle of poems, "Taliessin through Logres" and "The Region of the Summer Stars" make him the latest in the great succession of poets who have found in the Arthurian myth the supreme and satisfying language to express their experience of the meaning of life.

Braving the risk (even certainty) of distortion, it seems to me that the conjunction of Glastonbury, Arthur, and all this enthusiasm indicates something important about the nature of the Catholic thing, as it comes down to us. This is that it exists, and must exist, on the borderland of two worlds. It must strive to include not only all the conscious areas of human life, personal and communal, but all the dark, peculiar, unexplained areas that open out into the totally "other" world in which even the mystics are merely temporary guests, yet which is, finally, the most important of all. Life in this borderland is paradoxical and off-beat, full of contradictions and dangers. In this frontier region the Catholic enterprise has to struggle to keep a balance, to exclude neither side, to give to neither the supreme control, for as long as mankind is "bodily", it must live fully in the body, but not only in the body. The body requires a location for its spiritual searching, and having found one of the frontier-posts between the worlds, such as Glastonbury, the place becomes, as it were, a secure base on which to build the delicate and transparent yet extremely tough structure of myth. Old Welsh gods and Christian hermits and saints have attached their names and legends to the place, and it is not always clear which is which, nor — in the case of real historical figures — whether they actually lived there or even visited it. In some cases it seems wildly unlikely that they should have come there, yet the clustering of illustrious names is proper to the place. They are all names associated with the "odd" parts of the Catholic thing.

St. Patrick, for instance, is improbably claimed as its first Abbot. He is, as everyone knows, the patron of Ireland. His connection with Glastonbury may have no historical basis but it has a valid imaginative one, for Glastonbury and Ireland are both part if the extraordinary Celtic Christian culture which shows us in a thousand years of history a kind of church-experience startlingly different from the Roman model to which we are accustomed, yet unquestionably Catholic in both the narrow and the broader sense. This Celtic Christianity was one that lived in strong consciousness of that indefinable "something else" in religion and life which is symbolised by Glastonbury. Patrick probably never set foot in that place, yet he is properly associated with it. He came from Western Britain (North or South is disputed) and was educated and ordained in France after his time as a kidnapped slave in Ireland. He took back to Ireland British Christianity and French theology and learning. Ireland became, thereafter, a centre of learning and of a form of Christian culture whose unique character has come down to us in poetry and legends, and in manuscripts decorated with formalised symbolic figures of saints and animals, as well as in historical records, letters, and treatises, all of which convey to us the special character of Celtic spirituality. Yeats, and other revivers of Irish national feeling, tried to work within this context, and the phrase "the Celtic twilight" is a mocking description of the cult of obscurity in legend and ambivalence in symbols cultivated by the nineteenth and early twentieth century Irish intellectuals and patriots. But just as twilight is the ambiguous and mysterious region between daylight and darkness, so the Celtic culture, in some aspects, was a Christianity of the region between the worlds.

This "feel" of the Celtic culture for us is partly due to our historical distance from it, and sheer lack of information. The teachers and students who made up the hundreds of "schools" which made Ireland a home of learning were not trying to be "Celtic" or different. They were full of curiosity, and were making use of classical and Christian texts, trying to make good sense of their European heritage, but doing it with minds shaped by the traditions of the great Druidic teachers of Britain. The Celtic imagination was much concerned with places — hills, rivers, woods and springs — in which dwelt spirits of greater and lesser power. In areas of Celtic culture these pagan gods and goddesses and lesser spirits and heroes were accommodated quite comfortably into Christian folk-lore, unlike continental paganism which was feared and persecuted by the Church. But Western Britain was a long way from Rome, where the stark opposition between pagan and Christian, in terms of sheer survival, had made hatred and incomprehension inevitable. The especial Celtic religious sense has given us a link between the everyday world and the "unknown factors" — a link which has endured and come down to us as an essential part of the Catholic enterprise.

It did not live only on the shadowy side of the border. Its practical achievements were great and unique. They were unique because Celtic Christianity was a "system" that was never systematised but managed to be extremely efficient. It was a church without dioceses. Its centres were created by monks in search of learning and holiness, and around them Christians clustered, wanting education and religion. These monks, it must be said, were *laymen*, though they included men ordained to serve the community. This was predominantly a church of the laity. It was a church that was flexible, devoted, and produced saints and scholars as a meadow grows daisies. It was a person-centred church, growing around heroes and heroines, saints and sages, rather than within the pre-planned jurisdiction of a man chosen for the job by a central authority.

Celtic Christianity, as a Church and a style of thought and life, is being re-discovered in recent years, when the passion for uniformity, which a defensive post-Reformation church encouraged, has ceased to be necessary or sensible. The variety of local Christian cultures is newly recognised, still somewhat reluctantly in Rome, but then Rome is not the Church and — to its chagrin — never was. The new vernacular liturgy has encouraged people to delve into older local liturgical and religious customs, not smiling at them as quaintly primitive but appreciating their special local and national quality, sometimes with envy. The study of the Celtic world is suddenly fashionable and good paper-backs appear in book stores presenting the Great Celtic acheivement in poetry, story, art, mysticism and myth. History and archeology and literary criticism have their contribution to make, as well as religion and magic.

One special quality of Celtic culture was its delight in adventure. There was plenty of quite literal adventuring, for the Celts were enthusiastic explorers. Their pagan gods and heroes were travel addicts, as well as warriors, and the Christian saints who took over from them (sometimes acquiring their legends as well) were equally adventurous. By the seventh century, Celtic Christianity was essentially monastic in character; bishops were important and respected, needed to confirm and ordain, but Abbots, who were sometimes also bishops, and monks were the cultural, administrative and often political shapers of Christian and indeed all local life. And these monks were not Benedictines, stable and community-minded, but individualistic, even eccentric, full of curiosity about everything under the sun (or the moon) and extremely mobile. They lived, not in great buildings but in clusters of huts around a small church, and their lives were rigorous but flexible, and full of irrepressible delight in learning and craft and beauty.

They travelled both in fact and fiction. They travelled the country, preaching and teaching, but typically they travelled across the seas.

They had brought their kind of monastic life to Northern Europe most probably returning by ships from the Eastern Mediterranean, along with pottery and pilgrims from the Holy Land, so they were spiritually linked to the older, looser and very ascetic tradition of the "desert Fathers", from Asia Minor, Cyrenia and Egypt.

Their first monastery may have been Tintagel in Cornwall, and Cornwall is one of the great Celtic nations as well as one of the great "Arthurian regions". From there they moved to found monasteries in South Wales and then north, and thence to Ireland. By the early sixth century they had reached central and southern Ireland, in some cases by the same sea-routes as the earlier Cornish landings, but mostly from Wales. They did not stop there, either. The northern Irish aristocratic monk, Columba, sailed to an existing Irish colony in Argyll, on the West coast of Scotland, and an older Christian diocese, Whithorn in Galloway, was already a centre of Celtic monastic life. From there, they may have gone to the Isle of Man between Ireland and England. Northwards they went still, to Wester Ross in the far north-west, and on to the Orkney and Shetland Islands, out in the northern seas beyond the Scottish mainland. Meanwhile, in the South, the Cornish monks travelled across the sea to Armorica, now Brittany, where considerable British settlements already existed. The Breton culture is also one of the great Celtic ones, and seems to have sent offshoots even into Spain.

A Northumbrian prince called Oswald had been exiled to Scotland by the fortunes of the frequent wars between the kingdoms of Britain. He found himself in a Christian area where he learned Irish and Christianity. When he returned he brought St. Aidan from the monastery of Iona (off the coast of Argyll) back to Northumbria, to the Holy Island called Lindisfarne, off the east coast, and Celtic monasticism spread to form the other great monasteries of Northumbria (Melrose, Whitby, Jarrow, are only a few) and from these moved on to other kingdoms of Mercia, East Anglia and Wessex. These monasteries were centres for preaching and converting the remaining pagan Saxons, and they followed up this effort as far as the homelands of the (now well settled) invaders of Britain, travelling to Frisia, the Low Countries and many parts of Germany. Irish monastic foundations were made further and further south, in what is now Switzerland, and into Italy.

It was a formidable achievement, and it meant that the distinctively Celtic type of spirituality fed into the main streams of European culture, and the nations and cultures which absorbed it later contributed to the making of America. Although the great Benedictine and Roman type of Catholicism finally absorbed them and now dominates our imaginative view of Catholic cultural origins (because of its achitecture, its music and its continued presence) the lost Celtic Catholicism was uniquely important in its embracing quality, its feeling for the presence of the divine in natural beauty and in the unexpected, its single-minded devotion to the quest for God, and its sheer wealth of symbol and fantasy.

If the Celtic influence spread widely, it died out fairly soon in its far-flung homes, as the better organised and more explicitly formed Roman Catholicism became established. It survived longest in its North-western homes, in Brittany, Cornwall, Wales, Ireland and the Western Islands. The Celtic languages of Cornwall and the Isle of Man have now virtually died out. Scottish Gaelic survives strongly as a language, but as a culture has lost a sense of its origins. The language of Brittany is Celtic and so is much of its (still Catholic) folk culture and sense of nationhood. In Wales the language is alive and growing, and with it the heritage of poetry and song is preserved and loved and still grows. But Catholicism died out of Wales, for the Methodist Chapel culture, splendid as it was in many ways, distrusted its predecessor and all works of the fairies and the old heroes.

Even in Ireland, most proudly and self-consciously Celtic of all, the language has to be supported by law and the past promoted with festivals and grants. The culture itself has gone, except in remote areas and in a few tales. It can be recovered now in any of its old homes only in books and archeological sites.

There is no longer a Celtic type of monastery anywhere — and yet, it lives.

It lives in the stories, and the poems, whose themes became wound up with the Arthurian themes, for Glastonbury was a Celtic foundation first of all. It lives in the special quality of northern European poetry, which is haunted by inhabitants of the borderland world, talking animals, wood and water spirits, magicians and enchanted flowers. The passion for travel whose results I have sketchily traced in history was a constant theme of legend and poetry too. The monks who travelled across rough seas (in little boats most people would hesitate to use to cross a pond) to Iona or Armorica travelled in stories to even more remote places. The legend of the voyage of St. Brendan follows a pattern that links it with earlier, pagan legends of the hero Bran who travelled to a blessed Island, a sort of Paradise. Brendan really existed. In the sixth century he founded monasteries in Ireland and he was indeed an adventurous sailor, to Iona and probably to other places. But the legend takes him to explore the Atlantic ocean, searching for the "Land Promised to the Saints". In the story (there are several literary versions) he finds this wonderful land, but God tells him to return home. This earthly Paradise, full of fruit trees (which some think may actually have been America) is discovered by passing through a great bank of fog, recalling the "dark night" of mystical "ignorance" through which the searcher for God must pass. And like the mystics, the seer of bliss must return to his brethren.

This desire to explore and travel, physically and spiritually, gave some of its character to the tales of knightly adventure and questing, as we shall see. But these tough, dedicated men were part of a culture whose religious sense was remarkable for its human tenderness, and its delicate love of natural beauty and all living things. A lovely story from the life of Bridget, or Bride, of Kildare gives some of this atmosphere. St. Bride was foundress and Abbess of a double monastery of men and women. One of Bride's nuns, Dara, was blind, and one evening Bride and Dara sat beside the lake, talking of the beauty of God's world and of his other world of Heaven. They talked on into the night, not noticing the passing hours, until the dawn began to appear above the hills. Bride, full of awe at the beauty of the dawn-lit fields and hills, longed for her friend to share the wonder of God's beautiful works, and as the sun rose she laid her hands on Dara's eyes and prayed. The light of the rising sun dawned also in Dara's eyes, and she opened them and saw the light of morning on grass, on flowers, on lake and hillside. She looked and looked with joy and gratitude, and then she turned to Bride and said "Mother, close my eyes once more. I was content to love God in my darkness, and I am content to remain there with him." So Bride laid her hands once more on the eyes of Dara, and prayed, and the light died out of them, and the two friends went back to the monastery, talking of the beauty of God.

Again, from an unknown Irish author of the twelfth century comes this evocation of Columba in his hermitage on an island, with its typical blend of love of natural beauty, sorrow for sin and adoration of God:

"Delightful I think it to be on the bosom of an isle, on the peak of a rock, that I might often see the calm of the sea.

That I might see its heavy waves over the glittering ocean, as they chant a melody to their Father on their eternal course.

That I might see its smooth strand of clear headlands, no gloomy thing; that I might hear the voice of the wondrous birds, a joyful tune. . .

That contrition of heart should come upon me as I watch it, that I might bewail my many sins, difficult to declare.

That I might bless the Lord who has power over all Heaven with its pure host of angels, earth, ebb, flood-tide.

That I might pore on one of my books, good for my soul; awhile kneeling for beloved heaven, awhile at psalms.

Awhile gathering dulse from the rock, awhile fishing, awhile giving food to the poor, awhile in my cell."

There is also the tenth century Irish writer who wanted "to have a great ale-feast for the King of Kings", and the ninth century tale of St. Ide, who wished to have Jesus in the form of a baby, to hold to her breast; he came to her, and she sang, "Little Jesus, who is nursed by me in my hermitage — even a priest with a store of wealth, all is false but little Jesus. . . Sons of princes, sons of kings, though they come to my land, not from them do I expect any good, I prefer little Jesus".

And an undateable Gaelic folk prayer calls on Jesus and his mother:

"Virgin of ringlets most excellent, Mary, mother of miracles, help us, help us with thy strength; bless the food, bless the board, bless the ear, the corn and the victuals. The Virgin most excellent of face, Jesus more surpassing white than the snow. She like the moon over the hills, he like the sun on the peaks of the mountains."

It seems strange that this passion for natural beauty, this earthy yet ascetic spirituality, should have found artistic expression in entirely non-naturalistic art. While the poetry is full of reference to natural beauty, the intricate patterns in illuminated Gospels, in metalwork and stone carving, are made up of elaborately intertwined "strap work", coils within coils, where fabulous birds and animals crawl, never seen on earth. The occasional angelic or human form is drawn with the same convention, with hair like metalwork coils, robes making part of the restless pattern in muted colour. Perhaps the strangeness of a visible world in which God was as near as the sparkle of the sun on the wave top could only be expressed in these charged and vibrant patterns and strange beasts, linked to the older symbols of pagan worship, yet in their spareness and uncompromising clarity expressing the unworldly and aspiring thrust of Christian Celtic adventure, which must be hindered by no earthly thing.

This Celtic Christian culture could not, in the end, compete with the expanding Roman kind. It lacked, finally, either the strength of enduring organisation or the imagination of the great men and women who gave it life in its earlier days; but its power lives beyond its historical lifespan. The well-organised church system of southern Catholicism flourished because it was needed, as it was not in Celtic lands, to bring peace and order to powerful and warring nations. It prevailed because it established a network of consistent moral and legal and religious influence — clear, strong and reliable. This Europe needed. In the end, it discredited itself by clinging to a power-system no longer needed, and it may be that in our time — odd as it seems — the decentralised, person-centered, community-minded and non-territorial type of Church makes some sense once more.

Although as a way of life Celtic Christianity died out utterly it is still available to us, in our need, as the legendary Arthur is supposed to be ready, at his people's need, to return from his sleep under the hill and lead them to peace and prosperity. For our most vital link with that lost Celtic past is formed by the Arthurian legends which never died out, but continued to grow and put out fresh shoots of story. And at the root of the legend is Glastonbury.

The attachment of Patrick's name and spiritual prestige to Glastonbury was, as we have seen, "natural". When the glory had departed from Ireland, and the whole of England and Wales had come under a unified ecclesiastical system centred on Canterbury, Glastonbury still preserved the mysterious prestige of the Celtic church, for Glastonbury was the border between the Roman and the Celtic, the meeting of two worlds.

Where those two worlds met was Arthur. The Victorian debunkers of medieval records attributed the whole Arthur-Glastonbury link-up to monkish cunning, to the creation of a money-spinning centre of pilgrimage from some dubious bones and tatty legends adapted for the purpose. But more recent research has put together a corpus of evidence, none of which is conclusive in its separate parts but which, taken whole, points to a centuries-long acknowledgement of the significance of Glastonbury. It had in fact a special prestige and character, distinct from the other great ecclesiastical centres, and was definitely the locus of "the Matter of Britain". This "Matter" was important to English Kings. It reflected an indirect glory on royalty so they could somehow claim to be doing what Arthur did, by trying to create an "ideal commonwealth" of honour and truth like Arthur's Camelot. In claiming this as their aim they were claiming to do the Catholic thing, trying to discover the varied realities of human life — social and political and mystical as well — as expressions of the eternal kingdom.

Thus, Glastonbury was the place where the essential spirit of Celtic Christiantity was somehow felt to reside. And there the Celtic Briton, Arthur, was located — certainly in spirit, probably also in fact. Avalon, the mysterious place of his refuge and "sleeping" after his last battle, has been associated with

Glastonbury, but it may also have been his real burial place. He was a British Christian, and Glastonbury was the monastery he knew and respected (though he doesn't seem, from the scant hints, to have been at all saintly or even very pious). It would have been natural enough to take the dying warrior to the mighty shrine of Mary, and historians are no longer so scornful as they once were of the medieval monks' claim to have found his tomb there. But we can never know for certain. Wherever his body lies, and whoever this Arthur really was, his significance endures and is real, for Arthur is the embodiment of one aspect of the Catholic enterprise. He and his court and his knights and the Quest for the Grail form the myth which best expresses the longing and hope for a perfect Kingdom, the City of God among men.

The longing for the return of a Golden Age is typified by faith in the Sleeping of Arthur, to return at his people's need. It is a secular image of the faith in the Second Coming and its whole shape and detail express a sacramental view of human society, whereby the King not only serves but *is* the people, and his failure is their failure. The gathering of the Round Table, the adventures, the intrigues, express in symbolic language the human and Christian struggle to live with integrity on earth in the sight of heaven, even though it is a very vulnerable and brief achievement, flawed at its heart by pride and passion. It can be done, say all the Arthurian poets in their various ways; there can be a human city which is worthy of its heavenly archetype. But the poets know that it will fail, the King will be betrayed and will die — and yet not finally. There is no absolute end; the hope endures.

The Arthurian myth is a Catholic myth, not only in the obvious religious sense but in the sense that it only finds its meaning in the sacramental and integral terms of Catholic theology. Glastonbury and Arthur are the rendezvous for the Catholic enterprise at the very limit of conscious articulation.

The central symbol is the Grail, though the Grail only became linked to the Arthurian theme at a comparatively late stage in its development, in the poem by Chretien de Troyes called "Le Conte du Graal" written at the end of the twelfth century. Chretien died before finishing the poem; others finished it, extending not only the poem but the symbolism, so that the Grail became what Charles Williams called "the grand material object of Christian myth". About the same time another poet, Robert de Boron, used the subject in three separate poems, called "Joseph of Arimathea", "Merlin", and "Perceval" though the last is lost and only a prose version remains.

The reasons for the emergence of the theme at this point in history were two. One was the crusades, that immense and ambivalent enthusiasm for the liberation of the Holy Places from the Saracens. It is hard for us, now, to sympathise with this enthusiasm, knowing as we do how many horrors of greed and fanaticism it let loose. But there was a genuine horror in Christian minds at the idea of the scenes of Christ's life — and especially of his death — being in the hands of people whose religion did not acknowledge him as Son of God. The actual experience of the crusades taught many knights to respect the Saracens and their religion, but to the people at home they were the enemies of Christ.

The second reason has to do with the sacramental sense, the perception of the divine as inherent and verifiable in material things. This is something most of us have lost, but to the twelfth century it was an everyday and vital experience. The lively discussions (not only among theologians and clerics but among many educated layfolk) about the precise nature of Christ's presence in the Eucharist contributed to the emergence of the Grail theme. To the twelfth century it was not a technical point but one of fundamental human importance since it concerned *the* point of contact between the worlds. It was, therefore, a matter of daily importance, the exact place where the "unknown factors" of life touched the known and everyday, for although the almost superstitious respect often accorded to the Sacrament made the receiving of communion a rare event, the thing was *seen*, daily or at least frequently, and this sight was valued. The custom of elevating the host and chalice for the veneration of the faithful was the outcome of this hunger for the most precise visible sign of God's presence among men.

This lively concern for the material signs of Christ motivated the enthusiasm for the crusades and the enthusiasm for discussion about the Sacrament of the altar. The symbol that supremely expressed both these enthusiasms was the Chalice of the Last Supper, the very Cup which Christ handled and in which he consecrated wine to become his Blood, on the night before he died.

The Chalice is not a purely Christian symbol. The sacred or magical vessel is a recurring theme in myths and fairy-tales, and a thing called a Grail or Graal, a cauldron of plenty or a magic dish, is frequent in Celtic legends. A thing called a Graal, not a Cup at all but some sort of holy touchstone, occurs in Chretien's "Conte du Graal". This is the link between "old" Grails and the specifically Christian Cup which soon took over and eclipsed the others. It was bound to do so because it was a more inclusive, more catholic symbol; it referred to the feeding of the whole human thing, to the touching of worlds. It could be both a magical source of delicious food and the locus of ultimate visionary enlightenment. Its imaginative power was so much greater than that of any Celtic cauldron that poets (who are primarily poets, not anthropologists) no longer needed its precursors. As Williams says:

". . . the poetic inventiveness of Europe found itself presented with the image of a vessel much more satisfying to it — merely as an image — than any other. There is no need to suppose the poets and romancers were particularly devout; it is only necessary to suppose that they were real poets and real romancers."

The power of the Grail symbol has not failed since that time, though in the last century it came near to being romanticised out of existence and it also became, in Tennyson, more of a private and personal spiritual experience, exclusively for the pure and innocent. It ceased to be an experience of community, a uniting symbol, just as, at that time, all piety became very much a matter of personal search for God in domestic or conventual privacy. The pre-Raphaelite painters found in the Arthurian legends, especially those connected with the Grail, a powerful imaginative stimulus, a new language of the spirit, more vital than that of established religion, as we shall see in a later chapter. But this was a pale, over-refined version of the central symbol of medieval sprirituality.

For the Grail and the Passion of Christ were inextricably bound together and to them was linked the figure of Mary, Mother of God. The Cup of the Last Supper was the Chalice of Christ's sacramental Blood, but also, so a later legend said, that cup had been used to catch blood from the side of the dying Christ, and this priceless object had been magically preserved by Joseph of Arimathea. Joseph had escaped from persecution in the Holy Land and travelled across the sea, bearing the Hallows — the Cup, and also the Lance that had pierced Christ's side as he hung dead on the cross. Joseph, it was said, came to Britain and to Glastonbury, and built there a chapel dedicated to the Mother of God.

The Passion, the Grail, Mary — there is this connection and sequence all through. These three are at the core of Catholic spirituality from that time on. In the early thirteenth century, the anonymous writer of an Arthurian tale called "Perlesvaux" gives an account of Arthur, in which (it is the only time) the King himself encounters the Grail when he is out on a quest to restore his faded glory. He comes to a hermitage where, though he is not allowed to enter, he witnesses through the door the celebration of the Eucharist. He sees "a Lady so fair that all the beauties of the world might not compare with her beauty" and as the Mass begins and the hermit, purified by the opening "confiteor" of repentance, approaches the altar, the Lady takes on her lap "the fairest Child that ever was seen" and kisses him, calling him "my Father, and my Son and my Lord". When the hermit reads the Gospel the Lady takes her Son and offers him into the hands of the hermit, who sets Him on the altar. And as the Sacrament proceeds the King sees that the hermit is holding not a child but "a man bleeding from his side and his palms and his feet, and crowned with thorns", and "the King hath pity of him in his heart". But at the end the figure of the dying man becomes once more the Child, and He takes his Mother by the hand, and both vanish.

There are too many tales to quote or even to list. It is clear, both implicitly and explicity, that the vessel called the Grail was, in some sense, Mary, the vessel of grace, the God-bearer, and that the Passion of her Son, as well as his Incarnation, is presented through her (as woman and vessel) to the believer. But the meaning of the Grail is not simply the Christian Eucharist. The Eucharist is "every day" as well as high mystery, and the Quest for the Grail is a hard and problematic search in which only a few are successful, though all are affected. The Grail, in fact, is the symbol of the deeper, mystical experience of the divine which comes to only a few, yet is essential to the spiritual health of the whole enterprise. It is "contained" in the human body, it cannot exist in a disembodied world, it must be sacramentally conveyed to others. "Contemplata aliis tradere" is the Catholic motto: the unspeakable things must, somehow, be shared with others, as Mary had to give her Son, mysteriously and silently conceived, to the struggle and agony of bodily life and death. It cannot remain within. The Grail must be communicated. The shape of the Cup in Catholic iconography means both Body and Blood, for the container of the holy Bread is also cup-shaped. It is the holy Food, which is Christ, suffering and risen, presented to mankind by the "chosen vessel", Mary — herself, as Dante says in the last canto of the Paradiso:

". . . She by whom our human nature
Was so ennobled that it might become
The Creator to create Himself His creature."

The integrity of divine and human expressed in the body of Mary shows the need for the soul, seeking divine vision, to come to it through this ultimate humanness.

The Grail symbol, therefore, indicates the essential quality of Catholic mysticism. It may soar to the heights of heaven, but if it is real it will find there the transformed human thing, as Dante perceived, a "fourth", a human figure in the heart of the Trinity itself. This is the stumbling block for many people, who find Catholic spirituality altogether too "earthy" and can tolerate a Christ-centred spirituality only as an inferior stepping-stone to a higher, totally incorporeal experience. Many modern Christians turn rather to Buddhist forms of spirituality, for they can conceive of spiritual growth only in terms of *transcending* the body, while the Catholic tradition conceives of a divinely *transformed* body.

To many Christians the possibility of a physical experience of the risen Christ seems not so much logically or scientifically impossible as imaginatively inconceivable in the terms available for thinking about the possibilities of human experience. The re-interpretation of the gospel account of resurrection appearances takes the inconceivableness as its starting point, and one theologian recently expressed a fear that some of these texts encouraged a "crudely materialistic Easter faith". But the fact is that human beings are, in part, "crudely material" and it is at this point, in this inescapably material framework, that God has to touch people, or not at all. The "crudely materialistic" imagination of Catholic Christianity has always shocked people, and it can be very repulsive; but at least it reckons with reality, and it is because of this unrepentant earthiness that there is the possibility in the Catholic tradition of keeping an unbroken chain from everyday experience, through the "off-beat" and peculiar, or "psychic" experience, to mystical visions and finally to image-less mystical experience. These can live together as aspects of a total reality and be the healthier for so doing. There is always considerable danger of exaggerating one or the other at the expense of the rest, and to pick one as the only "real" life is to impoverish life dangerously, and sometimes to render it completely insane. But so long as a proper proportion is preserved, none are ruled out of human growth and some normally co-exist in the same individual, though for one person to experience all four stages is extremely unusual. (St. Francis of Assisi was one such exceptional person).

The point of the Arthurian myth and its later (but finally inextricable) connection with the Grail is that this is a myth which grew out of, and therefore expresses, the Catholic experience of spiritual development. Only certain people see the Grail, yet their attainment of it depends on their membership in a whole group. Arthur's Knights are in themselves a "church", containing many functions and many degrees of goodness, but in which all are dedicated to the common good and support each other in the Quest, so that those who cannot themselves achieve the Grail may yet somehow share in that achievement. The King is not among the holiest — in fact in the development of the myth his is a flawed character — yet his office is essential to the whole. Guinevere, his Queen, betrays him with Lancelot, his best friend, so there is sin at the heart of the commonwealth; yet this illicit passion has its own honesty and power. It "belongs", and though Guinevere is childless, Lancelot's son, begotten on Elayne in enchanted mistake for the Queen, is what Williams calls the "alchemical infant", the innocent one who can transform the base elements of his origins, and so come to behold the Grail. In a Church of very mixed human beings, the myth is saying, a Church where there is self-deceit, weakness, disordered feeling and thinking and self-love even at the heart of religious consciousness, there is always the possibility of the highest holiness, so long as the doctrine is "true and honourable", and so long as the "City" is not split up.

In the end of the story, of course, the City *is* broken up by attack from outside, yet Arthur is not dead; the City sleeps, and can be awakened. And the Grail, though withdrawn, is not destroyed. It can still be sought, it will, somehow, return to those brief "Camelots" which are made. Logres, the land on the frontiers of the other world, becomes merely Britain, the land of this world, yet Logres still "dwells" in it. The myth of Arthur and the Grail is the myth of Catholicism which is always trying to create a Camelot that will not be rent by sin, but can only fail and try again, and then fail, but never give up because the achievement of the Grail is certain, in the end.

There is another strand in this European awareness of the unknown factors in life, and it is closely woven into the Arthurian motif, though distinct from it. This is the Romance tradition, the carefully developed ethos of courtesy, of chivalry, of devotion to the sovereign Lady, which grew up so rapidly all over Europe. It was spread by the troubadours of Provence and the German Minnesingers, but it centred on the court of Champagne, where Mary, Countess of Champagne, daughter of Eleanore of Aquitaine and of Louis VII, presided over the half-serious games of the Courts of Love, in which the detailed and demanding "morality" of the code of chivalry was elaborated. This aspect of Western culture is, in fact, so familiar to us in its surviving forms that it doesn't seem at all strange to us. To a Chinese or a Navaho, for instance, it must seem very strange indeed. It is one case (and we shall discover more of them) in which the failure of the Catholic enterprise in its "Mother Church" guise drove men and women to explore for themselves, with the help of Sophia, some area of human experience which matters. The area of human sexuality has always been one of conflict for Christians, because it is so ambivalent. The "straight" medieval-Christian approach was a severely practical one, concentrating on the need for children and the mutual support of man and wife. It could be, and often was, leavened by tenderness and supported by laws designed to protect the rights of the poor and weak, but erotic pleasure in marriage was normally regarded as simply a delightful and legitimate compensation for the burdens of domesticity. Extra-marital sexuality flourished, of course. It was not harshly condemned by public opinion; it was even frequently accepted. But it lived in a kind of moral limbo, from which a person could emerge, with luck, in time to seek forgiveness and settle down, or at least die, in a proper state to face divine judgement. This meant that all speculation about erotic emotion, its meaning and nature, took place outside any kind of Christian framework. Yet it was the growing consciousness of Christian theology that human love must certainly be a mode of divine presence which made people explore this particular kind of human love more and more. It was not just sexual desire they were talking about, but sexual love — the intense desire of one person for another person, beyond any physical satisfaction. It has inescapably obvious links with such religious experience as conversion, and even with mystical illumination. It is a transforming experience. And if the official Christian framework could not provide a place and a language in which to explore and discuss this vital subject, then discussion had to go on somewhere else.

But the somewhere else where it did, in fact, go on, was not really outside the Catholic thing at all. It found a place to develop in that particular corner of Catholic experience in which it would naturally be at home, that is in the border-line area, the area of the not quite earthly and not quite heavenly, the realm of

117

Arthur and the Celtic twilight generally.

The links are cultural, geographical and apparently acciden-tal, but only apparently. The thing had to emerge somewhere; it could not be suppressed. There was an odd convergence of ap-propriate people at a suitable time and place.

Mary of Champagne was the grand-daughter, on her mother's side, of William of Poitiers, who had taken under his protection the minstrel Bledry, teller of Celtic tales. She in-herited both a taste for courtly love in all its elaborations, and a fund of Celtic poetry and legend, including the Arthurian ones. Philip, son of the Count of Flanders, came to seek the hand of the Countess in marriage, and Philip's father, Thierry d'Alsace, had himself brought back from the Holy Land a phial, so it was said, of the precious Blood of Jesus which, according to the apocryphal gospel of Nicodemus, Joseph of Arimathea had caught from the side of the dead Christ, receiving it in the Paschal dish from which the Lord had eaten the Passover. Philip brought with him to the court of Champagne a book, in prose, which he gave to the poet, Chretien de Troyes, suggesting that he put it into verse. The result of this was "Le Conte du Graal", the poem which gave distinctive form to many hints and legends of the Grail and intergrated it firmly into the Arthurian stories. But it did more than this. It cast the whole "Arthurian" myth in chivalric form and made it express the ideals of courtly love as well as of religious aspiration. "Le Conte du Graal" is a French Romance work.

The Romance culture was itself a strange mixture, and it is an important part of the cultural development of the Catholic enterprise. It is exclusively Western, and shaped by a Catholic pattern of thought even when it openly rejected the Church's teaching on marriage. That it did become so inextricably Catholic was not a foregone conclusion. Denis de Rougemont in his "Passion and Society" and "The Myth of Love" has traced links with Islamic poetry and spirituality, though it is hard to say whether the Romance movement grew from such contacts or simply produced similar ideas for similar social reasons. The fact remains that the Romance tradition took root and flourish-ed in Catholic Europe, and not in Islam. De Rougemont makes a more convincing connection between the Romance "religion" (for it became one, in all but name) and the Catharist heresy, and certainly there was a great deal of cross-fertilization, though again it is hard to maintain a definite sequence of cause and effect.

There are obvious and important similarities. Both movements arose from a disillusionment with the increasing worldliness of the Church structure and of churchmen. Religious feeling, for instance in the crusades, was being used as a political weapon. Warrior-bishops with little or no faith fought each other for lands and wealth. Monastic abuses were so great that they led to the reform at Citeaux, and later to the Franciscan movement.

Although the twelfth century ferment was at its height, or rather *because* it was at its height, men and women felt a longing for the "otherness" which the Church provoked but, as the thirteenth century dawned, increasingly did not satisfy. The crusades themselves were symptoms of this, deformed as they soon became, and the Catharist and other sects as well as the "orthodox" asceticism of St. Bernard and his followers, and the whole Romance movement, were the expression of the longing for a purer, more interior kind of spirituality. The Cathari (the word means "perfect") seized on a Manichaean type of theology, which opposed the principles of Light and Darkness — regarded as equal and at war — and consigned all bodily experience to the realm of darkness. The inner circle of the Perfect were vegetarian, they fasted frequently, and were strictly celibate. Sex, and more especially procreation which produced more flesh-bound individuals, was a work of darkness, preventing the release of the Spirit — the principle of Light — from the evil material principle. Their lives were in many ways beautiful. They lived poorly, gave alms generously and served one another devotedly. Their only sacrament was the "Consolamentum" which made a person one of the "Perfect". It was often postponed to the time of death, and signified the release of the spirit from all earthly and bodily bonds. Some undertook the "endura", a fast to death, in order to achieve final liberation all the sooner. This movement, with its unworldly purity and unmaterial love, offered a strong contrast to the less attractive aspects of a politically-minded church. It emphasised, as did many smaller sects, the primacy of an ecstatic and totally spontaneous experience of spiritual liberation. This freedom of the Perfect made unnecessary for them the codes of morality needed by more earth-bound mortals. They also refused belief in the presence of Christ in the Eucharist, for this implied that a material thing could be holy.

The Romance movement also sought spiritual liberation through ecstatic experience, but this experience was that of sexual passion — though mostly of unconsummated passion. It is not clear that the aristocratic disciples of courtly love foreswore sex, but at the heart of it was the cultivation of a single-minded and passionate service of the chosen Lady, who might reward her faithful servant by a chaste kiss, and even in some cases spend the night with him, but often without intercourse. It was the passion that transformed, giving a kind of sacramental significance to the relationship. Legal marriage was irrelevant; the Lady was never the wife of her knight, and in fact was often someone else's wife. The union of the flesh was obtained, after trials in the Lady's service, though there were different schools of thought about this. It was the *emotion* that mattered. It was expressed and developed through appropriate forms of asceticism, by "penance" for faults against the service of love, and by songs and poetry. The whole strange ethical system of Romance spread over Europe, at least among the cultured few. It endured for many centuries in the form of the rules of knighthood and later in the concept of the qualities proper to a "gentleman". The elaborate courtesy which, until quite recently, well brought up boys were taught to show to a woman, and the whole concept of "honour" in older schools and colleges, stems directly from the codes of chivalry of the Romance era.

The whole Arthur-Grail-Celtic culture-Romance-Mysticism relationship is strange and yet close. Just as the Court of Champagne was the place where the Arthurian myth and chivalric Romance met and fused, so Glastonbury was the place where the unique Celtic spirituality, with its passion for adventure and discovery, its intense fantasy and symbolism, encountered the

Roman tradition of ordered richness in law, ritual and religious sensibility. The four together found an expression in the Arthurian legends, and when the symbol of the Grail itself finally emerged as the focus of the whole thing (it was the lesser poet, Robert de Boron — protegee of Henry II of England and much involved with Glastonbury — to whom we owe that emergence) we find in this single symbol, in its Arthurian context, the potent and sufficient touchstone of emerging Catholic spirituality.

For the Grail is material. It is mysterious, surrounded by unanswered questions, magical and capricious in its appearances, yet it is a material object, from which the favoured are to be fed. In its presence, ordinary but more than usually delicious food appears on the plates of the assembled knights. It brings healing to physical illness. It is not identifiable with the Eucharistic vessel alone, though some commentators have suggested this. The Eucharistic reference is clear, but there is more to it than that: Geoffrey Ashe had plausibly suggested that it is concerned with the whole concept of incarnation, and closely linked, therefore, to the body and person of Mary. Indeed she appears in several of the Grail visions, not as an extra but as part of what might be called the Grail revelation.

The Grail, in fact, has to do with the especially Christian notion of God *in matter*, in the woman especially who has always symbolised the earth, the bodily but unconscious aspects of human life. This helps to explain the constant appearances in the legends of Mary, Mother of Christ, and of the "maidens" who, in Chretien's version, carry the Graal (much to the chagrin of at least one Catholic liturgical stickler). The transcendent spirit comes to human beings in material form, but in order to discover and partake of this transcendence a long quest, a purification, an Adventure of the fabulous Celtic type, is required. It is not a purely spiritual quest, in the sense of a non-material, flesh-rejecting concern. It is concerned with bodies and souls, with human behaviour as well as devotion, and this is shown by the pre-occupation with purity of life, compassion, honour and fidelity in the questing knights. Only Galahad, the perfect knight, enters into the ultimate mystery and is permitted (in "Le Conte du Graal") actually to gaze into the Cup itself, and returns trembling and overwhelmed, begging God that now he has seen "the object of all my desires", he might die in this state, for earthly life no longer has any meaning for him. And so he does. Here we touch on the area of mysticism proper. In fact we have been wandering through it frequently, for many of the great Celtic saints were true mystics, and they give us a good start in this area, since they walked in and out of it so naturally and with so little sense of any drastic break.

There have been great mystics in all religious traditions, and at the highest point they converge. But they cannot be glibly lumped together in the interests of some convenient "super religion". Each grows out of, and belongs to, his or her own tradition. Each was formed by it, and without that formation would not have reached such heights of vision.

To speak very broadly, the great Eastern mystical tradition grows out of a theology that treats the pursuit of spiritual detachment and perfection as the only real concern; the material world is "illusion", that is, not relevant to ultimate reality. Acts of charity and service are good as means of spiritual purification, but only incidental to the real life of the spirit. This means that the whole thrust of religious awareness favours a "monastic" calling, a professional and full-time contemplative life. Those who are not able to give themselves to this may look forward to doing so in a future life. Meanwhile they must reverence, and learn from, those who are on the way to enlightenment. This is why, as Thomas Merton noticed in the course of his final travels in Asia, Buddhists are really better than Christians at fostering the contemplative life.

Christian mysticism is rooted in a tradition that sees the final freedom not as a liberation *from* the material but as a transformation *of* the material, which has in it already the seeds of eternal life. To enable these seeds to grow requires long, hard discipline, longing and striving, yet the thing itself is of the Spirit. It is already divine. Thus there is no point at which the Catholic mystic can deny responsibility for, or involvement with, the material world or his or her own body, or the bodies of others. Creation itself is to be transformed, not set aside, and the Grail, mysterious and divine but physical, and visible (and meshed with legend and myth extending far beyond the purely Christian) is the adequate symbol of this kind of mystical stance. Those who can see into the divine vessel are few. They are at a point of sanctity close to the perfection of eternal bliss. But there is a continuity, there are degrees, there is a relationship at every stage and level with all other human beings, and their ordinary lives and concerns, hopes and fears, their own ways of holiness. Consequently there is an earthy quality about most of the great Catholic mystics, and an astonishing capacity for combining hard, practical work, profound and tender friendship, and efficient organisation with the highest mystical experience. Even the esoteric Meister Eckhart, the great Dominican preacher of the late thirteenth and early fourteenth century, who was so close to eastern forms of expression in his efforts to express the "otherness" of the ultimate experience that many have claimed that he left Catholicism behind, was (if you read him widely and in context, not in isolated texts) firmly Christ-centred in his spirituality.

Eckhart (and his Augustinian contemporary from the Netherlands, John Ruysbroek) made a peculiar but useful distinction between God and Godhead, conceiving "Godhead" — the "godness" of God — as the eternal Self which is the ultimate Being, and "God" as related to the human soul, as active, working and creating and drawing to himself. In Godhead all is potential, dark, unknowable, and the three-fold God is in the Godhead, yet flows out from it to be worshipped and to love. It is hardly surprising that Eckhart has often been misunderstood, both by the contemporary Church which felt uneasy about what looked like a down-grading of God, and by modern non-religious students of mysticism, who have seen in him a concealed atheist.

But Eckhart was firmly Christian and Catholic. His language, stretched to the limits of conceptual clarity (and a little beyond) is concerned with the same God as that of Catherine of Siena, visionary, mystic and prophet who used metaphor and poetic language to convey the inexpressible union of her soul with its Bridegroom, a union which drove her to involve herself passionately with nursing the sick and with the politics of her day. She once said that as a fish is in water, living in it and drawing life from it, so is the soul in God, its medium of existence.

To the author of the *Cloud of Unknowing* in the fourteenth century the experience of God is a darkness, an "unknowing" of the intellect in which only the blind will pushes stubbornly towards its love. "For of all other creatures and their works, yea, and of the works of God's self, may a man through grace have full head of knowing, and well he can think of them: but of God himself can no man think. And therefore I would leave all things that I can think, and choose to my love that thing that I cannot think. For why; He may well be loved, but not thought. By love may he be gotten and holden, but by thought never. Therefore — smite upon that thick cloud of unknowing with the sharp dart of longing love; and go not thence for anything that befalleth." Both this unknown author and Walter Hilton in his "*Ladder of Perfection*" combine this uncompromising demand for entry into the "darkness" with a homely common sense concerning human motives and behaviour, and an insistence that not everyone is called to this "Way" and that there are very good people whose calling is in the "Active Way". Hilton's attitude to "distractions" in prayer is an example of the straightforward and yet sensitive psychology of a school of mysticism which reaches to heaven but knows that the quest begins much lower down:

"Do not be distressed and angry with yourself and impatient with God (i.e. if your mind fails to concentrate in prayer) and be comforted . . . Recognize in this your own weakness, accept it readily, and humbly hold to your prayer, poor as it is. . . . Give up struggling against yourself, and do not worry about it any longer, as though you could force yourself to have these feelings. Leave your prayer and turn to some other occupation, either spiritual or physical, and resolve to do better another time. . . . Furthermore, a soul who never finds peace of heart in prayer but has to struggle against distracting and troublesome thoughts all her life, provided that she keeps herself in humility and charity in other ways, shall receive full reward in heaven for all her trouble."

Somehow, I can't imagine an eastern Master telling a disciple that enlightenment can be attained even if there is a complete failure to achieve mystical union.

The great medieval mystics have been re-discovered in recent years, but the mystical tradition did not cease with "the ages of faith". In fact I'm not at all convinced that there was more real faith then than any other time. For one thing, the English mystical style, with its special quality of understated, trenchant, yet often delicately lyrical feeling, was continued in the Anglican Church. And the troubled post-Reformation period of anxiety, defensiveness and embattled zeal cast up, as if in protest, Teresa of Avila, who was swept out of her senses in helpless passion for the divine. But she founded and guided until her death at a good old age the Carmelite reform, of women and then of men, with humor, ruthless will, and enormous compassion. She knew people's weaknesses, including her own, and pointed them out with vigour, but she could be infinitely gentle with the weak. She liked lavender water, and often danced with her nuns; she travelled all over Spain in a bumpy mule cart under blazing suns, endured calumny and persecution, wrote books that have guided seekers for God ever since, and lived through all this at a level of sublime mystical union that would seem to demand total solitude and peace. Hers was a true spirit of chivalry, for in Spain the chivalry that sprang up in France found its last home. (Don Quixote, after all, was Spanish). Teresa fought and adventured in search of the Grail, found it, and led others on the same quest.

There are too many names to mention more than a handful. Blaise Pascal, mathematician, scientist, and mystic, in the seventeenth century represents a completely different type, in whom a precisely, even passionately rational mind was no bar to intense experience of the God of fire — "God of Abraham, Isaac and Jacob, not the God of the philosophers". Augustine Baker, spiritual adviser to the exiled English nuns at Cambrai, drew them gently from the conscience-searching system of Jesuit direction of the time, and led them back to the high-way of contemplation. His huge book "Holy Wisdom" is only now regaining the respect due to it as a major spiritual classic. But the "counter-reformation" brought with it a fear of all emotional or irrational types of spirituality, as tending to dangerous "protestant-type" heresy. The soul was to be regimented, along with the armies of the beleaguered church. It must be scrubbed and inspected and equipped with formidable virtues to repel the enemy (the devil and the Protestants); it was expected to be neither comfortable nor winged. Fortunately, human nature (or rather, divine nature) worked out its own ways of getting around these fears, and people found their way to God in spite of all. In the nineteenth century, for instance, the letters of the Sacred Heart nun, Janet Erskine Stuart, are compounded of common sense and deep love of God and man. Abbot Marmion led the way back to a renewed monastic spirituality, and in France an obscure woman known as "Marie-Christine" kept a diary at the turn of the century (up to 1910) which revealed that sometimes God had things his own way:

"I see that notwithstanding the great discretion of those who surround me, they are very astonished to see that I always pray without a book. What can I do, O my God? I can do nothing, and no one in the world will ever be more astonished at it than I am . . . I went to see that poor soul who asked me to come and play a little to her on the piano."

Heaven and earth, the demand of God who drags the soul away from even the best books, and the need to play the piano to please a lonely person — that is the polar and paradoxical shape of Catholic mystical awareness.

Mystical experience in this sense is not necessarily associated with visions. Some mystics are also visionaries, and some know only the dark, imageless union. Francis, so transported in love of the Crucified that the seraphic vision imprinted the signs of the crucifixion on his body, is the most famous of all the visionary mystics. Teresa also saw visions, and the two Catherines, of Siena and of Genoa, described series of strange symbolic visions, beautiful and terrifying. In Peru, that extraordinary girl, Rose of Lima, grew flowers and embroidered to make money for her family, slept on a bed of stones, and treated her body hideously in passionate identification with the suffering of Christ and of the Indians, oppressed by her own people. She nursed the poor, had the gift of communion with insects and animals, and had visions of towering beauty.

Visions are a sore point with conventional Catholic piety. They happen, and are sometimes clearly of God. However, there is a chance that they might not be, and then the Church will be made to look silly: so says the traditional common sense of Mother Church. Therefore all visionaries should be treated with extreme caution, not to say suspicion. But visions are obvious ways in which the "unknown factors" in human and religious life break through the surface of every day, and they arouse a tremendous response. In our own time, the stigmatic friar, Padre Pio, attracted not only the merely curious but hosts of visitors whose motives were sincerely religious.

There are miracles, too, which, like visions, provide headaches for conscientious bishops. Inexplicable cures of severe and obvious diseases are not frequent but they happen, and less spectacular healings are fairly frequent. There is scope for fraud, self-deception, and self-hypnosis; nevertheless, well-attested healings should not really present a problem if we take seriously the premise of Christian faith, that man is body-soul, and matter is also in the process of being redeemed. It would be odd indeed if the spiritual power which expresses itself in so many forms — in myth, in legend and poetry, in romantic love, in the passion for adventure and the passion for God — were not able to make itself felt in the very flesh itself, in mystical experience, in the healing of sickness, or in those peculiar (but very well attested) cases where, for instance, food has been multiplied, or a person has been encountered physically in two different places at one time.

There is nothing especially Catholic about all this, and indeed many people can happily believe in the feats of Don Juan the Mexican sorcerer, or the responsiveness of plants to human emotion, while assuming that strange events heard of in a Christian context are unlikely to be true. But Catholic theology has a framework which gives them a proper, and proportionate, role in the drama of salvation.

The reason for building this chapter around the symbolism

of the Grail is that, as we have seen, it is the meeting place of so many aspects of Western, Catholic experiences of "unknown factors". It emerges from northern pagan myth, trailing Celtic adventure and faerie. It infiltrates and finally dominates the Arthurian legends, which themselves spread through the whole of Europe, and later, America, sprouting new tales and new symbolism as they go. From Chretien, through Robert de Boron, Wolfram von Eschenbach, and later Malory, taken up in due time by Tennyson and Wagner, and even Mark Twain, and finally in our own time still further developed in the Arthurian poems of Charles Williams, the Grail and its seekers, with the Court and the Round Table, express the deepest aspirations of Western spirituality. The legend takes many and even contradictory forms. In the prose work "Lancelot" it is the Romantic code of passionate, adulterous love, knightly honour and adventure, which dominates. Yet in *La Queste du Saint Graal* Lancelot is excluded from the quest by his sin and has to atone with much labour, many trials and tears. (Yet he *is* a hero, without doubt. The idea of a sinful and repentant hero is a purely Western and Christian notion). The *Queste* is about the longing for God, the mystical quest, yet it is not separable from the whole tradition, whose obvious context is not the "other world" of Heaven but the "middle world" of faerie to which Thomas the Rhymer travelled. It is a world which surrounds and penetrates and reflects the visible, everyday world, a world of goblins and demons (who are not really devils), of powerful but morally ambivalent wizards like Merlin, and goddesses-turned-fairy like Nimue. Magic is part of life, and the fringe of this dark wood opens onto the shores of that sea beyond which, symbolically, are the blessed lands of Eternity. Yet the influence of those "perilous seas and faerie lands forlorne" extends into human lands: the Grail descends on Arthur's Court and draws the Knights on the eternal quest. The world of politics and law, of organised religion, of daily work and war, of human love and grief, is inextricably one with the worlds of plant and animals and their spirits, of fairy beings good and bad, of high chivalry and demonic powers, of the supreme experience of God and the intermediate regions of visions and miracle. The Grail draws something from all of these and centres them in the Catholic sense of the Eucharist as *the* frontier post between earth and heaven.

It is dangerous territory. There, lost in the dark wood, Dante found a guide who would lead him, curious and terrified, through the darkest regions of the spirit where a false step meant destruction, before he could emerge to begin the long hard climb of the mountain of purgation, and come at last to the many levels of bliss and fulfilment. But to wander in the wood without a guide, or with a false guide, is spiritual suicide. Shakespeare's "Midsummer Night's Dream" shows us this moonlit, spirit-haunted region, where human beings are deceived and changed and pulled about by elemental forces, some merely mischievous, some great and powerful and frightening, yet not supreme or autonomous in their own actions. The book and the film "The Exorcist", crudely sensational as they were, stirred up a great tide of frightened awareness and fascination in people who had lost real belief in any "other world", good or bad, but still felt and feared its influence. Non-belief in fairies (or ghosts, or devils) does not affect their existence or non-existence, any more than non-belief in God makes God cease to be (except in the sense of Eckhart, to whom God *is* what is believed in, but Godhead resides beyond belief).

Whatever our attitude to the area "between the worlds" — the area of legend, magic, miracle, symbol — it has affected people since there were people, and still does. However you interpret the experience and the symbols, people have these experiences and find these symbols recurring, age after age, in story, poem, vision and dream.

Catholic life and theology have had to wrestle with all these, and have done so with varying success and little certainty. But no one can rule them out as irrelevant. Because the Catholic enterprise involves all of human life and experience, it has constantly to cope with these "unknown factors" as well, sometimes with a justified sense of danger, and sometimes with a kind of light-hearted humility, full of wonder at the strangeness of being human. The Catholic enterprise must never over-value such things, or try to make a whole religion out of them, or use them to prop up inadequacies in other areas. It must try to integrate them and live with them, because they exist, whatever they mean. It is, as always, an impossible balance to find.

For, meanwhile, whatever conclusions may be reached by conscientious researchers and theologians, people go on wanting God, by whatever name they identify that longing, and there are many false names. They want him not merely with their souls but with imagination, emotion, body. They go on pilgrimage, sometimes in odd places of the spirit, to seances, drugs, or witches' covens. Or they go in fantasy with the aid of Tolkien or Macdonald or their many followers. Or they get up and set out on their own two feet, and journey, as their ancestors did, to Nepal or Samarkand, or to Glastonbury. Pilgrimages are, it seems, "natural" to the spiritual search. The seeking out of holy places with actual geographical locations is a reminder which we cannot ignore that the human quest involves the whole person and is not a merely mental affair. The young pilgrims who camp out each summer at Glastonbury, earnestly studying the I-Ching, smoking hash, reading Thomas Merton, making candles, and discussing organic farming or the Second Coming are on the quest as much as young Parsifal. Like him they are apt to miss their chances, ask the wrong question, or not ask, and make the confusion worse. But at least they are setting out from their round table, and a few may achieve the Grail. It is a thoroughly Catholic quest, under the occasionally erratic guidance of Sophia. If, most of the time, they do not pay much attention to Mother Church, Sophia will no doubt help them to make contact with her when necessary.

Chapter 4
THE WORKERS

An enterprise that is trying to be universal cannot be elitist. Whatever other mistakes it may have made, the Catholic tradition has at least not made that one, though at times it has come perilously near to it, and at such times has been most noticeably unchristian. For the last three centuries, on the contrary, the favourite taunt of those educated Protestants who heartily disliked what they knew of the Catholic Church was that it was a religion for credulous peasants or Irish workers, who were controlled by a collection of subtle priests (especially Jesuits) who didn't believe all that stuff but found it useful for keeping the populace in a state of subjection. The accusation had, in fact, just enough truth in it to sting, but the reason it was not true was not because the clergy were more faithful and humble than in this version (though many were) but because peasants and Irish workers are not particularly credulous, and not in the least easily led. They may have accepted a good deal that a better education would have led them to doubt, but that was due to lack of information, not to intellectual or moral feebleness. Catholicism has always been a religion of the people, with all the good and bad that implies, but from our educated vantage point (one kind of education, anyway) we easily assume that this means a kind of 'popular' religion simplified for the masses, while the real theology goes on somewhere else. The theme of this chapter is the rather startling (but perfectly verifiable) fact that Catholicism is popular not only in the sense that it has always been a religion of 'the people' but in the sense that 'the people' *make* it. The experiences of ordinary people — peasants, industrial workers, immigrants, oppressed populations — have changed the Christian understanding drastically in a number of ways. It is the theologians who, afterwards, incorporate the insights gained by popular experience into the 'corpus' of Christian self-

131

understanding. That is their job, and their skill lies in their sensitivity to what is being expressed in the lives and words of everyday people.

In this chapter I shall try to spell out a little how this happens, and I begin with an idea of a Protestant writer, George Lindbeck, who, in an interesting article published in *Commonweal* in 1976, based his whole argument on the fact that, ultimately, "the Church" is not the clergy but the whole people, not just in a juridical sense but in the sense that the people have the last word. His article compared the relationship between Catholic and Protestant churches to that between an occupied country and its exiled freedom movement. The comparison deliberately implies that the homeland, the Catholic Church, is "occupied" by forces that have no right to govern; this means, in practice, that from this Protestant point of view at least some of the "structures" of the Catholic Church are "illegitimate" and therefore, according to traditional Catholic theology, the citizens have the right to try to get rid of them. It won't do to push any analogy too far, but there is clearly an important truth in this one. The suggestion that Protestants have been "freedom fighters" *abroad* makes a lot of sense from a Catholic point of view. In our time we have become familiar with the spectacle of people who have left their invaded or oppressed homelands in order to be able to work for the liberation of their country. Their intention has been, if all goes well, to return eventually to their liberated homes. Their exile is self-chosen, but it is exile, and it is intended to be temporary — yet there are examples in recent history of such exiled freedom movements which did not return home, because by the time return became possible they no longer wanted to. They had put down new roots.

This, says Lindbeck, is what happened to Protestantism: "The freedom forces have forgotten that the reason for their existence is to return to their homeland, a liberated homeland. Instead, they have tried to re-establish their native country abroad, alienated from the depths and continuities of culture, and tradition, from which they sprang."

This notion, as the author admits, is unacceptable to many Protestants, as indeed it will be to many Catholics. But it seems to me to establish a context for ecumenical discussions which is both realistic and hopeful. In terms of my own basic analogy, the other Christian churches need the homeland, and want it to be "liberated" and restored. But the reason why I find this comparison especially interesting is its premise that the "homeland" is *not* embodied in its rulers, but is more credibly represented by its constant popular culture and traditions, which are distinct from its government, whether legitimate or not. They are distinct, but of course not independent of it. The decisions of rulers shape a culture to some extent, but not to a very important extent. It has been observed, for instance, that the most radical cultural revolution ever undertaken, the Chinese one, has produced a culture which is at first sight completely new and without antecedents. Yet closer study shows that, under new names and within new forms, the "new" culture is distinctively and recognizably *Chinese*, rather than Communist, and that the continuity is real, even when unacknowledged. The changes are enormous but the cultural identity is recognizably the same beneath them.

In America, too, the Europeans of many cultures who emigrated to the New World were expected to lose their previous cultural identity and become American. The fact (unwelcome to many, baffling to most) is that in many cases they have not done so. Americans they may be, but they are also still Polish, German, Italian, Jewish or Irish; they still feel most "at home" with those of their own race. It is also interesting that whereas not long ago this cultural distinctiveness within American society was regarded as regrettable, or dismissed as a negligible and dying social factor, recently Americans have begun to see that this very diversity, and the deep roots of ethnic self-consciousness in each group, have a great value in both stabilising and vitalising American society. So, again, the acknowledged and overt political structures of a society cannot be used to define the nature of the country itself, though they are very important. It is the *people* who matter, in every nuance one can give to that word.

And it has many nuances. "People", first of all, means human beings as such. It can also have a contemptuous tone; for to the aristocrat or the politician "the people" are the masses who must do as they are told or can be manipulated by the powerful; yet even the most powerful and distinguished cannot do without them. Power has to have something on which to exercise itself, and an aristocracy doesn't exist except in relation to something below it. To the Marxist, "the people" is itself a power, a communal identity, with a recognizable "voice" and "will". "The people" is to be served and exalted, and if such phrases in the mouths of the Communist politician often mean, in practice, much the same as what the aristocrat or the capitalist politician means when he talks about "the common good" (that is, his own good), the idea does add an extra dimension. But in all ways "the people" are the ground from which everything else in a society grows. To be "a man of the people" means that one shares the attitudes and assumptions of the "ordinary" people, whose cultural continuity underlies whatever political, or artistic or intellectual achievements may occur at the upper end of the social ladder. Conquerors may come, and devastate, and settle, or leave. Governments may change, and be oppressive, or supportive, or irrelevant. But the people go on through it all, planting and reaping, making and selling and buying, marrying and bearing and burying, suffering bad harvests or huge taxes, conscription of the young men or destruction of the crops, standing in line at the employment exchange or the factory bench or the super-market checkout counter. The people endure, waiting for better times and enjoying them when they can, singing their own songs, making their own jokes, praying their own prayers and passing on their own bits of often cynical wisdom, learned from living and obstinately surviving in one land, one city, one tradition. The "gentry" or the "bosses" live in a different world, tolerated, resented, respected or hated. Whatever they are, they are irrelevant to the realities of life. They are not "the people".

When we talk of a "homeland", this is what we mean — the people, and their land (whether city or farmland), both together. People and place are woven together in webs of custom, enshrined in language, through the centuries. Extending this admittedly mixed metaphor, we may notice that a "web" is the name given to cloth being woven; and to "enshrine" a thing is to put it within a shrine, a specially made structure intended both to protect and display a holy thing. The prefix "en-" is medieval. It is impossible to use words without displaying one's own cultural roots.

The Lindbeck article mentioned above is concerned with a worry about the people — the Catholic people who, the author rightly perceives, *are* the Church. He fears (and he is not alone in that fear) that many sincere and fervent Catholics, in their search for renewed and up-dated Christian forms, have failed to realise the damage they could be doing at a level of whose importance they are either ignorant or contemptuous. "In their search for contemporary relevance or for Christian faithfulness, they have undermined that popular, traditonal, cultural Catholicism which, however oppressive and obscurantist it may seem to the upwardly mobile, the educated elite and the biblical purists, is still the source of meaning and life to the multitudes."

This, then, is the basis of the thing called Catholicism. It is the people on whom all depends, whether as the ground from which great trees may grow, or simply as the trampled soil over which armies contend. The Catholic thing is, and has always been a "popular" thing, a thing of the people, shaped and coloured by the continuity of popular cultures, whether of peasants or urban proletariat. It is a church of the poor, not only in the biblical sense (which has been, alas, not always evident) but in historical fact. Its strength and stability, its sheer, obstinate capacity for survival, have come from the poor.

I do not, in this context, necessarily mean people in want. I mean, rather, the people whose small livelihood is directly dependent on what they can grow or earn, those who are not cushioned against change and need and political oppression by wealth or privilege. The peasant, the small farmer, the labourer or craftsman, the artisan or factory hand, the family shop-keeper and the "small" professional people such as local doctors and lawyers, teachers, clerks and tradespeople — these are the "poor" in comparative terms, the "people" who have made possible the Catholic enterprise, and have made it their own. Such people, lacking the security of wealth or high social status, value and develop the security of continuity. Tradition and custom matter, for they give a sense of identity, a self-respect with which to face a future on whose kindness there can be little reliance.

It is the people, in this sense, who also form one of the strongest influences in the development of theology. This idea, odd at first sight, is quite uncomplicated historically. The economic and social needs of a large group of people present them with definite problems and possibilities. Over and over again, the demands of the Catholic people for better wages, freedom from exploitation, or for justice, have posed a challenge to existing systems with which the Church had identified itself not only in practical social ways but with theological underpinning. When times changed and these new social needs became obvious, some apparently immovable bits of theology had to be pulled down and re-built with consequent agonisings, anathemas and wranglings among the official teachers of Catholic religion, from the Pope down.

One extremely important example of this process grew out of the greatest of all "Catholic peoples" in both numbers and prestige — the American Catholic people. In a way it is quite misleading to talk of "American Catholicism", because there is not one form of American Catholicism but a number of them, according to ethnic origin. Although some have "melted" in the expected way, some have retained up to the present a remarkably distinct identity. With the exception of little groups of Hispano-Catholics, descended from the original Spanish settlers in the West, and the larger Mexican-Catholic people (both groups drastically separated from the rest of U.S. Catholicism by language and poverty) the bulk of American Catholic people, whatever their ethnic origins, have in their common background the experience of nineteenth or early twentieth century immigration. A few, usually German, brought a little money and were able to buy land and endure the early years by establishing farms. But most of the immigrants were extremely poor. They came because things were so bad at home that even the slender (and wildly exaggerated) possibility of better things in the New World was worth the horrors of the journey and the uncertainties of the future. They fled sometimes from religious persecution, like the Germans who came to escape Bismark's anti-Catholic policies, but more came to escape political or economic hardship.

The Irish were the first "wave". (The Anglo-Saxons, including the Catholic ones, had been there so long that they didn't really count as "immigrants", though of course they had been, once upon a time). They came in their hundreds of thousands, peasants driven out by economic distress, itself partly caused by English political exploitation, repressive legislation and religious restriction. They were desperately poor, but tough, clannish, and inclined to think that their version of Catholicism, which had survived persecution and derived directly (they said) from St. Patrick, was the only proper kind. By the time the Italians came in any numbers the Irish were numerous and strong enough to make it hard for any other brand of Catholicism to be respectable.

Italian Catholics, coming from a land where clerical privilege and corruption are indigenous, were naturally anti-clerical; they were also in large part devoted to lavish and exotic cults of saints with dubious antecedents. Many combined real piety with gross superstition and saw no contradiction between genuine faith and a rather elastic morality.

Different again were the Poles, profoundly attached to their homeland, strongly identifying Poland and Catholicism; they held strongly to national customs, religious and secular. The Germans, as I have said, were on the whole better educated and better off than most other immigrants. They were hard-working, cohesive, self-reliant and not at all inclined to be indentified with the swarming Irish or Italians of the eastern seaboard cities. The Germans moved west quickly and bought land, having the means to do so. The Irish, Italians, and others were slower to move, and for the most part they depended on eastern industry for a livelihood.

The majority of European immigrants shared the experience of being very poor in a strange land where none of the customs or structures of home were there to mitigate, explain or relieve poverty. Industrialists exploited this cheap labour. The city tenements into which they were crowded were, for largely rural people, a near approach to hell.

Many Americans feared and disliked these Catholic hordes who had invaded their almost entirely Protestant country. Discrimination kept Jews and Catholics from most public offices, and many private jobs were closed to them as well. They had little protection in the law of the land against the occasional outbreak of anti-Catholic violence or the more general prejudice and social and economic harassment. There was only one reassuring, recognizable thing around, and that was the Church. The priests who came with, or to serve, the immigrants were mostly men of courage, self-sacrificing and hard working. The parish church, however shabby, and the priests and nuns, were "our own". Each ethnic group tended to keep together in Irish, Polish, or Italian parishes with their own churches and schools. But they were all Catholic, and they were centres of the only kind of life that seemed comforting and hopeful. There, language, customs, ceremonies, and prejudices were familiar and home-like.

These extremely poor people went to extraordinary lengths of self-sacrifice to set up their own schools, hospitals, orphanages, and other necessary institutions. (This was not just a yearning for the presence of the familiar and reassuring. Some city authorities with large Catholic populations put all orphans, including Catholics, into orphanages where they were brought up as Protestants. This ensured that they would be subjected to a barrage of anti-Catholic propaganda). The Catholic people created nations within the nation, having had to do so in order to survive, not only psychologically but even politically and economically. With the strength of numbers, and with the leadership of energetic clergy, they could demand their political rights, work for better pay and conditions, and fight discrimination. It was the Irish who did the most fighting, not surprisingly, and there were at times violent reactions against all Catholics. The suspicions of Catholics as "Pope's men", out to subvert the state and subdue it to Roman domination, died hard.

My concern here is not with the history of American Catholicism, except insofar as it formed the American Catholic people. The story of the middle decades of the nineteenth century was, for Catholics, a story of patchy and hard-won acceptance, an acceptance won more quickly by the Irish than by the rest. In time it came to be accepted by most non-Catholic Americans that Catholics could be good Americans, and the reason for this was the attitude of the clergy, especially the bishops, who were predominantly Irish. They struggled not only to give comfort and support and every kind of practical as well as spiritual help to their people; they also never tired of telling them that they could be, and should be, good Americans. They had to show that they were just as patriotic, just as devoted to their new country, as non-Catholic settlers. They had to uphold American law and attitudes, including the fundamental one of separation of Church and State, on which was based their own claim to full citizenship.

The lesson was well learned. By the beginning of the twentieth century American Catholicism, though still a very homogeneous "world" with its "in" phrases and attitudes and its decided belief in the inferiority of other kinds of Christianity, regarded itself as totally and devotedly American. Catholics owed their newly won prosperity to the freedom of the American way of life. The church of the poorest had become the biggest single religious group, and it was rich. Its schools, convents and chanceries expressed even in their architecture this new, confident affluence. If they were not very beautiful they were openly opulent, a visible sign of the triumph of their Church in their land.

But there was a difficulty. Not only the Vatican but many European and some American theologians (especially those educated in Europe) heard with deep distrust the idea put forward that the Church should willingly forego her often asserted right to impose Catholicism as the one permitted faith, if she were able to do so. How could the Church discharge her mission if she had to accept a tacit equality with other churches and even other religions? How could good Catholics uphold the idea of democracy, rather than simply tolerate it because they had no choice?

To us, the suspicion with which many Catholics viewed the

139

American experience seems ridiculous, but it has to be seen against a European background. The eighteenth century "Enlightenment", which was expected to usher in the reign of Reason and Peace, crossed the Atlantic and found free space to develop and correct itself by experience. In Europe it could only develop by ousting older philosophies, represented by the Church and the "Ancien Regime," each supporting the other. To "progressives" in Europe, religion was the enemy. Therefore, to Church authorities, "Liberalism," "Democracy," "Progress" and "Science" all seemed to be the work of the devil. To hear these things being defended and even preached by American Catholics was an outrage to the theological sensibilities of many churchmen. It looked as if socialism and the forces of atheism were subverting the faith of the Catholic people.

In a sense, that is precisely what was happening — if you assume that "the faith" is the form of Catholicism which had been acceptable for so long that most people have never heard of any other. We are so far, now, from the "Ancien Regime" that we find it hard to see why any honest person could want to uphold it, let alone to regard it as practically God-given. But there had once been very good reason for the development of a theology of monarchy, a theology which explored the use of force and its limitations as a political weapon, and the relationship between the Church and secular power.

To give just one example: in the tenth century the degree of clerical and monastic corruption, backed up by the power of the nobility, was so great that a reforming movement was undertaken by churchmen who saw the urgent need for change and were brave enough to fight for it. They fought at the level where it counted, with Kings as allies. They moved in and forcibly reformed huge, rich abbeys and cathedral canonries, spring-cleaned the financial systems, tightened up the rules of monastic life, made elections of Abbots free and broke the tight hold of the great families on church appointments. (One family, for example, had controlled Papal nominations for over a century, and had seen to it that one of the family should be always on the throne of Peter). The reform was undertaken by men who were themselves usually of noble family but refused to profit by it. If they had not been, they could not have done what they did. They had as their allies Kings willing to be guided, and that was how the thing was done.

This single, too-brief paragraph compresses a fascinating story of which most Catholics have never heard, but the point is that in the process of pushing through desperately needed reforms, which saved the Catholic enterprise from becoming a business enterprise run by the great nobles of Europe, the reformers had to work out a theological justification for what they were doing and the means they had to employ to do it. They had to show why this King was right (because he helped them) and that King was wrong (because he let his nobles rule him, and opposed reform). They had to show that the Church had the right and duty to do this kind of thing, which might involve calling on men to fight in a "just cause". So a whole theology developed, showing the rightness of this relationship of the Church to the King and to secular government and power generally. It came to be taken for granted, not only that these relationships were right and necessary at the time, but that they were normative for evermore. From that time on, Catholic political thinking was based on such assumptions about the Church's political and social mission. No wonder that the American idea of removing secular structures wholly beyond the control, or even the guidance, of the Church struck many Catholics as dangerous and even heretical.

In the end, however, theology caught up with what was actually going on. The message got through that the Church could live, work, and flourish in an open, democratic society where it had no direct political role at all, or rather where it had the same political role as any group of citizens. That role was to give intelligent attention to political issues, judge them by proper moral standards, discuss, protest or promote them, and vote accordingly. The older theology of politics was quietly dismantled and folded away into the history of the Church. Many people now don't even know it existed.

All this was done not because any talented theologian wrote books about it, or religious leaders saw a need for change, but very largely because the Catholic people of America, including the clergy who worked for and with them, experienced a new kind of Catholic life. They found that it worked, and just went on living it. Most of them never even realised that Rome was in a turmoil about what they were doing. They were getting on with trying to be Catholic Americans and American Catholics, and doing it pretty well.

They created, in the process, what came to be known as "ghetto Catholicism". The ghetto is disappearing rapidly and is generally despised — not, I think, with good reason, for it was needed and at least for a while provided a life support for the new arrivals. Religion is a curious mixture. Not all of it is as "spiritual" as we would like to think, and one of its functions has always been to validate the necessary life-style of a society, to reinforce cultural and moral norms and attitudes, and generally to give people a sense that the way of life which the community has evolved for its survival is a good one, worth upholding in spite of personal suffering. It gives a sense of communal self-respect; it provides outlets for emotions that might otherwise do damage, and it helps to reduce the impact of inevitable structural tensions — for instance, envy of the more prosperous by the less prosperous.

The ordinary Catholic American family, once settled, had the job (over several generations, naturally) of finding a way of life that made sense both of America and of Catholicism. This was a very big job, and it had to happen while the family was also struggling to achieve financial stability, education for the children, and some kind of future. To do something like that requires support, and it came from other Catholics, including the clergy and Sisters who were the heart of the Catholic community, its interpreters to the rest of America, and America's interpreters to their congregations and pupils.

This interpretation went on in the schools, first of all. Catholic parochial schools (without any State support, of course) sprang up by hundreds. The process continued throughout life, in higher education, in Catholic newspapers and reviews, but also in all kinds of societies and movements — in church "guilds" based on European models, in the Christian

Family Movement, in retreats, courses, and associations for learning everything from needlework to the Church's "social teaching". These groupings were purely Catholic, but in many cases they existed, tacitly at least, in order to help Catholics to do, as Catholics, things that other Americans were doing. Catholic professional associations had the same purpose. From the pulpit many priests (taking time off from upholding sexual purity and demanding money for the school) helped to form a pride in being Catholic and American, and to develop a sense of the basic unity of the two. The idea that a conflict might develop between the demands of the American government and the conscience of the American Catholic was one that did not occur to most people. Patriotism and Catholicism were one glorious purpose. The agonies of the Vietnam protestors, draft-card burnings and imprisonments, were part of an unimaginable future.

The Catholic "ghetto" was in fact a considerable cultural achievement which had far-reaching consequences for the whole Catholic enterprise. It broke down once and for all the notion that the Church could only operate fully under one kind of political regime, patiently tolerating others when it had no choice. Together with the experience of the loss of the industrial working class of Europe and the loss of political power in its old strongholds, the American experience offered a fresh self-understanding which later enabled the Church to realise a new kind of mission in a war-torn world, a world suffering from extremes of riches and poverty and subjected to every variety of government from exotic neo-feudalism to communism. American democracy came in time to seem pleasantly reliable and respectable. Even its sins were predictable and this must have been a relief to harassed Vatican officials.

That particular kind of American Catholicism has almost disappeared, as have parallel European experiences. The Second Vatican Council, or rather those who set out to implement its decisions, pulled up cultural roots all over the Western world and left many Catholic peoples reduced in numbers, uncertain of their purpose, angry and anxious.

But in the early days of change, when the experience seemed to be one of simply loosening too-tight bonds, there was a tremendous revival in America and (to a much lesser degree) in Europe, of interest in old "Catholic customs", often of European peasant origin. It was a mainly middle-class movement. The comparatively secure were searching for a symbolic framework which would give meaning to lives which seemed (among all the new comforts) curiously arid and un-beautiful. This was a domestic, family movement, and hardly touched church structures, though it did creep into some of the schools. It was an attempt to give to daily home life a quasi-liturgical shape which would sanctify it. Some strongly ethnic Catholic groups in America had some of this living symbolic tradition, so the new movement learned from them, as well as from European travel and books, using these "new" customs and rituals without having had previous experience of them. Much of the enthusiasm for this kind of thing has since faded, but a minimum did become established "Catholic family custom", helping Catholics to feel real links with the past, and with Catholics in other countries.

The phenomenon was interesting, because it betrayed a deep longing for roots in a world thought of as more stable and "natural" than the industrialised Western life most people know. It was the same longing which has motivated many families and communities to undertake "back to the land" projects. Most of them have not endured, for the same reason that the self-conscious, domestic, liturgical type of Catholic piety has endured only in a much reduced form. That reason is a failure to understand the way a culture operates. Above all, a particular culture works the way it does because it has to. It is, as I suggest, a way of "humanising", making meaningful and manageable, the requirements for survival. Common rituals celebrate the things that are of vital importance — the lambing season in pastoral cultures, harvest in arable ones, marriage wherever family stability is vital to the continuity of agriculture or craft. And the moral emphases which receive specially strong religious validation are those which underpin the economy — martial fidelity matters because a disrupted family means a disrupted farm or workshop; diligence at work matters where productivity or high quality of goods maintains the standard of living; obedience and respect are important where a strong authority system is needed to hold the community together.

So the rituals and customs which modern western Catholic families revived didn't really belong to their secular culture. But they did at least partially belong in the "separate" Catholic culture, and they worked as community-building experiences, to some extent at least, just as they had in their original settings. For the customs of European Catholic peasants were the customs of a Catholic peasant economy which drew the particular symbols, beliefs and moral principles it needed for its survival from a Catholic source, and not from (say) a Hindu or Islamic one. These peasant cultures were selective in the aspects of Catholicism which they developed as their own, and they differed greatly, even though the basics of both life-style and religion were the same. They took what they needed, and more widely educated and zealous parish priests were sometimes driven to despair in their efforts to persuade a cautious peasantry to take the Christian obligation of charity to strangers, for instance, as seriously as preparations for the procession of the local patron saint. Strangers are, on the whole, irrelevant to peasant societies, and often regarded with absolute hostility, whereas the local saint "means" the life of the village, its spirit and value, so to celebrate the feast day with ceremony and proper jollification was and is a matter of great psychological importance. The rivalries between the cults of saints in neighboring villages, or even of the Mother of God under differing titles (Our Lady of the Mountain in competition with Our Lady of the Valley) were not as ridiculous as town-bred, half-educated post-Christians would like to think. Religion, as an understanding of the meaning of life and death, expresses itself through things that affect the actual experience of life and death. Local identity and communal feeling are among the most important of these, especially so in a peasant culture in which life means life on this bit of land, and no other.

Millions of people flocked to see the musical film "The Sound of Music" which was a sentimentalized and adapted version of the real life story of a remarkable Austrian Catholic family of great natural musicality. They developed their talent as a group, first of all as amateurs and when they left Austria secretly to avoid working as musicians under Hitler's regime they came to the United States and earned a living as singers, finally becoming U.S. citizens. The film took the story only up to the point of the flight from Austria, and distorted even that in the interests of suspense and phoney romance, but the real story told by the mother, Maria Augusta von Trapp, showed both the origin of the family's strength and the way it developed in the new country.

The values and strength were peasant ones, though the father was a Baron, and an ex-naval officer. And though the author's own background was not a peasant one, she had lived among peasants as a child. Later, studying to be a teacher, she learned to value peasant art, custom and culture. Her vision of folk ways was therefore a little on the rosy side, and she learned the folk songs of her country not so much in the village as among other students. After a few years in the monastery of Nonnberg she found that hers was not a monastic vocation, and eventually she married the widower Baron to whose children she had been governess for a while. She brought to the aristocratic household a strong, solid, country Catholicism, with its sense of the importance of a stable family community, love of the land, and celebration of both in yearly rituals and customs in which religious and secular are so intertwined that it becomes impossible to tell clearly which is which. She taught the children to sing, with remarkable results, and this, too, grew out of her knowledge of Austrian folk-songs, which she recognized as deeply embedded in the whole culture. Whether they were pious songs, drinking songs, love songs or just jolly songs about the harvest or the birds, they had (as everyone knows who has joined in folk singing) a remarkably uniting effect on the group that used them habitually. Later the von Trapps extended their skill and repertoire not only to folk songs of other countries but to the full classical repertoire; yet it was the peasant culture and attitudes which gave the whole extraordinary enterprise its strength.

It is indicative of the source of the von Trapps' strength and stability as a family that, although they became musical celebrities in America, and had to travel widely, their one ambition was to have a bit of land of their own, and when they finally bought some in Vermont neither the house they built themselves nor the life they chose to adopt bore any resemblance either to those of their new compatriots or to the dignified, aristocratic household which had been theirs before they left Austria. Instead, the life-style they developed (apparently without any doubts about it) was as nearly as possible that of Austrian peasant culture. To get their own place was only the necessary and longed-for outward expression of the "interior" culture which had sustained them for so long.

Maria von Trapp believed that it was their Catholic faith that kept them together and warded off despair and disintegration, and she was right, but in a special way. To her, Catholicism and the culture of her native countryside were one. She could, and did, live her faith, and help her family to live it, in alien conditions. She could, and did, understand the moral imperatives of her faith, in demanding resistance to Hitler at whatever cost, in a way that few peasants did. Yet her faith was formed by a peasant culture, and naturally and necessarily expressed itself in the symbols, and even the life-style, appropriate to it.

This shows very well the way in which a Catholic people both shapes and is shaped by the Catholic enterprise. A faith *must* have "a local habitation and a name" before it can become a live reality. The expression really is local and particular, because people's lives are local and particular, but that is not all it is. What anthropologists call "first order" religion is related to particular needs, fears and structures, and at that level this religion tends to be superstitious and "magical" in its ways of thought, but the "higher order" level of over-arching religion is needed to make a coherent meaning-pattern out of the elaborate network of pragmatic charms, folk-wisdom, pagan survivals and the sheer conservatism of peasant populations

The Catholic enterprise has been remarkably well-adapted to the needs of peasant cultures at both these levels, as even the least pro-Catholic observers have noted. Even when Victorian agnostic or severely Protestant travellers considered this kind of

Catholicism as merely a sign of the unenlightened condition of the peasants, they recorded (with disapproval) that poor and over-burdened populations spent a great deal of time honouring gaudily dressed "Popish idols", processing about the village streets or "telling their beads" in church, instead of using the time sensibly to earn a bit more money.

There is a level of poverty, however, where the thing doesn't work. Continuous, grinding hardship wears out confidence in any but the most deeply personal and heroic faith. The habit of some French nineteenth century peasant farmers, for instance, of getting their hay in on a Sunday no matter what the priest said, and sending only the women to church, is an example of the point at which a religious culture is no longer relevant to experienced reality. That by then the Church was politically discredited had something to do with this, but to the peasant it is his immediate local experience that matters.

To set the record straight, we have to notice that village communities were not really idyllic places. For example, they indulged in ritual warfare between gangs of young men from rival villages and the weapons were as horrific as those used in modern urban gang fights. Tales of incest, rape, child-abuse, wife-beatings, bullying and carefully hushed-up murders are to be found in every village. That is how people are. Yet such a culture has a remarkable ability to contain and modify violent behaviour, keeping it within recognized bounds. The gangs, for instance, only fight on certain days, like football teams. The religious culture is part of their ordering and regulating system, even sin is clearly recognizable and has a "place", and is therefore less generally disruptive.

So the faintly self-conscious middle-class people who tried to re-create the sense of the sacramentality of daily life which belongs to peasant Catholic culture were doing the right thing, in a way, though it tended to become a decoration added to the real necessities of a culture incompatible with the peasant one. It did, at least, help to show up the un-human values of a newer culture which seemed incapable of finding sacramental expression at all. The people who tried it, as those who still try do, sensed also that a religion integrated with daily life is the only kind that can establish a base strong enough to enable people to break away, if conscience demands it, even from that daily life itself, with its routines and hopes and fears. This is well illustrated by the story of Franz Jagerstetter.

About the same time that the von Trapps decided to leave their country rather than work for the Nazis, this young peasant farmer was beginning to face an even more difficult decision in another part of Austria, the small village of St. Radegund in Upper Austria. His cultural background was the same as that of Maria von Trapp, though his family was a truly peasant one. Born in 1907, an illegitimate child, he had grown up with the same yearly celebrations, the same village festivals and church fasts and feasts, learned the same religious beliefs, though he had no "higher learning". After a fairly wild youth, he married, had a family, and was on the whole indistinguishable from the other hard-working young married men in his village. He was, however, more serious, both about his religion and about the political situation, than most people felt to be necessary for a practical farmer. In fact, when he re-organised his farm work in order to have more time for religious duties his neighbors disapproved, for, as his biographer, Gordon Zahn, put it in his book, *In Solitary Witness,* "the peasant views religion as part of the established order of his life, not as something that interferes with it", and later on this was interpreted as showing that his "extremism" had made him a bad farmer and neglectful of his proper duty to his family. (A close relative said, though, that she thought his revised system was really more efficient). Hitler invaded Austria in 1938, and thereafter unpleasant stories filtered through, even to remote mountain villages, but the change in the rulers didn't at first affect the country people very much, as long as they kept quiet and did what they were told. What was happening to intellectuals and Jews was happening far away. Even when war was declared and men of military age began to be called up for the German army most peasant families submitted, angrily but resignedly, to the drafting of their sons and husbands. It was bad, but governments were like that. Hardships and oppresive rulers are no novelty to peasant populations, and traditionally they submit because they have no choice.

Franz Jagerstetter refused the draft, not because he was a pacifist, nor because he was a patriot, but because, as a Catholic, he held that Germany was engaged in a war of aggression, which was clearly unjust in the Catholic definition. The people of the village treated his doubts with contempt and even hostility. He would make trouble for them all, they thought. The parish priest sympathised but felt that Franz would do best to obey lawful authority, and to be of use as a "Christian influence" among the men in the army. The bishop, too, counselled conformity to orders of legitmate government. Franz listened respectfully but could not agree, and he confided his interior struggles to a diary. He loved his family, his land, his home, but he had no choice, he felt, but to obey his conscience. Eventually, after months in prison, he was executed. The village blamed him for leaving his family in economic hardship and probable danger of harassment by the Nazis. At best he was a fool; possibly too much religion had that effect. They put him out of their minds and kept on as before with the observances of religion and the routines of husbandry.

Many commentators have used this story to illustrate the spiritual bankruptcy of traditional peasant religion. But Franz Jagerstetter had precisely the same religious formation as the other boys of his village. Do we give the credit for the spirit of martyrdom to an exceptional man, or to his religious formation? If he was so unusual in his resistance, is his religious culture quite irrelevant? It seems impossible to say that it was irrelevant, because the principles for which he was prepared to give his life were drawn from the religious teaching he shared with the other village boys. He had no other source. Yet the other boys couldn't see what all the fuss was about. It isn't possible to say, either, that the rest of the village had ignored its religious heritage, for it remained, overall, an observant and believing community, according to its own interpretation of the right and proper degree of observance and belief.

This, of course, is the crux of the matter, and it is a basic and inescapable problem for a Church which calls itself "Catholic". To be Catholic must mean, if it has any meaning at all, that Christian religion is not the affair of an elite. It must, somehow, embrace humankind in at least a minimal willingness to take the gospel seriously, while always pointing at the same time to the heights of holiness. There can be no moral test, nor even a credal test except an extremely rudimentary one: the one requirement is that a person should be aware of the need for salvation, and be prepared to seek it in company with the Church. Even then it won't do to enquire too closely into motives and meanings, for who are we to probe our brothers' eyes for specks of moral or theological dust? A Catholic Church must therefore include people of all kinds. If it includes a number of saints and sages it will also include a number of hypocrites and cynics. It will also include an even larger number of insensitive, cowardly and self-seeking people who don't love too much, in case they might get hurt. They cannot, must not, be excluded, not even mentally. They are not "fringe" members of the Church, they *are* members. The call is for them, the message is for them, and must be available in all the fullness possible, which means in whatever way it is possible to present it to them, each one in his or her time, place, and personality. It must reach people where they are, in their own cultural milieu, whether that be an Austrian village or an American city, and in the process the message will be restricted, scaled down to meet their level of love and understanding. If it were not, they could never realise that it was for them, let alone have a chance to respond. That is what "Catholic" has to mean in its cultural context.

How little or how great that response may be depends on both the culture and the person. There have been cultures, like that of the respectable Victorian middle class, which restricted the message to a point at which it was scarcely recognizable — yet it still was just recognizable, and out of that milieu, also, grew people who heard the message with unmistakable clarity, and lived it with splendour. In an Austrian village, the daily symbols of transcendent faith were much better expressed, even if the verbal teaching was probably narrow. Many just went through the motions, their consciences un-stirred, or so it seems. But who can judge the value of moral action in another, or presume to know how hard it may be for one to do something that comes easily to another? The fact remains that the thing was

there, the gestures and words were used, the message was proclaimed. Each culture which encounters Christianity takes it and
shapes it to its needs, and sometimes it seems almost to absorb it,
so that, as a distinct type of awareness, it disappears. Certainly it
is never possible to say exactly where "culture" ends and
"religion" begins. Yet the two are not identical. As a culture
modifies Christianity, so Christianity modifies the culture, and
implants something which can never be wholly neutralized by it,
but retains an unpredictable, heavenly vitality, a steady flame
which glows through the daily, yearly round and is always liable
to light a bonfire of sacrificial love if the right fuel is available.
Franz's grandmother, for instance, had clearly been a woman
with exceptional gifts of prayer, though we would never have
heard of her if her grandson had not met a martyr's death. There
are always some who discover what lies behind the routines of
religion.

The little fire of routine Christian religion certainly blazed
up in the case of some of the English Catholics who lived under
Elizabeth I, and continued to burn throughout the seventeenth
century. These heroes and heroines sprang from another
recognizable Catholic people, those known as the "recusants",
meaning the ones who refused to conform to the new religious
rulings, or attend the new services. I shall be studying the particular genius of Anglicanism later; what I am concerned with
here is the special and peculiar religious culture which
developed among people who saw in the new church simply a
betrayal of the old faith, the faith of their fathers.

Comparatively few died for their faith, and of these most
were priests. One hundred and fifty-six of them, on one estimate,
died during Elizabeth's reign, out of an estimated total of about
four hundred priests who were "on the English mission" during
this time. The government of Queen Elizabeth wanted to stamp
out Popery, which contained the threat of political coercion by
Rome. It used the threat and the fact of the death penalty for
this purpose rather than as an attempt to wipe out all priests, let
alone all Catholics. The government was quite prepared to turn
a blind eye to the old religion, where that was convenient. Lay
people were as courageous as the clergy, but priests "ordained

abroad" were the government's chief target. Those laity who died, like the butcher's wife, Margaret Clitheroe, and the bookseller James Duckett, did so usually for harbouring a priest, for the government rightly assumed that the recusant population relied on its clergy for support and encouragement. The number of lay-people who died was fifty-nine, three of them women, but imprisonment and fines were the usual penalties for recusancy, together with loss of the possibility of political or professional office. There were exceptions, even here. The composer William Byrd was openly a Catholic and wrote both Catholic Masses and music for the new Anglican services, and in the reign of James I the Prebend of the Council of the North was a Catholic, Sir Marmaduke Wyrell. Sir George Calvert was Secretary of State from 1619 to 1625, though openly sympathetic to Catholicism. Although he had to resign his office when he declared himself a Catholic, this did not prevent his being raised to the peerage as Lord Baltimore, and becoming, with royal patronage, the founder of the colony of Maryland. It was a matter of knowing the right people, keeping a cool head, knowing when to keep out of sight, and other techniques familiar to disadvantaged minorities.

I am not concerned here with the rights of and wrongs of Elizabeth's attempts to wipe out Popery. As E. I. Watkin has pointed out, the government persecuted Catholics for political, not religious reasons, because their allegiance to the Pope (and, by association, to Spain) represented a threat to the unity of the nation at a time of national danger. But Catholics resisted the government for religious, not political, reasons. With few exceptions they disliked Spain, loved their country, and wanted only to be left alone to worship as they had always done. Without attempting to follow the ins and outs of the struggle, we can see that the very pressure of persecution was bound to create a new kind of Catholic people, no longer simply inheriting traditional values and customs but forced by circumstances to make a conscious decision about religious allegiance.

For, whatever the merits or demerits of the new Church order, it represented the line of least resistance for everyone. There were some people who changed to a Protestant type of

Christianity for genuine reasons of conscience, but they were mostly on the Puritan wing of the new church. Most ordinary people had little idea of the issues, were ill-educated religiously and bewildered by the rapid changes in religious and political life. They and their forefathers had always worshipped in the parish church, and so (the penalties for not doing so assisting) they continued to worship there. The younger people soon got used to the new services and were not interested in whatever their parents remembered of the old ones. Those who did not "go to church", therefore, were usually people who had thought about the issues seriously (it was a very serious matter) and decided that their faith mattered more than their prosperity. Admittedly, in the early years of Elizabeth's reign the changes were so new and the political outlook so uncertain that it was reasonable to suppose that Elizabeth would change her mind, by whim or perforce. It seemed contrary to nature that the custom of centuries should be permanently altered, and in those early stages there were probably a great many of all classes who conformed only outwardly, expecting the old faith to be reinstated. Some priests from the previous reign continued to say Mass in private for those who wished, while celebrating the new service in the church. The Benedictine Augustine Baker, at the end of the following century, wrote that thousands who sincerely professed the Catholic faith, as time passed "unawares to themselves became neutrals in religion, neither true Catholics nor yet mere Protestants." Their children knew nothing of the old faith, and so it died out. But not altogether. Some held on, in spite of every active and passive discouragement. After a long, long time, the claim to belong to a recusant family, became a claim to a remarkable tradition of quiet, unassuming heroism.

Because those who chose not to go to church had to make a hard decision in a matter by no means obvious to all, they were usually people of at least minimal education. They were not generally labourers or small farmers and artisans, but were for the most part rural "gentry", urban craftsmen, small business people, or professional people. The exceptions were the people who lived on the land of a Catholic landowner. In such cases the landowner would provide support for his tenantry, protect them as best he could. He would often have a "mass centre" where a travelling priest might come from time to time, as Edmund Campion did. The owner of the place therefore had the job of allaying official suspicion that he might be harbouring priests; in any case he had to pay huge fines for not going to church, and sometimes went to prison for years.

So the landowner and his family often became the ordinary "ministers" of this strange Catholic culture. They were the ones upon whom the faith of those in their care depended. It was a difficult and dangerous vocation, requiring not only courage and compassion but a mixture of shrewdness, toughness and common sense. This was necessary to cope with the probability that a discontented servant would at any time turn informer and that to demand too much of some temperaments would be likely to make them give up rather than to stiffen their courage. Such virtues were needed in order to decide when discretion was the truer courage, and gestures of defiance a luxury the oppressed could not afford. There was continual harassment and stiff fines were frequently levied. Sometimes the strain was too much, and a landowner conformed. This meant, in practice, the death of Catholicism in that place, for with no Mass and no encouragement it could not survive.

I described in my sketch of Edmund Campion the strange network of such Catholic families, geographically isolated but linked by a common faith and a common work — that of keeping the faith alive. The thing became a sort of system. The country was covered by a network of "reliable" houses, where priests could find refuge and could celebrate Mass. It was rather like the network of homes which protected Jews or escaping prisoners in World War II. In time many of these houses were equipped with expertly concealed hiding holes built, for instance, between floors or under staircases or into the thickness of some great stone chimney.

Messages would be sent by reliable people to let local Catholics know that a priest, referred to as "Mr." So-and-so, would be at such-and-such a house, on such a day, and the people came in by ones and twos, long before daylight. Lookouts were posted while confessions were heard and Mass said, and then everyone dispersed quietly before the neighborhood was awake. Often the neighbors knew what went on, but would not tell, either because they did not want to make trouble for old friends, or because they sympathised, but were not hardy enough or convinced enough to join the obstinate groups who would not "go to church".

It was a strange life that the households lived. The great nobles could get away with a good deal, for the crown respected property. Although some suffered greatly and lost lands to pay fines, they were not harassed if they kept quiet and had friends at Court. The smaller gentry had to be more careful, and the fine line between heroism and foolhardiness was often hard to discern. Since it was forbidden to teach children the faith, and universities were barred to them anyway, many adolescents whose parents could afford it were sent secretly to France or Belgium to be educated, for both religious and secular professions. This was a great expense, and a further drain on family resources already reduced by fines. If it was discovered, this sending of children abroad was punishable.

Punishments were not consistent. The government's idea was to discourage Catholic allegiance, not to make martyrs. So prosecution was sporadic and inconsistent. Nobody knew if, when, or whom the law would strike, or if it did how severe the penalty would be; the tensions of uncertainty as well as fear were part of life. A time of apparent security might end with a sudden raid, a search for hidden Mass vestments or books, and might or might not be followed by arrests.

One effect of the accumulated experience of persecution, mild and severe, was to make Catholics very dependent on the family circle and household concerns, since this was where all of life had to be lived. These "recusant families" were understandably clannish and exclusive. All that was needed to maintain daily life had to be found within the household, which included trusted servants. Education, entertainment and religion all had to be found there. Younger children were taught at home. Sometimes books of classical learning or of a pious nature were printed abroad and smuggled in. Among the books that came out of the first half century of recusant history was Father John

Gerard's vividly written memoirs, recounting his work, escapes, captures, imprisonment and torture. In a quite different vein various pamphlets came from France, either denouncing the Queen (in earlier days) or protesting loyalty to her, or trying to offer comfort of some kind to the bewildered adherents of the old faith. Different again were the works of the martyred Jesuit John Southwell. He wrote a devotional book, "Mary Magdalen's Tears", and an "Epistle of Comfort to the Persecuted Catholics". He is best remembered as a poet, however, and his reputation in that field does not rest only on his fame as a saint and martyr. His recurring theme of the Holy Child at Bethlehem must have meant a great deal to the defenceless households which read and circulated the poems, for he stressed the power of the feeble Babe, whose "weapons" were those of the politically powerless —

> "With tears he fights and wins the field,
> His naked breast stands for a shield;
> His battering shot are babish cries,
> His arrows looks of weeping eyes,
> His martial ensigns cold and need,
> And feeble flesh his warrior's steed . . .
>
> My soul, with Christ join those in fight;
> Stick to the tents that he hath pight;
> Within his crib is surest ward,
> This little Babe will be thy guard;
> If thou wilt foil thy foes with joy
> Then flit not from this heavenly boy."

His readers needed to hear such things, and many of them did indeed "foil their foes with joy", not only by going cheerfully and even jokingly to prison and death but by maintaining a remarkable cheerfulness in the long endurance of uncertainty and hardship. Among weightier spiritual books, to encourage steadfastness by prayer, were those of Benet Canfield, whose "Rule of Perfection" taught the Christian to perform *every* action solely for the love of God. Stories were told and later written, detailing the heroic adventures of fellow-Catholics all over the country. Letters containing accounts of martyrdoms were read, re-read, and passed on secretly from home to home.

The devotional life of these tiny "churches" (for that is what they were, very like the earliest Christian groups, who met in family homes) was fed by these stories and books, as well as by editions of older English spiritual works. But there was a big gap in the "spiritual life" of these churches. Their central devotion, the Mass itself, was a rare privilege, and nothing else could take its place. Also, the spiritual sensibilities of the recusant culture clustered, as it were, around the Mass, because it was obviously for the Mass that martyrs died and they themselves were provoked and harassed. To "go to church" did not mean just attending *any* of the new services. It was compulsory for everyone to receive communion in the new (and to Catholics invalid and heretical) rite. To avoid this act of betrayal (as they saw it) they suffered; therefore the Catholic Mass was the focus of their thinking as Catholics. Eucharistic devotion was intense. When a priest could say Mass, and people gathered secretly to hear it, the atmosphere was charged with an awe even greater than that of medieval eucharistic devotion, because it was bound together with the sense of the high courage demanded in order to carry on this worship. There was the powerful sense of communion with each other, as well as with the Lord, which comes from a shared loyalty in face of danger.

It was at least in part because of this tremendous concentration of Catholic popular piety on the Mass itself that some of the scope of Catholic sacramentality was lost. The Eucharist is certainly the "touchstone" of a really incarnational faith which knows God in created things and experiences, as well as in the experience of the sublime and unearthly. The Eucharist should be the key to the whole range of bodily experience of the indwelling God; but circumstances made it, in the popular feeling of this Catholic people, almost the only one. On the other hand, the "instinctive" and fierce concentration on the uniqueness of the Eucharist did preserve that touchstone intact: it prevented it from being dissolved into a merely symbolic presence, comparable to other symbols, in a culture which has, in any case, an impoverished notion of what symbols are.

This impoverishment means the loss of any sense of the

dwelling of God in flesh. The sense of the meeting of earth and heaven easily becomes a dissolving of heaven into earth; then earth loses its glory, its potentiality to reveal "something else" within itself, becomes nothing but earth, and any sense of the realities of life which can be thought of as Catholic is lost. Reality becomes one-sided. The recusant churches, and also all the later Catholic peoples who have felt themselves beleaguered and have become defensive and conservative in consequence, did at least preserve the one thing that could never cease to challenge awareness of the inner radiance of fleshliness. It kept them from despair. It even made them unaccountably happy.

I referred earlier in this chapter to the Irish Catholic refugees from religious persecution, who swelled the flood of American immigrants. They, like the English Catholics, suffered from penal legislation. Not only was it fiercer in the case of the Irish; the marked differences in the two situations also produced very different effects on the Irish Catholic people, and on the culture they took with them across the Atlantic as well as on the version that developed in Ireland itself.

It is a terrifying chapter of history, a long tale of oppression which easily accounts for the modern horrors of the struggle in what is now "Northern Ireland". Catholics and Protestants of Belfast and Londonderry are the successors of two races (for the whole struggle is racial in origin, only incidentally religious) whose antagonism was deliberately fostered for political reasons, from the time when King James I, first joint monarch of England and Scotland, settled "reliable" Protestants in Ireland with the express purpose of keeping the Irish powerless. The settlers had every incentive to do this, since they were living on land seized from the Irish, who naturally hated them. For although there had been an English presence, and consequent anti-English hostility, in Ireland from the 12th century onward, it became particularly oppressive with the Protestant Reformation in England. Attempts to drive out Catholicism were made, mild at first, later brutal. Both the native tongue and Catholicism were forbidden, but the hunger for these was fed by Irish Franciscans at Louwain which was a home away from home (with Douai and Cambrai) of so many exiled British

Catholics, and a centre of spiritual renewal and hope for them. They published catechisms in Irish and had them smuggled in. Irish property was confiscated by Protestant settlers, and the consequent resentment burst into rebellion in 1641, starting in Ulster. Protestant settlers were murdered, people were tortured, graves desecrated, and in England a wave of anti-Irish and anti-Catholic feeling began to spread. In 1642 Irish Catholic lay-people, military leaders, and bishops set up a provisional government, the Catholic Confederacy, which confirmed its allegiance to the English monarch, but refused to be governed by the English parliament. The Catholic Confederacy was recognized as the legal government by France, Spain, and the Holy See.

But the Confederacy was split between those who were truly loyal to the crown and those who opposed it as the possession of heretical kings and queens. This division and internal fighting made the Confederacy too weak to withstand the English reconquest, which was undertaken with genocidal intent. "Even in a time and country where brutality was no rarity," de Breffny writes, "Cromwell's ruthlessness was extraordinary. Thousands of Irish were butchered at Drogheda, many in St. Peter's Church where they sought sanctuary; a few wretched survivors were deported to the West Indies to be slaves. The barbarity was soon repeated at Wexford, where over two thousand priests, religious, soldiers, and townspeople were slaughtered. When Kilkenny fell to the Cromwellians the eighty-year-old Catholic Bishop David Rothe, the author of *Analecta,* was stripped and humiliated. Throughout the country, churches were desecrated, sacred books and pictures destroyed, priests hunted down and banished . . . Cromwell felt himself anointed to smite the Catholics, whom he considered idolators, as the God of the Israelites had destroyed their idolatrous enemies." Cromwell was a great man who excites deserved admiration, which has led some biographers to play down the horrors of his Irish campaign. But it is not possible to excuse them, any more than it is possible to excuse the atrocities of the Inquisition. There are some things which cannot be smoothed over by talking about religious motives or the less sensitive feelings of our ancestors.

We have to acknowledge that it is indeed possible for extreme evil to co-exist with genuine faith, and the faith does not excuse the evil, nor the evil make the faith unreal. I doubt, however, that Cromwell's victims were much impressed by his faith. His actions have endured as a burning and unquenchable hatred at the heart of Irish self-consciousness, a hatred reinforced by the fact that the English government and people appeared to be perfectly satisfied with his actions. Following the re-taking of Ireland, far from showing any sign of shame or revulsion at Cromwell's action, Parliament confiscated *all* Irish land, which was distributed among English soldiers and adventurers. Irish families were forcibly evicted from their homes, and landowners were resettled. Following Cromwell's death the prejudice against the Irish Catholics remained, but no attempt was made to interfere with their worship, and Irish education was allowed.

After the Battle of the Boyne (in which there was the irony of Papal support for the Protestant King William III) the King, largely because of his need for Catholic continental support, agreed to assure Catholics freedom from religious persecution. Once he was free of his obligation to Catholic allies he repudiated this promise and instituted the Penal Laws during the years 1702 to 1715. All the Catholic hierarchy were ordered into exile under pain of imprisonment or deportation; religious orders were banished; priests were registered; Catholics were banned from all public office and from the university; Catholics were not allowed to teach or keep schools. Any Catholic who apostatized was allowed legally to claim all of his family estate, to the exclusion of his father and brothers.

This was the background to what happened during the great potato famine, when the failure in several successive years of the potato harvest brought death to millions. It did so because the bulk of the Irish population worked such small patches of land that no other crop was possible on it, and so when that failed there was nothing to fall back on. They did not even own the land they worked, but held it on various kinds of temporary bases, with few or no rights in relation to the landlords who (with some honourable exceptions) regarded their tenants as so many beasts and treated them as they would not dare to treat a valued animal. The iniquities which resulted from application of the laissez-faire economic doctrine to a starving population make such appalling reading that the difference between Cromwell and those who refused to budge from their adherence to a "market economy" appears to be merely that Cromwell did the killing himself, while the Government in the eighteen-forties let hunger and disease do it for them. Even if their motives were not obviously religious, it is fairly clear that the fact that the sufferers were Irish Catholics, and not English Protestants, made all the difference in the world to their attitude.

Compared with such gross sufferings — from persecution, from economic oppression and from lethal inaction — the ordeal of the English Catholics looks almost genteel. But such comparisons are not much help. Each group coped with its suffering in a characteristic way; each, in consequence, produced a particular kind of popular Catholic culture which had theological effects as well. In England the beleaguered Catholic community withdrew into an entirely private world, divorced from political concern, but still feeling themselves very English. In Ireland, where one race was oppressing another, lack of political power led to the growth of a political concern amounting to obsession, and mostly of a negative kind. There is a curious irony in the fact that one place in British culture where the Irish were truly valued and felt "at home" was the Army. Irish soldiers were known to be among the best and bravest, because fighting someone — almost anyone — seemed a "natural" occupation. There is the story, told by Abraham Lincoln, of the shipwrecked Irishman wading ashore towards an unknown land and shouting, "Whatever government this country has, I'm against it." It's a funny story, but what lies behind it is not funny at all. The mentality that it represents has produced in the Irish, as a Catholic people, some odd results. On the negative side, Irish Catholicism has produced a brand of stubborn and unreasoning conservatism which makes the Roman Curia look like a meeting of the local left-wing students' organisation. This clinging to the past springs from the experience of a Catholicism which was oppressed, and which was once whole and their very own. So every detail of it is precious, even if, in fact, the tradition from which it springs is comparatively young.

On the positive side, this often quixotic intransigence has made a very special contribution to the Catholic enterprise. Travellers in Ireland, in the days before the worst of the famine, remarked on the gaiety and courtesy of people who lived, even then, in conditions of the direst poverty. This capacity for getting a great deal out of life in most unhelpful conditions has created a kind of popular religion which is humane, durable and irrepressibly cheerful. The priests who fought for the civil rights of their immigrant flocks in new American cities were the cousins of the heroic men who struggled and suffered to save their people at home, and the people who managed to laugh and sing in New York slums were the same who danced in their rags in the Irish villages, and shared a cup of water as if it had been champagne. It is the culture of a very poor people, even when they have ceased to be poor, with the defiant and often bawdy gaiety of people who are born and wed and die in overcrowded rooms. It is not much concerned with the future, or with the kind of verbal accuracy that people fuss about in more "respectable" circles, but much concerned with loyalty and generosity, with imagination and with adventure, both real and fantastic. If the form and custom of the ancient Celtic Churches have gone, at least some of the same attitude to life persists. As long as there are Irish Catholics, there will be a popular culture which clusters around colourful personalities and great adventures rather than around buildings or schools of thought, and that is a very important contribution to the Catholic enterprise.

Writing as a European, it would be impossible for me to do justice to the kind of popular Christianity which has been developing in countries whose experience of Christianity is comparatively recent. It is for this reason only that I have dwelt mainly on popular religion in Western countries. But it seems clear that these non-western countries will play an increasingly important part in the development of insight into the meaning of the Christian message, and they will do it the way people always make Christianity their own. They will live it and change it and hand it on.

Among the most interesting Catholic popular cultures of the

immediate future are those emerging in Africa, where some of the new African nations have large Catholic communities. The African Catholic experience is a whole new world. In some places where the Gospel has been newly preached the rate of conversions has staggered the European missionaries, accustomed to sceptical Westerners who had to unlearn so much before they could come to perceive the stark and joyful simplicity of the Gospel demands. New African Catholic communities have brought to their Christian allegiance a whole-hearted, deep-rooted piety, strong enough to outweigh the unfortunate effects of the efforts to impose a Roman type of liturgy on entirely non-European cultures. African music, African dance, African sprituality with its rich sense of the indwelling Spirit, found in Catholicism a satisfying expression at every level, and the Catholic enterprise itself has received a much-needed inflow of new life, wherever it has been willing to accept it. Bernard Haring, a moral theologian from a very traditional European world, who has shown remarkable sensitivity to emergent ideas, believes that the future of the Church might be found in Africa, and he spends as much time as he can there to renew his appreciation of Catholicism. He tells one story about the transforming effect of the Christian message on one tribe. Their tribal custom had led them to divide men and women at mealtime, the men eating separately from their wives because the presence of women was thought to be a degrading (maybe even a defiling) thing. A priest was able to visit this tribe only occasionally, spending enough time to instruct catechists, and once he found that during his absence the tribe had dropped the custom of separating the sexes. When he asked the catechist the reason for this his answer was, "The Eucharist taught us. If we can share God's body and blood with women, we certainly must share our meals together."

In parts of Africa the Christian community lives under threat of persecution, and for Uganda it is not the first time: the extraordinary heroism of the martyrs of Uganda in the last century is not forgotten. But all over Africa, perhaps more than anywhere else in the world, Catholicism is truly popular. Nowhere else, probably, do worshippers pour in from the villages to celebrate Easter with a vigil that goes on all the day before, and all evening, erupting after the liturgical Paschal ceremonies into a celebration with dancing and music until daylight, the local bishop joining his flock in the dance. This is the life of a Catholic people, one doubtless as divided into good, bad, and tepid as any other, with mixed motives and rivalries and sins, yet strongly Catholic, embracing the whole person, body and soul, private and public, brain and heart.

It seems likely that when eventually Catholicism in China comes to the surface once more we shall see yet another totally different Catholic people. The experience may prove as powerful a stimulus to theological and structural change in the whole enterprise as that of the American Catholic people. (It seems unlikely, for instance, that a future Chinese Catholicism would accept an all-male ministry, and that in itself would produce new patterns and new ways of thinking.)

In Latin America Christianity is going through a painful rebirth, a re-discovery of its roots and its meaning through the ordeal of bitter persecution in police states. In these countries the Churches have been forced to re-think their political allegiance, inherited from a Spanish colonial past, and to learn to identify with the poor and the oppressed. Since this brings them into conflict with the rich and powerful they are labelled communists and agitators, and their leaders "disappear" into secret prisons. In the torture rooms and cells of many countries, the Church is recovering her identity with the crucified. The much quoted saying that "the blood of the martyrs is the seed of the Church" may be verified yet again. When it comes to fulfillment, this new and truly popular Latin American religion will surely have a splendour seldom equalled.

This book is mostly about the Western, and especially English-speaking, Catholic enterprise, because Europe is where it took root on a large scale and learned its first ideas and flourished exceedingly; and England is my home, both physically and intellectually. The English patterns are the ones I understand best. It would have been artificial and untrue to claim for myself a universal empathy, but the Catholic enterprise can and must claim it, and it seems more than likely that it will find its

165

major future impulses and philosophies outside the area of Western culture. Wherever it is rooted, it will be the experience of Christian peoples that will shape the self-understanding of the new churches, churches which will certainly have forgotten some of the old denominational boundaries. They will be cared for and interpreted by their ministers; they will be inspired by men and women of outstanding individual quality. But basically it will be the shared, common, everyday experience of living and loving and dying as Christians in a particular environment which will count, as it has always done.

The important thing to remember is that "popular" Catholicism is not a kind of second best, a background for the more enlightened. Among many inadequate and halting expressions of Christian awareness, all kinds of "popular" Catholicism must be inadequate also, in particular ways. But they are the real thing, they are part of the enterprise, they are the stones laboriously chipped and hauled to build the cathedral, and suddenly what it all means becomes visible, in a person like Jagerstetter, a place like Lourdes, a cause like the Pilgrimage of Grace — none perfect, all flawed, yet strong, genuine and aspiring.

A story was told by von Hugel about a very ordinary, conventional parish priest who had been thrown out of his customary prim stride by an encounter with the results of just such a crude form of "popular" Catholicism. No kind of "popular" Catholicism has been the subject of more easy contempt than the Irish variety; among some Christians it is almost a synonym for priest-ridden, unthinking, superstitious religiosity. So it is fitting that it should be an Irish girl who gave the good man a shock that shook him right out of his usual categories and let him glimpse "the heights and depths of holiness." I can only let von Hugel tell the story:

"He had been called, a few nights before, to a small pothouse on the outskirts of this large and fashionable town. And there, in a dreary little garret, lay, stricken down with sudden double pneumonia, an Irish young woman, twenty eight years of age, doomed to die within an hour or two. A large fringe covered her forehead and all the other externals were those of an average barmaid who had, at a public bar, served half-tipsy, coarsely joking men, for some ten years or more. And she was still full of physical energy — and of the physical craving for physical existence. Yet, as soon as she began to pour out her last and general confession, my informant felt, so he told me, a lively impulse to arise and cast himself on the ground before her. For there. . . .lay one of the sweet, strong, simple saints of God at his feet. She told him how deeply she desired to become as pure as possible for this grand grace, this glorious privilege, so full of peace, of now abandoning her still young, vividly pulsing life, of placing it utterly within the hands of God, of the Christ whom she loved so much, and who loved her so much more; that this great gift, she humbly felt, would bring the grace of its full acceptance with it, and might help her to aid, with God and Christ, the souls she loved so truly, the souls He loved so far more deeply than she herself could love them. And she died soon after in a perfect rapture of joy — in a joy overflowing, utterly sweetening all the mighty bitter floods of her pain. Now *that* is Supernatural."

Chapter 5
MAKING IT A BIT BETTER

One perennial need of the "Catholic Thing" has been for people who would take on themselves the task of making it a bit better. There can never be, in human time, a point at which the enterprise is complete, nor is it a question of adding bits. To meet new needs, it has to change; methods and structures that worked in one set of circumstances don't work in another set, so new ways must be found.

Where are they to be found? We shall find, in studying this aspect of the enterprise, that over and over again those who wanted to change old ways in order to do the old work better looked beyond the obviously Catholic context for ideas and inspiration. This is natural enough. If the existing forms of Catholic thinking and action proved inadequate, those who wanted something better had to look elsewhere.

The questions this raises about the nature of the Catholic enterprise, about what is 'Catholic' and what is not, are obvious and important, indeed in a sense the purpose of this book is to raise those questions, and I shall be examining them in detail in the last two chapters. But in this one I am chiefly concerned with the way in which those within the main-stream Catholic tradition, driven by conviction to pursue different ways of being Catholic from those currently regarded as 'normal', found ways to be radical and Catholic, radical because Catholic and (in the last resort) Catholic because radical, though not Catholic in the way most people expected. I could have written, instead, about people who did not regard themselves as in any way Catholic, in the usual sense, but whose ideas and actions did become, in time, part of the thinking which urges on the Catholic enterprise. This is a fascinating area, and names such as Calvin, Wesley, Marx, and Jung spring to mind, but then if I pursued all the areas of experience in some way connected with my subject I would have to write not a book but a library, and I have to be, reluctantly, selective and particular. My choice, in this instance, has been to concentrate on people who grew, as it were, from the inside outwards, in relation to the Catholic tradition (though this did not necessarily mean they 'left the Church', whatever that means) rather than (at least in their effect) from the outside inwards.

I have chosen a handful out of possible hundreds, and my 'radicals' begin with Camilo Torres, and travel backwards to include Abbe Pierre, Maritain, Mounier, Lamennais, Matteo Ricci, and a few others. In fact what I want to do here is to illustrate what I can only call the 'radical tradition' within the Catholic enterprise.

In doing this, two things are obvious. One is that much radical thinking which grew from study of the state and needs of the Catholic church, referring it to the Gospel standard and seeing where it failed, was so unpopular with the entrenched Catholic system that people felt forced to respond by moving out of the official unity of the Roman Catholic Church. This happened either because of revulsion at the refusal of opportunity to put into practice the needed innovations, or because the proposers of innovation were forced out by officials fearful for their prestige and their accepted forms. The other thing is that innovators within the official unity, whether they remained within it or eventually left, frequently drew their inspiration from sources outside the Church and even outside Christianity. This has become more obvious since the eighteenth century, but Renaissance innovators like Erasmus drew from pre-Christian classical sources and even from Islamic thinkers. So we have a traffic in two directions — people going out of the Church, and ideas coming in. The results have been confusing, ambivalent — and essential to the health of the whole enterprise. It is difficult not only because of the ambiguity of the reformers' relationship to the visible Catholic Church, but also because there are so many innovators, reformers and even revolutionaries in the story of the Catholic thing that an attempt to disentangle a few for inspection becomes almost ridiculous.

For instance, every religious founder was starting something new and usually did so in reaction to a failure in the existing religious or secular establishment. These men and women almost always aroused violent opposition. Many mystics and saints attracted suspicion and persecution because their message seemed to the Church of their time scandalously new and different. Every major theologian is now regarded as major precisely because he broke new ground. One could almost (but not quite) say that *every* great figure in the long Catholic tradition belonged among the innovators. Popes, theologians, missionaries, teachers, Queens, Kings, writers, politicians, social workers, visionaries, tramps — there are some of each sort among those who drastically changed the church of their time, and so affected it for the future. If the definition of a radical is someone who goes back to the roots to re-discover the true meaning, then there have been Catholic radicals by the thousands in every generation, leavening the lump of those who were happy to use such bits of Christianity as could be comfortably accommodated in the existing ways. If a revolutionary is someone who is aware of sins against honesty, justice and humanity and seeks the means (almost any means) to create a more human society, then the list includes men and women, known and unknown, who have really listened to the revolutionary social message of the Gospel in every century, and tried to apply it in their situation. And their struggle has been not just against obvious social injustice but against the dishonest ideas that breed and perpetuate it.

So where does one begin? What I have done, as I suggested at the beginning of the chapter, is to choose a few people who exemplify a number of different ways of being radical, not only in order to show how various they are in themselves but also to show how different circumstances dictated different, even opposite, strategies aimed at the same end — that of human wholeness. And I have taken these examples "backwards," beginning with a famous modern revolutionary and tracing his antecedents, both theoretical and human.

Yet even when one realises how crowded are the radical ranks, it seems at first sight perverse to talk as if the radical tendency were a central expression of the Catholic enterprise, when the most superficial acquaintance with history shows the ecclesiastical powers generally on the side of the status quo, both politically and intellectually. We always see "Mother Church" as the Church, and in describing the radicals and their struggles it will be obvious that, over and over again, the "villain" of the story is this "institutional Church." So it is easy to conclude that all those who can be described as defending the institution were, therefore, either stupid, cowardly or corrupt. In many cases they were one or more of these things, but (apart from the foolish arrogance of supposing that we can competently judge another person's motives, especially after hundreds of years) two mistakes must be avoided.

One is the tendency to read history in terms of our own particular experience, and with the benefit of hindsight. Pius IX, for instance, is a popular Aunt Sally, as we shall see. But his reactions — though not very helpful — make much more sense if we don't assume that the word "liberal" means the same now as it did in the middle of the nineteenth century.

The other is to forget that it is the *whole* Catholic thing — saints and sinners, Popes and housewives, bigots and simpletons and scholars — all these who carry the message from one generation to another, the message which the great (and lesser) radicals recognize and revitalise. Such a method of transmission naturally scrambles the message at times, but it is because the thing is catholic in this sense, also, that it is worth revolutionizing. It is a people's faith; and the people are of all sorts. Most of them have enough of ordinary intertia, timidity and greed to keep from being altogether delighted at plans to open up their cosy, familiar Church to the vigourous breeze of the Spirit. It is not villainy which makes most Christians resistant to zealous reformers, but simply their condition of being in need of salvation, and rather scared of it.

But it is also necessary to remember that the "villains" are sometimes right. Sometimes the most important thing has been to sit tight and resist change, even change that is, in itself, valuable, because the time is not right. Reluctant as we may be to admit it, Mother Church is sometimes wiser than her sister.

Finally, we have strenuously to resist the historian's habit of always saying "the Church" when what he means is the hierarchy and their advisers and followers. It is easy to fall into this mistake, but the Church is the whole people, and sometimes the Church's true spokesmen have been very obviously "the people," rather than the official teachers. When laymen and women have spoken out in the name of the Gospel, and acted on its principles, then this is the voice of the Church, and the protests of politically-minded clerics are the voice of the "world." This is, of course, another kind of over-simplification, since real people don't divide up so neatly into cops and robbers, but some such effort of theological imagination is needed to correct mentally the question-begging historical assumption that the higher clergy are "the Church."

We come up against the need for this kind of internal corrective in the very first example I have chosen, a modern revolutionary martyr-hero, the guerilla-priest Camilo Torres, who is close enough to us, and to issues that really affect us, to demonstrate clearly how hard it is not to oversimplify great issues. Was he a martyr or a hot-headed fool? Did he do the only possible thing as a Christian, or was he misled by his own character and education? Was he justified in his action, or did he, in fighting against manifest wrong, take a path that came to a dead end? Most people will answer such questions on the basis of their own political prejudices, but history will take longer to evaluate his career. His importance is not in doubt, however, and he demonstrates the inevitable tragedy of the radical vocation.

Camilo Torres emerged from a situation of political oppression, and felt driven to confront it. To do this he needed a type of analysis that would show both what was wrong and the action that fitted the analysis. In this, also, he helps us, because the effort to "make things a bit better" has to have an adequate theoretical underpinning, if it is not to make a bad situation worse. Radical thinkers are as important as active reformers. Camilo was both. He moved from personal concern through theoretical study and analysis to committed personal action of an extreme kind, because the situation he was reacting against was also extreme.

It is possible to trace his dramatic intellectual development in his essays, speeches and letters. The change was not, as some observers seem to feel, from inaction to action, as if his earlier years had been wasted. His final decision to join the Colombian "guerillas" in the mountains grew out of his years of working and thinking in more conventional situations. A man who dies fighting for freedom has a tremendous symbolic impact, but many people have died for causes which were unworthy or ideologically one-sided, or just plain bad. Martyrdom is a prophetic action, but there is more to be done than to prophesy. To be a part of the Catholic radical impulse martyrdom must be driven by the need to recover a wholeness that is threatened or lost. Some human value is under attack, something is going on that so impoverishes the human spirit that it is no longer capable of the wholeness of the gospel vision. Therefore something must be done to heal the wound, to restore the lost integrity. To die for this is the ultimate affirmation of its importance, even though there is so much else to do.

Sometimes this sense of being in a damaged, sick society produces a desire to withdraw, not just for one's own sake, but in order to get to grips with the evil at the basic level of common humanity — Jacob wrestling through the night with the Angel of God. This is a radical action in a very proper sense, as the Catholic ethos has always recognized, but people who do this are not necessarily engaged in the radical enterprise, in the more obvious sense. Some mystics have been radicals, however, in company with theologians, reformers and popular leaders, and it is interesting that Camilo Torres' early impulse, when he first began to look seriously for a life that had meaning, was first of all towards solitude.

Born in Colombia in 1929 of a professional and very intelligent family, he was sickly as a child, a bit spoiled, and he grew up a clever but "wild" young man (not unlike Augustine). He wrote and published a newspaper while he was still at school, mostly to denounce his teachers. He was about to study law, then got into a group which was interested in religion. He fell in love, but the girl entered the convent. His "conversion" surfaced soon afterwards during a holiday, when he visited a region of tropical forest. The hugeness, the silence, the sun, seemed to shrivel up his previous life to a point of utter triviality and pointlessness. He wanted to be "useful," yet the obviously useful professions somehow didn't appeal. He knew he wanted more, wanted God, and he wanted to find him in "silence, meditation, tranquillity," as he said later. His intention to look for all this among the Dominicans was thwarted by his mother, a formidable lady who clearly wanted to keep her son within reach, much as Monica did with Augustine; but unlike Monica, Camilo's mother caught up with him before he could escape, and Camilo, faced with a scene in the middle of a crowded railway station, compromised. He went to the local diocesan seminary intead, to study for the secular priesthood, where his outstanding intelligence and his interest in social questions made the church authorities decide to send him to continue his studies at Louvain, in Belgium, after ordination.

The time at Louvain was of decisive importance. He was trained in the usual Western type of sociology, which aims at "objectivity" and had not then discovered that "objectivity," in the sense used by modern scientific disciplines, means not acknowledging one's own hidden pre-conceptions, only other people's. It took him a long time to realise this. Eventually he began to use the available methods to analyse conditions in his own country (deprivations of the poor, the restriction of students and trade unions) and discovered that the categories he had been given were not adequate to the job. At a time when "liberation theology" was an unknown phrase, he tried to work out the Christian implications of the situation he saw — of a State which consisted of landowners, businessmen and military men who controlled the Colombian economy and were able and willing to prevent any increase in living standards for the poor majority; indeed they were very willing to depress them further if that would increase profits. He saw Church officials accepting this situation, from a fear of communism, and from self-interest, since most of the higher clergy came from the oppressing classes.

Camilo was one of the first to spell out the fact that violence does not mean only the random force used by criminals or terrorists, or in war. It means any use of force greater than that legally controlled minimum which is necessary to ensure the ad-

174

ministration of law. Force used to prevent the poor from being heard through newspapers or local leaders, force in the form of artificially maintained economic deprivation, force that keeps people in a state of servility against their will — all this is as "violent" as armed rebellion. Victims of police torture can testify to this. And it seemed to Camilo, as it has seemed to many others, that in situations of oppression, when nothing else will do so, force is justified to put right manifest wrongs. A number of medieval theologians would have agreed with him.

After some months of working with the United Front to bring about revolution for social justice, he became disillusioned and joined guerilla forces in the mountains. Peaceful political action appeared to him to be ineffective; he saw participants quarrelling and failing to produce results. By then he had asked to be laicised; he felt that his identification with a church structure that had no sympathy with the necessary revolution could only impede, not express, his real Christian faith, as well as the priestly office. The phrases he used are now familiar: "Violence is not excluded from the Christian ethic, because if Christianity is concerned with eliminating the serious evils which we suffer and with saving us from the continuous violence in which we live without possible solution, the ethic is to be violent once and for all in order to destroy the violence which the economic minorities exercise against the people."

"The Catholic who is not a revolutionary is living in mortal sin," he told Colombian Catholics.

"I took off my cassock to be more truly a priest."

On October 18, 1965 he was killed during a guerilla raid, and his death made him a symbol of the Christian need to resist injustice and to identify with, and stand up for, the oppressed. Since that time we have witnessed a phenomenon which most people would have considered inconceivable only a few years ago. In Latin America, and in many other parts of the Third World, it is Catholic clergy — even bishops — who are most often the spokesmen for the poor, and therefore the chief targets for abuse and persecution by oppressive governments. "Communist" is, of course, the label which is attached to such people. It can be counted on to produce a panic reaction among the tiny minority of the wealthy who own these countries, and also in the United States. This is important because many oppressive but commercially useful regimes now rely on the U.S.A. for support in trade, in training the armed forces, in "security" methods, even for armed intervention on behalf of the ruling class. (This is, however, no longer likely to be as easy to obtain as it was in the past. It is too expensive, and too unpopular.)

"Communist" is a difficult label to shake off, partly at least because many revolutionary Christians have come to rely on a Marxist interpretation of economics and history, in order to explain what they see and experience, and so enable them to make decisions on appropriate action. As in the case of Torres, this reliance can be quite uncritical, as uncritical as the mouthed phrases of the other side about the rights of private property (that of the rich) and the holiness of the family (the families of the rich). It is only very recently that Christians engaged in this world-wide struggle for the sake of the oppressed have been able to discern the limitations of this Marxist analysis, as well as its advantages. Alexander Solzhenitsyn, for instance, for all his romanticizing of suffering, has spelled out the basic flaw in Marxism as a language about human life: it excludes the area of the experience of the spirit. The Marxist language is relevant, clear and forceful. It was for long the *only* language available to analyse the situations of oppressed peoples in terms that allowed effective redress, but it is, in the end, inadequate to articulate the total situation. This was never a problem for people like Camilo Torres, who *lived* the other side. And it is not a problem for those who deal with these things in books and articles, at a purely intellectual level. The inadequacy only becomes apparent when the lack of any moral imperatives — other than what is good for the revolution — leads to a contempt for human life, negating the ideals which inspire the real struggle. This can allow a cynical exploitation of power which, once achieved, ends by being as oppressive as the power it replaces.

Violence "once and for all" does not happen. Violence breeds violence. The philosophy is inadequate, unreal and therefore finally inhuman. The wholeness is lost — yet wholeness has been lost before. To develop the passionate Christian vision of men like Torres towards a greater wholeness must be a long, long work, but some are working at it. Chief among them at present is Dom Helder Camara, a Brazilian who is a good example of one type of Catholic innovator, the sort who is in some ways less spectacular than the single-minded martyr, but who has a broader and longer view. With other South American bishops, he was responsible for the astonishing Medellin Statement, which lined the Church up on the side of the oppressed, putting the responsibility for oppression where it belonged. Since then, Dom Helder has been a primary target for the powers of oppression in Brazil — not only in a figurative sense, for bullet marks adorn his shabby little house. He was denounced to the Pope as a Communist. "The Pope knows very well what I'm doing — we've known each other for some time," said Dom Helder, grinning. "He calls me his 'red archbishop'." He has been harassed by every bureaucratic method, his closest colleagues have been assassinated or imprisoned and tortured. He himself is alive mainly because he is too well-known to be disposed of without uncomfortable publicity. In Brazil the press has been forced to be silent about his words, activities and even his existence. His constant service to the poor and support of their cause is known only by word of mouth, even in his own diocese of Recife in northern Brazil, the poorest and most neglected region of the country.

But the Brazilian government cannot silence the media outside its own borders. Dom Helder has, despite everything, become a symbol of hope for the oppressed. He makes it clear that he has great sympathy and admiration for the young who, like Camilo Torres, feel obliged to take up arms to oppose intolerable injustice. But he believes that real change can come by "peaceful violence" like that of Gandhi and Martin Luther King.

His references to Gandhi are an example of the way in which Catholic radicals have learned from sources outside their own tradition — or is it really outside? Gandhi learned his ideas in Europe, before he wedded them to Hindu wisdom. Here we have the paradox which is increasingly familiar: Christians recover their own deepest principles as they are reflected back from the teaching and experience of other religions and other cultures. Dom Helder's politics are, as he says, "socialist", and socialism is hardly a Catholic invention; yet his definition of socialism might provide a few shocks for Russian or Chinese experts. "Of course I am a socialist!" he told a reporter, "God created man in his own image and likeness, because he was his co-creator and not because he was a slave. How can we allow the majority of men to be exploited and live like slaves? I don't see any solution in capitalism. But neither do I see any solution in the socialist examples that are offered us today, because they're based on dictatorships, and you don't arrive at socialism with dictatorship. My socialism . . . respects the human person and goes back to the Gospels. God is not unjust and wants that there be no privileged and no oppressed, he wants each to receive what's essential for living — while remaining different . . . Marx should be interpreted in the light of a reality that has changed, and is changing. I always tell young people it's a mistake to take Marx literally; Marx should be utilized, while keeping in mind that his analysis is of a century ago. Today, for instance, Marx wouldn't say that religion is an alienated and alienating force. Religion deserved that judgement, but such a judgement is no longer valid; look what's happening with the priests of Latin America. Everywhere."

The situation, as Dom Helder says, has changed, and Christians make use of critiques and inspiration from many radical thinkers who are not Christian. Yet Christian revolutionaries are not, as most people imagine, a twentieth century phenomenon. Even Dom Helder, immersed in the present and with a just anger about the more recent past of the Church, shows little awareness of the roots of his own protest as part of the Catholic enterprise. "The Church belongs to the mechanisms of power," he says, and this is true but not the whole truth. The tradition of radicalism in the Catholic enterprise has, as the name implies, long roots, as indeed the constant New Testament references of its exponents show.

Camilo Torres, and others like him, did not get their ideas new and entire from Marxist sources. He himself went looking for a usable language to express his Christian awareness of poverty and oppression, and the incentive to look for it came from earlier contacts with men who were experiencing the same kind of anger at the sufferings of the poor and at the muddle and compromise in the Church. During the years when he studied at Louvain he spent some vacations working in Paris with Abbe Pierre, the priest whose work for the homeless roused the conscience of France and also roused a hatred, as well as an enthusiasm, as violent as that surrounding Torres himself.

Abbe Pierre's approach was quite different. He was uninterested in ideology, and began his radical career as a practical politician. (He was a Deputy of the French Chamber for a time, and used his salary to buy and repair the home which became the first home for his strange community of down and outs). His interest was very direct: he wanted decent conditions for ordinary families who could not afford inflated rents and were sleeping in cellars, in gaps between houses, in tents (if they could get them) or, when they were lucky, crammed into a single squalid room, until the money ran out and they were on the street again.

Abbe Pierre is a familiar type of Christian revolutionary, but the pattern of his revolution does not follow that of Camilo Torres. Camilo made no attempt to serve the poor directly, or to alleviate their suffering by (for instance) organising strikes or by the sort of "consciousness raising" Caesar Chavez and his Farm Workers' Union have done. Torres' concern was real, but he was a middle class intellectual, and his action was the result of using purely intellectual tools to reach an understanding and then a decision. Abbe Pierre represents a type which is more familiar, partly because (unless they happened to be martyrs, like Camilo) people who work for "structural" political goals are less easy to identify with and to admire than those who work in more direct fashion.

Yet Abbe Pierre, and those in his tradition, are just as revolutionary, sometimes more effectively so. Direct help for those in need is often dismissed by the politically-minded as "putting Band-Aids on a cancer," but although this argument is, in any case, usually carried on in incompatible categories, there is an important point which is never mentioned, because the vocabulary used excludes it. This is the effect of such direct confrontations with a social evil on the consciences of those who witness it.

Abbe Pierre stirred up the conscience of France. It did not happen suddenly. His dilapidated old home had been used, at first, as a weekend conference or retreat centre, but there drifted into it, and into his life, a strange group of down and outs and ex-convicts who had nowhere to go. One day, an evicted family also arrived there and were given rooms in the old house. When news got around the homeless continued to come. When the house was full, the Abbe began to realise both the extent of the problem and the utter indifference of the housing authorities. So, driven by necessity, he and his strange community began building small, primitive but solid little homes for these people, meanwhile housing them in old caravans, tents, or whatever could be found. The houses, lacking permits, were illegal, and the authorities were outraged. "Find them something else," said the Abbe, and carried on. The "Compagnons d'Emmaus," as the group of men called themselves, financed this unique housing scheme by "rag-picking" and by house-to-house collection of junk, to be sorted and sold. They picked over rubbish dumps, looking for reclaimable and saleable material. They tried to publicise the plight of the homeless, but few believed in the frightful conditions the Abbe described. Only tramps and people who don't work have no homes — not decent people, said the majority, and shut their purses. And although the little homes were built, one by one, the work was slow — too slow for the homeless in a terrible winter. One night, a baby in one of the "waiting" caravans died of cold.

Next day Abbe Pierre demanded broadcasting time, and got it by sheer force of personality. He then told the nation what happened. He flayed the legal hypocrisy, the indifference of the comfortable, the political careerism that ignored the real needs of the people. He challenged the Minister responsible for housing to come to the baby's funeral, and see for himself. To his credit, the Minister did. The response was immediate. There were, of course, those who cried "Communist," but money came in, and action was finally taken at government level to authorise the use of land for public housing schemes, on a scale more in keeping with the need. Permission was granted for a temporary "village" of Nissen huts for the interim period. The Abbe was a good propagandist; he knew how to reach people. He had other methods of persuasion too, such as the housing of homeless families in tents adjacent to new luxury flats, so that the press photographs could not fail to reveal the contrast. He organised a program of squatting in empty buildings, and then challenged the authorities to evict the squatters — in public, with journalists and cameras on the spot. The Abbe's eloquence was considerable. He made people squirm, but first he went right into the mess and shared it. He got people to help themselves, and one another. He was outraged that it was illegal to build a decent house for a family unless it accorded with regulations no normal working class family could afford to comply with; yet there was no law against letting children die in a tent, or a hole.

Abbe Pierre's method was that of direct confrontation, forcing change by attacks on conscience in his action and in his words. Was his achievement greater or less than Camilo's? The fact is, neither "succeeded" in the ordinary sense. The social conscience of France stirred and then went to sleep again, but meanwhile thousands were saved from despair, and a practical precedent was set. In Colombia, no structural change took place, but the death (rather than the teaching) of Camilo inspired many to continue the struggle for the oppressed, and to find practical ways to achieve it. The theological justification for both is clear, and it was expressed by a violently atheistic old builder who slanged the Abbe for an hour, denouncing the "hypocrites in cassocks," the Church that cared nothing for the poor except for the money they paid for funerals. Finally, the Abbe managed to get him to understand that he wanted building blocks to build homes for the homeless. Grumbling all the time, the old man produced the blocks, and then, as the truck was about to leave, he seized the Abbe by the shoulders and spoke unforgettable words: "If God exists, it's in this sort of thing that you're doing." The kingdom of heaven is within you. If you have done it to the least of my brethren, you have done it to me. The bad-tempered old man was a sound theologian.

There has to be a theology if real change is to happen. The structure of thinking determines the action which is possible, as the structure of a building determines what it can be used for. Torres, and Abbe Pierre, and all the others in the active radical enterprise, each used a very specific kind of theological structure to give the meaning and force to their action. Without it there could have been no effective action. But they did not design it. They took existing designs and re-organised them to fit new situations, and it is not surprising to discover that Camilo Torres worked in France on his vacations and studied in a French-language University, for France has been the centre of the radical Catholic tradition since the early nineteenth century. The man who represents the intellectual effort of innovation in the early twentieth century is Jaques Maritain. He was, in fact, one of the influences in the formation of Camilo Torres, as he was in the lives of so many young Catholics who were restless and searching for a dynamic Christian role in a world which they felt had lost both its sense of direction and the will to discover one. Maritain was a major influence on Emmanuel Mounier, whose "Personalist" philosophy became (through the Frenchman Peter Maurin) the foundation of the Catholic Worker movement, but Mounier was even more profoundly influenced by the writings of Charles Peguy, who had been sometime earlier of great importance in the formation of Maritain's thinking. The three — Peguy, Maritain and Mounier — and the others associated with them, span the period of growing disillusion followed by drastic economic and social change in Europe, the time from the end of the nineteenth century to just after the Second World War, and they prepared the way for the "theology of liberation" in a time with even less reason for hope. The towering figure is that of Maritain. He made Catholicism intellectually respectable after a period when "all educated people" took it for granted that Catholicism was in process of rapid dissolution, and that its continued activity represented merely the twitching of a corpse. But Maritain makes sense only if we understand how he developed and from whence he drew the ideas which he adopted, developed and handed on.

Maritain's generation was the "fin de siecle" age of intellectual disillusion, of old nations deteriorating politically, of self-assured scientists pontificating like medieval Popes, while aesthetic young men followed fashion and doubted everything. Rising commercial prosperity lived alongside gross poverty at home, and based itself on the exploitation of colonies abroad. It was a time when young people who "had a concern," to use the Quaker phrase, looked to socialism for some hope of political salvation. They were generally atheist or at any rate indifferent to established religion, which was identified with the ruling powers and seemed to have nothing to offer a new age. Like many others, Maritain was ashamed of his own comfortable, bourgeois background. Socialism had at that time an atmosphere of spiritual dedication and intensity which compensated for its doctrinal materialism. Even in his teens, however, Jacques Maritain had an attitude to his new creed that shows exactly where he would, later, discover its inadequacy, for there is in his account of it a sense of spiritual fervour, a sense of sin, and an eschatological aspiration which could not be satisfied by the kind of socialism which prevailed. "Do I have the right to be a socialist and to enjoy, consequently, the joyous socialist hope — I who enjoy at the same time bourgeois privileges — since socialist joy . . . should be reserved to the oppressed worker alone . . . the only real mankind? . . . Everything I will think and know I will consecrate to the proletariat and to humanity." The tone is religious; it is not that of the practical politician.

But while pouring out socialist aspirations expressed in terms of apocalyptic symbolism he continued his bourgeois education officially and unofficially. With his fiancee, Raissa, he went to every lecture, concert and exhibition for which he could find time. Like other students, these two despised their teachers and the institution of learning. They looked for a "real purpose" for learning. Unlike many, they found it, first of all in the person of Charles Peguy, a mystic and fervent nationalist, who died in one of the early battles of World War I. Peguy was ten years older than the Maritains, and at the time he met Jacques and Raissa he was at a crisis in his own life. He had defended the cause of the unjustly accused Jewish officer, Dreyfus, when the "affaire Dreyfus" split French society from top to bottom. When the case went against Dreyfus, on a wave of anti-Jewish feeling, Peguy was disillusioned. This battle for Dreyfus had been his crusade for the soul of France. When the socialists, in whose cause Peguy had seen salvation for France, refused to support Dreyfus for fear of causing a split in the party, Peguy moved away from socialism. He moved away, in fact, from all available labels, and became a kind of errant prophet, an announcer of doom. It was Peguy who took the young Maritain, with Raissa, to hear a lecture by Bergson.

Bergson came at the right time to inspire the young and hungry intellectuals. His own search for a way of understanding human knowledge — a way that could break through the deterministic stranglehold of nineteenth century science — gave to those who came to hear him a quest that appealed to them. The "enlightened" materialism that had claimed to liberate the human race from superstituion had only succeeded in imprisoning men and women in industrial and moral squalor. The voices of men like Bergson and Peguy, and of Leon Bloy — castigator of all things modern, a John-the-Baptist calling France to repent — were like trumpet blasts. They were piercing and imperative, they summoned to a wider mission, one in which politics was a part, but only a part, of national and human salvation. Raissa and Jacques became Catholics. Jacques found in Catholicism the satisfaction of his need for an imaginatively coherent system of symbols, his longing to escape from the bourgeois world, his desire for self-dedication to a worthwhile cause.

Maritain applied himself to the vast theology of Thomas Aquinas. The stuff was solid and satisfying. It opened doors. He soaked himself in the Catholic past, but made it new in himself. Here was a tool for understanding his world. Later it made him a sturdy support for thousands of young men and women from the middle classes and the newly educated working class to whom the bourgeois Church offered merely a stuffy theatrical performance at excessive prices. They wanted a new France, a new Europe, a new World, but the Great War had left Europe demoralised and defensive. The old social structures, among them the Catholic Church, were in disarray.

New movements sprang up, like mushrooms in autumn, for the War had discredited, potentially, almost all previously held ideas. But among them sprang some with sturdier roots, including the Jeunesse Ouvriere Chretienne, a genuinely working class, lay movement of young people, dedicated to bringing Christ into daily life as it was really lived, in factory or field; later the movement spread to the colleges and universities. The J.O.C. is an example of a whole movement dedicated to making things better. It began in Belgium, grew strong and flourished. The J.O.C. (Y.C.W. in England and America) was not alone, but it is the best known and most lasting of many movements, a symptom of a new, lay consciousness on the Catholic scene. It had minimum but very efficient organisation, and a balanced programme of meetings for study, discussion and prayer, both on the Gospel teachings and on specific local or global issues, from the conditions in the factory wash-room to the rise of Nazism, applying Gospel teaching to each issue and making practical decisions for action.

But the necessary study and personal formation as an effective Christian demanded more than just a reading of Scripture. Intellectual leadership was needed, and was to be found. Members of this new generation of lay Catholics were finding that their Church had, after all, some astonishing sources of wisdom on social and political questions. Maritain was one of them. His wide learning, his love of his country, his compassionate anger at what was wrong in his world, and his ability to give a real hope for a better future based on Christian values, helped to form a generation whose hopes were, in short term, doomed to terrible disappointment, but which had resources of courage and faith deep enough to survive even the strain of the Vichy regime and the horrors of the Nazi occupation. His romanticism offended many; he could be insensitive to areas of human feeling outside his own experience. But even his unpopular emphasis on the need for symbol and authority needs to be honestly thought through, and answered.

Maritain was by no means an isolated giant. France, between the wars, saw a renaissance of the Catholic enterprise. Long before most people had heard of liturgical renewal the old church of Saint Severin in Paris was drawing the congregation into the eucharistic celebration, making a whole district aware of itself as a Christian community. Students learned to respond at a "dialogue" Mass, to sing plain chant, and to face the priest over an altar no longer fastened to the east wall. Study in common, prayer in common, lay action in common, were normal in many places in France. This grew side by side with a religion of traditional "Premieres Communions" complete with lace, candles and plenty of photographs, and the splendour of black plush funerals (mourning black was supplied in twelve hours by the cleaners and dyers in every street) embellished with black gloves, wax flowers and rivers of doleful crepe. A church still in the nineteenth century, prop and ornament of the bourgeoisie, co-existed uncomfortably with the eager and noisy Catholic students and workers who read Maritain, St. Thomas and Marx, organised demonstrations, and held open air rallies. Emerging from this ebullient but anonymous crowd were the writers, artists, scientists, poets, philosophers — Catholics, many of them converts — only a generation after the Catholic enterprise had seemed about to collapse from sheer inertia and petty-mindedness. Cocteau and Marcel, Gilson, Riviere, Bremond, Blondel, Mauriac and Bernanos succeeded Bloy, Claudel, Peguy and Huysmans. They are names which mean little to a post-war generation, but to their contemporaries they meant that the Catholic thing was not only very much alive; it had a radical social and intellectual message. To be Radical meant to them to turn away from a corrupt democracy in the search for a more human structure based on ancient loyalties. It left out of account many things which the next generation had to reckon with. It was certainly "reactionary," but the meaning of that depends on what one is reacting against.

Among Maritain's younger listeners was Emmanuel Mounier, whose philosophy of "personalism" contributed so much to the American Catholic Worker movement. He also was reacting against what he saw as a bankrupt, amoral pseudo-democracy without human values or direction. A crisis greater than any since the Middle Ages was building up, Mounier felt, and with crisis came the opportunity for a new advance. "We are witnessing the cave-in of a whole area of civilisation," he wrote in his "Personalist Manifesto" in 1936, "one that was born towards the end of the Middle Ages, was consolidated and at the time threatened by the industrial age, is capitalistic in structure, liberal in its ideology, bourgeois in its ethics. We are taking part in the birth of a new civilization whose characteristics and beliefs are still confused, mixed with decadent forms or the convulsive products of the civilization that is disappearing."

The new historical ideal which was to take the place of one-sided philosophies like Marxism, as well as the ego-centred individualism of the intellectual world, was what he called "Personalism." He wanted a pluralist state, de-centralised, regional, derived from and answerable to local needs. The huge sovereign State was to dissolve into a service to "particular sovereignties." He demanded an international organization whose job would be to defend and uphold the rights of the human person. His vision, in fact, was close to the ideal of "Christendom" pursued by the twelfth century, but according to a new and much less unitary ideal, one in which the spiritual and moral action of the Church presides over a temporal order composed of culturally and politically heterogeneous people whose religious diversities themselves are not about to disappear. Human society was to be understood in terms of the Incarnation, as existing in time and place and body, yet as spiritual, therefore culturally located and formed. The programme was not a practical one, in the sense that Marxism provides a practical analysis leading to specific action. The importance of Maritain and Mounier and those who worked with them was that they tried to provide a vision of the values of a human society which would be worth living, and possibly dying, for. It was not a programme but a prophetic announcement.

The coming of the war confirmed the diagnosis of cultural crisis and impending disaster; it created, Maritain and Mounier felt, new opportunities. They believed that their Church could give a lead in re-creating society. It did not, and the post-war Catholic political parties proved weak, ineffective and often corrupt. In fact the inner contradictions of Catholicism in the post-war period were so great as to make clear concerted action impossible. When the contradictions finally found expression in the Second Vatican Council and its aftermath, it seemed unlikely to some that the Church could survive the experience. In retrospect, it is clear that a Church which was sitting on top of such a volcano, and unwilling to admit it, was not in a condition to provide the dynamic leadership which the French vision demanded. But this failure points up a failure of language more than a fact. We find it hard to say "church" and *not* mean the ecclesiastical structure. That structure can, but often does not, lead the Church in the true sense of the whole body of believers. Maritain and Mounier and others assumed that the first sense could subserve the second. The Catholic enterprise is not created by an official church government of whatever kind, although, historically, Popes and Bishops have been among those who shaped its development. The great upsurge of awareness of the meaning of the enterprise in France between the wars, was one example of how, somehow, the genuine vision re-asserts itself to re-form falsified values and redress a lost balance, even though the new expression will inevitably prove, in its turn, inadequate.

If France, "eldest daughter of the Church," was the heart of the Catholic enterprise in the first half of the twentieth century, that development was not a chance one. "Liberty," said Maritain, "flows in her veins." For two centuries, French intellectuals saw France, not without justification, as the centre of Europe's culture, the source and preserver of civilization in the face of Northern barbarism and Southern superstition. Paris was the heart of the world, the only place to think or to dress. France *was* culture, was reason, intelligence, taste, and — for the new Catholics — faith, too. This sublime national conceit had good historical foundations dating from the time when, in the eighteenth century, France led the break-up of the old order in Europe and ushered in a new age, for good or ill.

The intellectual restlessness that produced the "philosophes" of the eighteenth century and the doctrines which underpinned the Revolution of 1789 also inspired those in the early twentieth century who, whether in sympathy or in reaction, were aware of the dangerous narrowness of the Enlightenment mentality which they had inherited. They looked to the Catholic inheritance for some understanding, some hope for a truly human future. But whereas the officials of the Catholic Church in the early twentieth century were begining to be aware of the need for an understanding of new cultural experience (however cautiously and nervously) Church officials during the "Enlightenment" period were rigidly convinced that the only possible political option for faithful Christians was total opposition to all new ideas combined with absolute adherence to the "ancien regime." Radical Catholics, therefore, had a hard time of it. Most of them ended out of the Church, or in demoralised submission for the sake of unity.

The name of Felicite de Lamennais, born seven years before the Revolution, is central. Here again is a name which means little to most people nowadays, because it is not the name of a bishop, or of an anti-Christian revolutionary, these being the kinds of representative figures which are expected to embody the history of Church and State. He is an example of the romantic-idealist type of innovator, and he will have to suffice as representative of a movement, or rather two movements, for Lamennais was both a liberal Catholic and an Ultramontane, which seems at first sight an odd combination. "Ultramontanes" were Catholics who wanted a strongly centralised Catholic system, totally dependent both doctrinally and administratively on Rome, the place "beyond the mountains" of the Alps. In our century, a strong allegiance to the Papacy as the final arbiter, guide and governor of the Catholic enterprise, is a mark of the conservative, of people addicted to older ways and forms and suspicious of change and democracy. The notion that a strong papal allegiance might be a liberalizing ideal seems paradoxical, to say the least. But those who want to improve things must make judgements on the basis of what is actually happening. If Lamennais became a strong papalist, an "Ultramontane," he did so because he thought that the "Gallican" idea of the Church, located in the nation and administered by the secular monarchy (itself once a liberalizing tendency), had become an obstacle to the proper growth of the enterprise. His insight doomed him to tragedy because the official Church was quite unable to sense what he was trying to do.

To make sense of his ideas and his tragedy we have to understand what was going on. The French Church, before the revolution, was not corrupt so much as it was lukewarm and dull. The bishops and higher clergy were, indeed, usually extremely rich, worldly, and interested in nothing but maintaining their comfort or advancing a political career. But, just as in the late Middle Ages, the ordinary parish clergy were generally worthy of respect. They were often poorly educated, and certainly very badly paid, but they were hard-working, conscientious and devoted to their people. The religious orders were tepid and declining in numbers, prestige and enthusiasm, but they still existed and they were quietly producing a few who, when the time came, were ready to accept martyrdom. When Louis XVI called together the Estates General in 1789 for the first time in a century and a half (because he needed them to vote him money to cope with a drastic financial crisis) there were great hopes of using this opportunity to reform both Church and State; nobody was thinking of sweeping away the Church. The clergy lined up with the bourgeois against the aristocracy, and expected great things. "No day in my life has been as happy as that which I now see dawning," wrote a very old parish priest at the time. It is to be hoped that he died before he could see the full horror which actually followed. For even fairly drastic reform gave way soon to revolution, in the hands of stronger and more ruthless leaders. For a while a "Constitutional Church" devised by the King was allowed, though only about half the clergy took the required oath of allegiance to the State which set it up. Soon, even this was under attack, many were killed, others went into exile or survived in hiding. The State was formally de-Christianised and the Goddess Reason proclaimed.

When the worst terror had passed the priests who were left gradually took up their work again, with surprise at the strength of the basic Catholic feeling among the people. This Catholic sensibility had survived generations of a tepid worldly Church, followed by State persecution. However, the faintly reviving Church was still the "Gallican" church created by the strong earlier monarchy of Louis XIV, one in which appointment and finance were entirely controlled by the State, without reference to the Pope, though "without prejudice to the unity of faith . . . with the visible head of the universal Church." Many Catholics approved of this as a state of affairs which was healthier for the real life of the Church and its mission than too much dependence on an Italian potentate whose political needs and plans swayed his ecclesiastical judgement. The Gallican idea, broadly, left doctrine to the Pope but kept finance and administration under control of the nation — that is, of France.

When Napoleon rose to power he, naturally, approved of this policy. Religion, he knew, was essential to keep the country together, but he also knew he could not carry the clergy with him unless he had the Pope's approval, so he set out to get it. He got his own way: a Church reformed and restored, in communion with Rome and at the same time firmly under his own control, because he not only restored confiscated Church property, but also arranged to pay State salaries to the clergy. As soon as the Concordat on this basis had been signed, however, he himself drew up a set of regulations to restrict the exercise of Papal authority in France. Napoleon thought he could make a usable tool out of the Church, and he partially succeeded. But he irritated the Pope, who finally proved far less compliant than expected, and dependence on the State also irritated the clergy. The Gallican recipe was not quite baking the cake Napoleon expected; French Catholics found they didn't like the taste, anyway.

When Napoleon fell, the French Church heaved a sigh of relief. Napoleon, for his own ends, had given the Church a chance to recover from the revolution, and so it had, but it was like a person weakened by a long, debilitating illness. It lacked energy, enthusiasm and ideas, as indeed did most of European Catholicism. Many French Catholics hoped that the restored Bourbon monarchy which followed Napoleon would strengthen the Church, for, like many people in the wake of a tremendous social upheaval, they longed for the stability of a respected authority, guiding and ordering life in the proper way. The Bourbons, however, were timid and interested only in staying in power, which they therefore failed to do.

Lamennais was one of the previously royalist Catholics who, realised at this time that an irreversible change had taken place. To try to restore the old order was not only futile but wrong, since the ideals of the revolution, however misapplied and narrow, were those of justice and liberty. The Church, therefore, had to free itself of dependence on the State. In its mission to create a better society it must be prophet and teacher, not administrator. It must look for its leadership and integrity to the Papacy, as symbolising a supra-national, un-worldly faith, not tied to any State, yet with a mission to all. He was prepared for the Church to forego privileges and exemptions granted by the State, in return for moral freedom to carry out its mission.

Lamennais drew disciples. His personality was attractive and his ideas made sense in a confused and demoralising situation. Among the most famous were the Dominican Lacordaire, and Montalembert. With them, he founded the review called, ambitiously, "Avenir," but its "future" was short — only thirteen months. In it they advocated ideas which have since become so totally acceptable to "all right thinking people" that it seems tedious to list them. They rejected the divine right of kings, and talked of the sovereignty of the people. They wanted freedom of conscience, separation of Church and State, no State payments to clergy, freedom of education, of association and of the press. These reforms were to be led by a Papacy freed from dependence on Catholic sovereigns and relying solely on its spiritual authority.

It is hardly surprising that the Pope didn't see it that way. The role thus designed for him was altogether too uncomfortable and risky. The Bishops disliked intensely the high-minded penury proposed for them by "Avenir," and the new "citizen king" thought it was all very revolutionary and dangerous. Rulers newly in power after a violent change of regime are seldom advocates of very much freedom. So "Avenir" was condemned by the Pope, Gregory XVI, who was afraid of losing the Papal States (of which the Popes were still secular rulers) if he did not placate the great powers. Lamennais submitted for the time being, but in bitter anger and disappointment, and before long he left the Church to devote himself to the republican and democratic cause.

It is possible, at this distance, to realise that there was another side to the matter. Pius IX's policy of solid resistance to all innovation was not as totally idiotic as it seems when his words are read out of context and given a late twentieth century meaning. The polarisation of ideas that took place during the nineteenth century, with liberals on one side wanting democratic institutions and freedoms, and traditionalists on the other wanting firm authority, was quite unrealistic. If the traditionalists were unduly afraid of "anarchy" the liberals had a touching but misplaced faith in human perfectibility, which it has taken the West a century and a half of mounting horrors to un-learn. "Pio Nono," once an eager reformer, turned his back on reform and became an entrenched conservative because he could see no hope for a truly human society in the aspirations of the Italian liberals. So although Lamennais and "Avenir" were good prophets they were, arguably, not good politicians. They grasped the principles which had to govern the enterprise in a new era, but they lacked sufficient knowledge to judge the right way, and time, to apply them. Yet the vision was needed, and if Lamennais himself gave up in despair he had inspired others.

Lamennais was influenced by the eighteenth century prophets of enlightenment, Rousseau and Voltaire, and their predecessors of the "Age of Reason" in France and England, but he was also the inheritor of an older tradition of radical analysis. The Catholic enterprise has a built-in self-correcting mechanism: the doctrine itself, the incarnational demand for an ever-renewed search for wholeness, pushes people to look for new ways to do the job if the older ones are not working well. The need for repentance and reform, and the inevitability of occasions for them, are clear in Christ's parables. Innovation to meet new circumstances is demanded by them, and the gospel command to "teach all nations" means adventure and newness. However much normal human inertia and fear of risk try to disguise it, there is a doctrinal presumption in favour of the reformer and the pioneer which can be strong enough to outweigh the obvious advantages belonging to the known, the accepted, and the established. This is why the eruption of radical innovators and revolutionaries is a regular occurrence, and yet always seems to be exceptional. Each one has to struggle against the weight and power of established tradition, yet the tradition *itself* contains the argument for innovation. Sometimes the balance is very fine; whether the pioneer is accepted as a hero or rejected as "rash" or worse is decided by small details of temperament and circumstance, like the tantalising case, referred to in the first chapter, of Erasmus and the Pope, in which the fate of religion in Europe was (it seems more than likely) altered by the slow delivery of a letter.

One of the saddest examples of an extremely successful innovator whose work was finally destroyed by bureaucratic failure of imagination was Matteo Ricci, apostle to the Chinese. He is an example of the curious blend of pragmatism and principle which is typical of the Catholic thing at its best, neither applying fixed formulae blindly, nor melting into circumstances as they change, but working to discover in a given situation the eternal verities, waiting to be newly expressed and lived.

It is salutary to remember that Ricci's lifespan extends from the late sixteenth to the early seventeenth century, the era of the Counter-Reformation, of wars of religion, of the Inquisition in Spain, and of Topcliffe in England, when intolerance of other systems was the mark of sincerity in one's own. To realise just how unusual Ricci was we should remember that in Latin America even the most dedicated missionaries assumed that to become Christian meant to become pseudo-Spanish or pseudo-Portuguese. Patriotism and religious loyalty had become closely identified, as were spiritual and political authority in the mentality of Roman ecclesiastics. The famous Jesuit "Redactions" in Paraguay — born of a genuine concern for and devotion to the Indian converts — showed little respect for the indigenous culture, but organised these little communities on enlightened but "paternalist" lines. The missionaries protected the Indians from rapacious merchants and estate owners and made them self-supporting, but everything was done under the guidance of the missionaries. In the circumstances this was probably the best that could be done. The local culture, though admirably adapted to its own circumstances, was quite unable to cope with the sophisticated weapons of the Europeans. If the Jesuits had not used their spiritual and political prestige to protect them the native peoples would have been (as others were) enslaved or wiped out. There was no time for adaptation of local culture to Christian ideas, or vice versa. It was a brutal encounter in which dedicated men managed to salvage some human dignity for the Indians from conquerors whose sole motive for undertaking the very considerable risks and discomforts of colonization was the hope of huge profits.

Matteo Ricci encountered a very different situation. The Chinese Empire was ancient, sophisticated and powerful. The Chinese had a poor opinion of the barbarous people from the West with their coarse features and coarser manners. When he first arrived there, Ricci, who was a truly humble man, at first assumed that simplicity of life and behaviour must be proper to a man of God. He found that although he gradually gained friends and was personally respected, few took the Western teaching seriously. It was at best an interesting curiosity, and after many years there were only twenty converts (in contrast to thousands in Japan). In the end, Ricci realised that in order to gain a serious hearing in China it was necessary to compete with the highly educated and cultured leadership of the country on its own ground, by proving oneself acceptable and worthy of respect at the highest level. In the attempt, he gradually wore out his health; he died at the age of fifty-six. But he had succeeded. Ricci studied and mastered that most difficult of languages, Mandarin Chinese, with its complex and subtle calligraphy. He studied Chinese science and religion, and finally achieved the supreme honour of an audience with the Emperor, to whom he showed a chiming clock. His reputation for erudition, impeccable courtesy and profound wisdom grew. He drew maps showing areas until then unknown to the Middle Kingdom, which had considered that any lands beyond its own boundaries must be minimal in both size and importance. He discussed philosophy and religion over endless cups of ritual tea, and developed headaches which grew worse with the years.

But his plan worked. The beliefs of this wise and learned

scholar commanded the attention of virtuous and intelligent people. Conversions increased as potential converts learned that Confucian teaching and respect for ancestors were regarded by Ricci as worthy foundations on which a higher faith could be built. He presented Christianity as the fulfilment of all that their own great culture had developed, and it became acceptable as such. After his death others carried on the work. One of his successors was the Court astronomer responsible for a revision of the calendar which was in use until this century. But the European ecclesiastical system had meanwhile become ever more suspicious of anything unusual. "One Lord, one faith, one baptism, one God and father of all" was not enough. There had to be one rite, one inflexible credal formula, one method of evangelization, and no compromise. Franciscan and Dominican missionaries, raised in the Spanish and Portuguese traditions, were outraged at the accommodation to Chinese "pagan" custom and thought. They reported angrily to Rome. In the end, the long, slow, imaginative and catholic work of the Chinese Jesuit mission was destroyed, and Christianity in China became a despised and outlawed sect.

In the nineteenth century, access to China was once more possible for Western missionaries, but they came by the power of superior armaments, not by the power of learning and virtue. It is hardly surprising that the Communist revolution had nothing but hatred and contempt for a Christianity associated with the greed of business men and the cynical power-politics designed to keep them in business. But Matteo Ricci's body is buried in China, and his work was vindicated long after, when Chinese rites were once more promoted and Chinese philosophy studied with respect by Western Christians. It was too late for Chinese Christianity, but Ricci's experience has had its effect in other places.

It is worth remembering, too, that though Ricci was remarkable in his time he was not unique. In India the Jesuit Roberto di Nobili studied under a sannyasi, dressed and lived as a Brahmin ascetic, wrote in the Tamil language about the ways in which Hinduism and Christianity complemented each other. He wrote poems on Christian subjects in the manner of Vedic hymns. He used Hindu rites and feasts, and even conformed to caste prohibition in a way which, while it reassured the Brahmins, was barely compatible with the preaching of universal love. This is one example of how the innovator is sometimes faced with previously unimaginable moral dilemmas. He has to deal with them as best he can. To be radical is not always to be right.

There were others who were feeling their way to a wider interpretation of the Christian message, realising that the Word could be spoken in many cultural modes. It took another two centuries for these ideas to become articulate enough for general acceptance, and another century still before assumptions about "savages" were got out of the Christian system. Now, when Christian evangelists take it for granted that they must, like Paul, be "all things to all men that some may be drawn to the Lord," they are acting on an understanding that met some of its earliest severe challenges in the sixteenth century. We see because of those experiences that the Catholic reality is what it says it is — a way and a word for all peoples, everywhere, and therefore capable of expression in many cultures.

The inspiration that drove men like Ricci and di Nobili to seek Christian meaning in distant cultures, and Lamennais, Maritain, Helder Camara and so many others to recognize it in men and ideas "outside" the Catholic tradition, was already present long before these later opportunities could even be imagined, creating at each stage a new synthesis, widening the scope of the enterprise while giving new life to "converted" ideals and ideas.

When William Langland wrote his "Vision of Piers the Plowman" his evocation of human society was confined to the fourteenth century England he knew, but the principles he expressed embrace all of humankind, and the book constantly castigates people who attempt to narrow down the scope of God's Kingdom to those who possess (for instance) learning or good sense, or choose the celibate life, or even embrace an ascetic life. He allows no short cuts to salvation: it is heavy work plowing the field of Piers (Peter) the Plowman, yet he is convinced that men and women have the truth in them, by their created nature. "So that one can recognise love by natural instinct, it begins by some power whose source and centre is in the heart of man. For every virtue springs from a natural knowledge in the heart, implanted there by the Father who created us." Therefore Truth, known by Love, is available to all but it must be valiantly safeguarded, and this is the job of Holy Church. This is, however, a task frequently left undone, as Langland points out without mincing matters, because of the greed and callousness of Church officers, even the highest, who make war when they should give service and good example, and claim fat fees for corrupting consciences. Langland saw the Church as the body commissioned to show the way to the wholeness of heaven by the road of a just and merciful social system. He saw it failing, but also saw that the job needed doing. His remedy was repentance and re-discovery of the Gospel ideal of brotherly love, which makes all men equal in mutual service, whatever their work, be it clean and pleasant or heavy and foul.

And what William Langland wrote, others knew too. In England, after the Black Death had decimated the labouring population, some labourers were demanding better wages and conditions. A law was therefore passed to "peg" wages, even though prices rose. Then a "poll-tax" was collected for the king from each man, regardless of income. The better off (including the higher clergy) generally did their best to keep the labouring classes under control, fearing their new power. While "the Church," in the history-book sense of the clerical bureaucracy, was naturally on the side of the wealthy and powerful, the Catholic enterprise was most clearly apparent in the cause of the peasants. The bishops and wealthy churchmen simply tried to keep their wealth, but the champion of the people, the priest John Ball, based his case on the equality of all men before God. He wanted "no villeins nor gentlemen" but "everything in common" like the first disciples, for "we be all come from one father and one mother, Adam and Eve; whereby can they say or show that they be greater lords than we be, saving by that they cause us to win and labour for what they spend?"

The language may be less sophisticated than that of Camilo Torres but the message is recognizably the same. John Ball preached to the members of what they called "the Great Society" on the theme that God had created all men equal; serfdom was the invention of proud and sinful man, and contrary to God's law. The "proud and sinful" were, as usual, stronger, and they won. Force was their argument, and that alone. Promises of reform were made, then broken as soon as the rebels had disbanded. The leaders were executed. Nothing was gained, except that another link had been forged in the long, strong, chain of the development of Catholic radicalism.

Inevitably, attempts to put egalitarian ideas into practice are strongly opposed by the existing powers (even when they claim to be egalitarian themselves) and that has meant, all too often, Church powers as well. This is why radical movements in the Middle Ages tended to be labeled (and to *become*) "heretical" sects, because it was only in separation from the Church structure that they were free to develop their ideas. Once separated, however, their emphasis on their points of separation easily unbalanced their understanding of life. None, therefore, survived for long, though their ideas often contributed to later development. The Lollards of the fifteenth century were followers of John Wycliffe, who saw the Church's riches as a betrayal of Christ, and suspected things would be better without a Pope. They were only accidentally heretics in the doctrinal sense (they wouldn't seem heretical now) but they were politically radical, too much so for the churchmen and the nobles. Wycliffe's preachers were poor, as the Friars had once been. The people listened to them. They were persecuted and, as their teaching was denounced, it became gradually more extreme.

In Italy, in the mid-fifteenth century, the Dominican friar Savonarola represented a type of radicalism which is more familiar as evangelical revivalism. Deeply serious and ascetic, shocked by the cynical and even atheistic worldliness of the Pope (Alexander Borgia) and Cardinals, and appalled at the limitless rapacity and tyranny of the great Italian families who ruled the Italian cities, he struck a responsive chord in the hearts of his Florentine hearers when he preached against wealth, vice and oppression. He was small, ugly and awkward. His power as a preacher stemmed from his violent sincerity rather than from

199

any natural eloquence. He shocked people into listening to him. For a while, by his own single influence, he transformed beautiful, luxurious Florence into a kind of monastery, living at an extraordinary pitch of puritanical piety. It was an egalitarian monastery, with a vote for every citizen. This was not a new idea but a return to the ideals of the earlier republics. In Savonarola's mind it was an expression of Christian allegiance, a return to gospel patterns. Some of his reforms were very practical, like interest-free banks to provide loans for the poor, but the emphasis was religious. Highly emotional conversions — sobbing, howling crowds confessing their sins out loud — abandonment of games and finery — distrust of non-religious learning — all show the close resemblance to more modern revival movements and "crusades." There was a huge bonfire of luxuries, games, finery, and "frivolous" art, into which famous painters, inspired by the fervent Friar, threw paintings regarded as indecent or irreligious. Books of bawdy poetry and other "worldly" works were added to the vast pyre. Children were organised into a kind of "vigilante" corps, and searched out improper or frivolous pictures and books in people's homes. The sound of psalm-singing and the sight of religious processions filled the streets and crowds for Mass overflowed the churches. There was an emphasis on justice and compassion. In times of famine, Savonarola sent his followers to feed the starving.

But the movement was far too one-sided. Its fervour depended on one man and increasingly required penalties and religious stunts. It had no sufficient basis for development; it asked too much too quickly. Savonarola became so obsessed with his role as prophet and saviour that he could not see what was lacking. Although his downfall was brought about by the order of the Pope and the powerful nobles, furious and frightened at his influence, his kind of radical programme was inherently unstable. After his execution, the whole thing collapsed, and a reaction of wild gaiety and licence followed, itself an indication of the lack of balance in the movement and its inability to put down roots in people's lives.

Savonarola died a Catholic, but his ideas were in many respects very un-Catholic. Wycliffe rejected the Church and so, in the end, did Lamennais and many other reformers whose inspiration was indeed Catholic. Successfully "orthodox" radicals like Bernard of Clairvaux, or Francis of Assisi, were canonised, but it is possible to be fairly certain that the definitions of heresy and orthodoxy depended much more on the political climate of the time, the personality of the Pope or his advisers, and the theological fashion of the moment, than on any fool-proof test of Catholicity. This is why the Catholic enterprise is so hard to outline. Its thrust and its nature are clear, but its membership is not always so. Newman became a Catholic in his search for the genuinely Catholic, but he developed his ideas of what that must entail in his Anglican days, and he brought with him into the Roman Catholic enclosure a vision which it needed, but did not easily accept. Newman's work took a long time to bear fruit.

The radical impulse has always been there, because the endeavour has always been in need of renewal, re-direction, or drastic re-structuring, if it is to be true to its mandate.

The impulse to change has been present from the beginning. Ireneus, convinced that the immutability of a united Church founded on the Roman See was the only possible hope for the preservation of truth and a humane society; Tertullian demanding a purified elitist minority Church as symbol and example to the evil world; Clement of Alexandria seeing the main thrust of the Catholic effort as an educational one, with pupils of quite varied quality: all have their later counterparts. At one time it is the secular power that pushes reform, like Charlemagne (whom Alcuin addressed as "ruler of the Christian people, in power more excellent than the Pope or the emperor . . . in the dignity of your rule more sublime,") who issued regulations for the behaviour and duties of bishops, enforcing their authority but keeping them up to the mark — which had to be his mark. Kings (whose coronations were quasi-sacerdotal consecrations, with holy oils, laying on of hands and commissioning) were indeed for good or ill the spiritual leaders in many countries. When this power was abused, and rulers used their power over the Church as a means to their own ends, the initiative in reform had to be taken by Church officers themselves. The "Gregorian" reforms of Gregory VII have already been referred to, and Thomas a

Becket of Canterbury did not die for the right of the clergy to be tried by separate ecclesiastical courts, as most people imagine, but for the right of the Church to pursue its mission as it saw fit and the Lord guided it, not as the King willed. The business of the church courts was, as a part of this autonomy, merely the point on which the dispute came to a head.

Later, it was often a religious or an ordinary parish priest who turned prophet and led the demand for reform and renewal, and later still radical leaders and teachers emerged from the laity, whose effort can often take a secular form, if that is what the enterprise chiefly requires at that time. Our own time has seen a diverse lot of radicals: Mother Teresa of Calcutta creating a new and extremely radical religious role to serve the poorest in total poverty; Thomas Merton, a contemplative monk of an ancient Order, gaining a following from every religion and country and leading his unseen but devoted disciples towards a "hidden wholeness" (as he called his book of photographs of roots, paint-cans and old gates); E.F. Schumacher, one time follower of Gurdjieff, of Buddhism and Gandhi, drawing from all of these a Catholic vision which enabled him to preach to the world (in his "Small is Beautiful" and other books and lectures) the hope of a more human future through a technology and a politics designed for human beings. Dorothy Day has already appeared in this book, as well as Helder Camara and Caesar Chavez. Danilo Dolci, like many before him, took the Catholic initiative on behalf of the poor of Sicily out of the Catholic Church structure, when he could no longer make the two work together. "The more things change, the more they remain the same." It really does change, but the innovations are essential to the enterprise. Without them it would collapse into ancient rubble.

Chapter 6
OBSERVERS AND TOURISTS
AND PILGRIMS

The preceding chapter made it very clear, if it was not before, that the Catholic enterprise is often more catholic than its official Roman persona likes (officially) to admit. It has been forwarded, amended, challenged and even guided by ideas that grew up among very definitely non-Roman Catholic people whose ideas were, in fact, Catholic in the sense that they contributed to an understanding of the wholeness of which the Catholic Church had temporarily lost sight. But it works the other way, too. This chapter is concerned with some of the people who, while not belonging to the Roman Communion, have found in the Catholic tradition something essential to their own search for a truer human or religious catholicity. A few of them were eventually converted to Roman Catholicism, but most of those with whom I am concerned here never felt any inclination to join the Roman Church.

The particular group of people discussed here have, however, a peculiar importance, one which shows the inter-relatedness of the varied material I have used. My immediate subject is the nineteenth century movement to recover the forgotten medieval heritage.

The most obviously important development took place within the Anglican tradition, and I shall be giving this great tradition the centre of the stage, but along with the tremendous recovery in the Anglican Church of its own Catholicity went a discovery of Catholic culture, values and ideas among people who were not essentially religious at all — men like William Cobbett, and the odd, evanescent little group which called itself the Pre-Raphaelite Brotherhood. The particular significance, from my point of view, of this complex cultural development lies in the fact that it occurred first of all in England, a country which had been officially Protestant in its recognised State religion for two centuries, which is a long enough time for the "folk-memory" of an older system to have died out almost completely. It was also long enough for a strong and definite anti-Catholic bias to have become more than a matter of religious orthodoxy. It had come to be taken for granted as one of the principles of national life that 'Popery' was an un-English, corrupting influence, even if one happened to know a few odd Roman Catholics who seemed harmless. Against this background the revival, in the last century, of passionate interest in the medieval experience takes on a peculiar importance.

The movement cannot be written off as motivated by a romantic nostalgia in reaction to the new age of Industry, Science and Commerce. Rather it was the beginning — a minority beginning, narrow and misunderstood — of a great effort in the West to recover a sense of wholeness in human life.

Recently the threat of destruction by nuclear power or by unchecked pollution has caused a more far-reaching search for an understanding of human life on earth which would unify, rather than fragment, ethical and social and religious concerns, and so seek to heal the wounds caused by divorcing business from morality and science from spirituality. But small groups of nineteenth century English (and later American) men and women of the Protestant tradition discovered the medieval enterprise in their search for this unification.

They were a strangely assorted collection, varying in religious attitudes from atheism to profound piety, and in temperament from the riotously bohemian to the prim and scholarly. In fact they had nothing much in common except a conviction — which they themselves sometimes found rather shocking — that the prosperous, scientific, rational, progressive world of the nineteenth and early twentieth centuries had lost something which was vital to proper human life, and that this something had been known to the Catholic middle ages, in spite of all its barbarities.

If they had all picked on the same things in the medieval world to admire one might reasonably dismiss as mere romantic idealism this tendency to turn that period of history into a Golden Age, and to compare it with the modern world, to the disadvantage of the latter. Their ideas were, in any case, mostly not very firmly based historically. These medievalists evoked a world that never actually existed, not because they lied, or invented, or consulted inaccurate sources, but because they were selective, as people ardently supporting a cause tend to be. But the things they referred back to with such nostalgia, and tried, or longed, to re-create, were real things, distorted only by isolation. And they were all different. It is this variety of reasons for trying so hard to get behind two or three centuries of history which makes the phenomenon interesting. Even allowing for all the wishful thinking and the lack of complete information and the blindness to the less attractive aspects of the medieval world, it is clear that what these men and women perceived was a world with saner, more human values, less narrow in its understanding of what matters in human life, less dominated by inhuman ethics dictated by capitalism, closer to nature, bringing human beings closer to each other, capable of artistic achievement unsurpassed before or since. They discovered, in fact, a more catholic vision of human life; they longed to bring it to life once more. If that could not be done, they felt, it would at least provide a standard by which to judge the failure of the industrialised commercialised present.

By their struggles and arguments and experiments they created a new hope which, though sustained by a minority, continued unquenched until now, when their insights are once more given full value, and a chance of real growth and influence. The people, therefore, were an integral part of the Catholic enterprise, since they shared its values and tried to forward its aims. They drew from it, enriched it, and gave it a new impetus both at the time and also now, when the perspective of time has given their work greater value than ever, and we can see more clearly the central thrust of their achievement.

William Cobbett, one of the earliest and certainly the most idiosyncratic of these lovers of the Middle Ages, had little time for religion of any sort. "Your religion, Mr. Cobbett, seems to me to be altogether political," a parson wrote to him reproachfully. Cobbett replied that it must be so, since he had been furnished with a creed by Act of Parliament. This was a typical dig at the Established Church, for which he had little respect. "The fact is," he added, "I am no Doctor of Divinity, and like a religion — any religion — that tends to make men innocent and benevolent and happy, by taking the best possible means of furnishing them with plenty to eat and drink and wear." Listening once to a Methodist preacher calling on a house-meeting to seek for "houses not made with hands," Cobbett remarked that the girls in the room didn't seem much interested, and conjectured that they were probably more interested in "getting houses in this world first: houses with pig-styes and snug little gardens."

"Houses with pig-styes and snug little gardens" for each labourer, a piece of land large enough to grow vegetables and keep a cow, with the use of a bit of common-land for extra grazing and to collect firing — these were Cobbett's symbols of a decent society in which the Englishman would not be a wage-slave, forced to live on potatoes. (Potatoes were, to Cobbett, pig-food, and a symbol of the degradation of his countrymen.) He was a farm labourer's son, self-educated, a large, strong, compassionate, intelligent, obstinate and angry man, who moved from violent conservatism to violent radicalism, but always for the sake of the country people whose way of life he saw being destroyed by the new businesses, by a callous, conspiracy-obsessed government, and by paper money, about which he had a phobia. He hated the passing of his boyhood, which he idealised, but he was right about what was happening, as the tragic and abortive labourers' revolt in 1830 demonstrated. He denounced the "false gentility" of new farming families, who had to have a parlour with a carpet and a piano, and no longer ate in the kitchen with the farm hands and maids. He taught his own children at home, for schools were another of his abominations, along with Methodists, Quakers, and "the Great Wen," by which he meant the rapidly expanding fashionable London of the newly rich businessmen who, he said, grew fat at the expense of the working people. But he was not a socialist. He was convinced that the continuity and stability provided by a landed gentry and a monarchy (however stupid and contemptible its individual representatives might frequently be) was essential to the welfare of his beloved countryside and its people. The wealthier people must, however, recognize their obligations to the poor. People who lived on investments he regarded as parasites. He said so, which did not make him popular when he became a member of a Parliament heavily populated by businessmen. But even more than these "rogues and tyrants" he despised the preachers of revivalist religion, whom he regarded as hypocrites, encouraging the poor to accept their misery as God's will, while they themselves ate the little the poor could scratch together. The accusation was not altogether unfounded, but it was wildly exaggerated like almost everything Cobbett said. Being himself a man of enormous self-confidence as well as strength, he could not understand anyone needing "the comforts of religion." (Once, at a meeting where he had, as usual, uttered very frank criticism, someone suggested throwing him out of the hall. He stood up in his place, and the suggestion was promptly dropped).

It was no interest in Catholicism as a religion that made Cobbett look to medieval England for his Golden Age. He was looking for a concrete example of something he knew inside his head. He was never a theorist, and constantly moved from one opinion to another (both held with the certainty of absolute rightness) when he saw and experienced things which caused him to re-think. So he needed something solid and real as a model to hold up to his oppressed, misled, or feeble-minded con-temporaries, something to show them what English men and women could be, when they had the chance. To him, the medieval world was one in which society had been held together by a strong conviction of mutual responsibility at every level, when the land produced food for those who lived on it, when craftsmanship was valued and sturdy peasants lived in wholesome simplicity under the care of humane landowners. It was a selective picture, yet it was very much the picture that the medieval idealists themselves had in mind, and in places actually achieved. Cobbett's chief reason for fastening on the medieval period as his ideal England was, however, a negative one. That England was, he felt, destroyed by the rise of a market economy run by a class of greedy capitalists who cared nothing for the land or those who lived on it. These were the causes of the evils which were quite clearly bringing degradation and "pauperism" to the people who lived on the land. What went before must therefore, have been a Golden Age.

His "History of the Protestant Reformation" is an extraordinary book. There he traces the continuity from the Reformation to the American and even the French Revolutions, because he thought that the taxes levied under Protestant William of Orange in order to fight the Papist French (taxes designed, he said, specifically to make Englishmen associate Popery with Foreigners and hate both) were the origin of the taxation which by his time was becoming so intolerable in England. This was transferred to the American Colonies which, Cobbett noted approvingly, had bred "a clever sharp-sighted and a most cool and resolute and brave people," who would not put up with this arrangement. It was part of Cobbett's attempt to show that all the evils which had since afflicted his country (and the Colonies) stemmed from the Reformation, which he saw as a purely political affair, intended to enrich the King and his servants at the expense of the poor. It did this first by taking away the property of the religious orders which had relieved poverty and distress, and secondly by seizing the funds of the trade guilds, part of which had been set aside for the same purpose.

When the book was published Cobbett's violently expressed vindication of the old Church, and his attacks on the hypocrisy of Protestantism, roused not only anger but complete disbelief. Belief in the degraded, superstitious and poverty-stricken state of the Middle Ages, and in the glorious freedom and prosperity created by Protestant Good Queen Bess, was too deeply ingrained in the national mythology to be so easily refuted. But historical studies have vindicated Cobbett. His account is one-sided, intemperate, and full of splendidly imaginative sequences which no one can take very seriously, yet he said things that were true and needed saying. Here is his thesis:

"that the 'Reformation' as it is called, was engendered in lust, brought forth in hypocrisy and perfidy, and cherished and fed by plunder, devastation, and by rivers of innocent English and Irish blood; and that as to its more remote consequences, they are, some of them, now before us, in that misery, that beggary, that nakedness, that hunger, that everlasting wrangling and spite, which now stares us in the face, and stuns our ears at every turn, and which the 'Reformation' has given us in return for the ease and happiness and harmony, and Christian charity, enjoyed so abundantly and for so many ages by our Catholic forefathers.''

There was quite another side to this story, of course, but the contrast that Cobbett noticed was a real one. It was one that had, indeed, been glossed over or explained away or denied outright by earlier historians whose class privileges made it essential for them and their readers to believe that the lands and funds and prestige they enjoyed had rightfully and necessarily been taken away from the Church organizations or guilds of the Middle Ages. The degree of communal self-deception involved makes modern readers of history blink, though of course it is not unusual for a group that seizes power to do its best to blacken the reputation of its predecessors. Cobbett, to his credit, saw that this was indeed the motive of most of the 'no-popery' agitation, though he himself was "born and bred a Protestant of the Church of England," as he wrote at the end of his book, "having a wife and numerous family professing the same faith, having the remains of most dearly beloved parents lying in a Protestant churchyard." He never suggested or implied any interest in changing his allegiance, though one cannot help wondering whether an invitation to become Pope might not have given him pause. His strong defence of the faith and practice of the medieval Church sprang from the fact that it seemed to him to have been a religion of real and practical justice and charity, whereas he saw his own Church, and the government of his country, failing to practice anything of the kind — not, he knew, from the lack of power but from motives of combined fear and greed. He saw that the great monasteries had spent their revenues on the land where they were built, whereas landlords of his time (and ours) could and do spend them purely on themselves. As he saw, this brings poverty to those who live on the land and often leads to eviction. He saw in that distant age hospitals, poor relief, shelters for travellers and the aged, free schools for the children of the poor, and contrasted them with the lack of all such benefits in his own time. He concluded that the social system brought into being under the influence of the medieval Church was directed according to just and humane, and also economically sound, principles and that everyone would be better off by returning to them.

Cobbett was one of the most outspoken, and most whole-hearted of those who in the nineteenth century re-discovered the medieval world. But his was not an isolated voice. He was at the beginning of a great cultural awakening which had the medieval world as its point of reference.

The medieval ideals of Thomas Carlyle were just as historically selective as Cobbett's, but his reasons were quite different. Cobbett evoked a time when the "yeoman" was secure, free, and self-respecting, and when the rich and powerful were under a moral obligation to do their duty to their tenants and to the poor. Carlyle, who thought that England was going to the dogs for lack of respect for Heroes, had no opinion at all of the Vote. While Cobbett campaigned for the Reform Bill to give more just representation, and pinned his — largely unfounded — hopes of improvement upon it, Carlyle longed to bring back a time when, he thought, England was content to obey Heroes. Oliver Cromwell was one of Carlyle's great Heroes (Cobbett hated him), but Carlyle looked to the medieval period as an ex-ample of an ordered society, by which he meant one under orders from wise leaders, doing what it was told. He saw the medieval Church, for all its faults, as the creator of that har-mony in which men did not starve in the midst of plenty, as he saw them doing in the countryside and in the great new in-dustrial cities. To the monasteries, as good landlords who pro-vided medical care for the sick, schooling for clever children, and relief for the destitute, and to the craft guilds which upheld good work and controlled profits, Carlyle contrasted the ex-ploitation of the poor and the unbridled mania for profit at all costs which seemed to govern his own time.

This was the time of the rise of the Chartists, the forerunners of the Trades Union movement. It was a time for the stirring of anger and despair among the poor. It was the age of Industry, and of revolution, of unbelief and of profit. The "bourgeois King" of France Louis-Philippe was driven to take refuge in England, and Mazzini, the Italian revolutionary, left England to rouse Italy. There were riots in Berlin, Munich, Milan and Madrid, and barricades in Paris. Revolt was in the air, but revolt needs more than rioting crowds: it needs an ideal. In most of Europe, and in America, this ideal was seen as either anti-religious, rejecting the Church as essentially tied to tyranny, or simply, as in the new United States, ethical and non-religious. There was no past model to turn to, only a possible future Utopia such as many New World groups were trying set up. England, being Protestant, could use its Catholic past as both a model and a useful polemical weapon. So Cobbett stood for Parliament and promoted radical methods of reform (provided they were organised by himself) holding up a sturdy medieval peasantry as example, while Carlyle longed for a return of a sense of orderly responsibility under the guidance of Heroes. Both looked to the Middle Ages, and essentially to its Church, as shaper and guide of society, as model and ideal. Neither considered for a moment joining the Church whose past cultural and social achievement they admired. Carlyle, in particular, had the profound distrust of Popery and "ritualism" that one might expect from his Scotch Presbyterian origins. (Cobbett, as a matter of fact, would have been quite happy as a certain kind of Catholic, the Belloc and Evelyn Waugh type — chauvinist and aggressive.)

Both these men looked to a Catholic past for political inspiration. So, in a different way, did Ruskin, Carlyle's contemporary — art critic, amateur geologist, artist and sociologist. Ruskin influenced enormously a quite different group of people who saw the medieval world as offering an aesthetic ideal. Their enthusiasm was not merely that of the new fashion for Gothic architecture as a purely aesthetic experience. Rather, it was the other way round. These were people who looked to the Middle Ages for artistic inspiration because it seemed to them that medieval art was not isolated from the rest of life. It seemed to them that in that period art had not been a special and extra bit

211

of culture for the well-to-do. It was rather an integral part of everyday life, an expression in paint and stone of a whole understanding of life, material and spiritual. Pugin, the leader of the Gothic revival in architecture, whose works and ideas stamped the Victorian religious scene, thought of the Gothic in architecture as the expression of a God-oriented society. He and others responded to the sense of the wholeness of human aspiration in the Gothic forms. It was also this sensed catholicity of medieval culture that attracted the slightly muddled devotion of the young "Pre-Raphaelite Brotherhood."

Pre-Raphaelitism became a big cultural movement. Many of those who are associated with its ideals were not members of the Brotherhood, which, in any case, did not endure for long. In its early days, though, it drew a great response, especially from the young of the newly prosperous middle class whose sons, and even daughters, were acquiring an unprecedented degree of education. No longer burdened by the eighteenth century notion that learning was out of place for those with social pretensions (unless one were *very* rich or *very* noble; then even the eccentricity of erudition was permissible) these young people were exploring, with the awe and delight of those venturing into virgin territory, the history and art of the past, that "Gothic" past dismissed by their immediate forbears as barbarous and not worth attention. The "Middle Ages" had been thus labelled dismissively to indicate a worthless interim period between the departure of the glories of classical learning with the fall of the Roman Empire, and their revival at the Renaissance. It was now this despised period which became, for a new generation, an enchanted, secret realm, their very own, untrodden by crass and elderly people, though a small elite of sages from the older generation were their guides in the new land.

Only a few years earlier the Oxford Movement (of which more later) had aroused in some an interest in the pre-Reformation past, while producing in others a reaction of fear of "Romanism." As one of the sages of the young Pre-Raphaelite Brotherhood, Ruskin was careful to divorce his praise of the culture that created the Gothic cathedrals from the religion that informed it. This emphatic separation may have saved some from a precipitate flight to the Roman allegiance, but the young artists and poets who belonged to, or were influenced by, the pre-Raphaelites, were not really in danger of doing anything so drastic. Their religion, when they had one, was completely bound up with their pursuit of artistic integrity and, in some cases, of social renewal. If they had tried to discover the medieval Church in the forms of contemporary Roman Catholicism, they would have been disgusted and distressed — not without reason — at its stuffiness. It took a Newman to be able to see the wood for the trees, and the pre-Raphaelites were busy concentrating, precisely, on trees. To them, "truth to nature" and honesty in art meant to delineate every detail in a picture with the minuteness of a monkish illuminator and the directness and simplicity of vision which they thought of as characteristic of the early Middle Ages. This simplicity, they believed, existed before art became contaminated by the un-spiritual "worldly" attitudes typified for them by the Renaissance painters, of whom Raphael was their special abomination — hence the name of the movement.

That the artists of the twelfth century were men of great aesthetic sophistication, who knew what to put in and what to leave out, when to distort and when to "tell it straight," and that the soaring cathedrals were built under the guidance of great architects, using teams of highly skilled and disciplined craftsmen, they did not know. They were themselves too ar-tistically and historically naive to discern the signs of this in the works they adored and strove to emulate. Ruskin taught them, and they taught others, to believe that the "roughness" and simplicity of medieval work, as compared with the finish and elaboration of the eighteenth century, were the signs of healthy, independent craftsmen, "the life and liberty of every workman who struck the stone," instead of the "slavish copying" from pattern books of the previous century's workers in wood and stone. Ruskin tried to disentangle this excellence from any taint of Romanism by attributing it all to the better social status of the workman, in this way blending his art criticism with his sociology and economics and it was this synthesis, arbitrarily labelled "medieval," that later inspired the Utopian socialism of

William Morris, the most important figure in the movement from an historical point of view.

None of them were *very* important, for all of them, like Maritain and Mounier later on, were swimming against the cultural stream. It took another century of experience to demonstrate that their anger at the effects of industrialisation, at the worship of "Science" and "Progress" and at the pursuit of affluence as the only proper human goal, was not caused by mere nostalgic sentimentality but by a true, if ill-informed, awareness of a disastrous gap at the heart of the great new commercial prosperity. It is not really surprising that the last twenty years have seen a revival of interest in the pre-Raphaelites, in Morris, and even in Cobbett. The mid-Victorian "aesthetes" were mocked by the satirical weekly *Punch* and cold-shouldered by the literary and artistic establishment. They were indeed, in the terms of the political realities of the time, of negligible importance, yet even if their information was defective and their concrete suggestions naive, their sense of values was right. They were looking for an expression of those values in the right place, though their rosy perceptions were quite out of focus.

The medieval world came to them through its art and poetry, especially the poetry of Malory and Chaucer. The Arthurian legends claimed new devotees: the paintings of Burne-Jones, Morris, Rossetti, and even the early Millais, as well as the poetry of Rossetti and Morris, were for a long time concerned with a world of knights and ladies, angels, dragons, and heavenly visions. These themes were expressed in paintings which followed the pre-Raphaelite doctrine of "truth to nature," meticulously painting each leaf on a real bush, patiently enduring in the cause of art the discomfort of damp trousers. In doing so they also proclaimed that the division between the artist and the non-artist was purely artificial. *Anyone* could be an artist if he would be a good craftsman, they said, and some with small natural talent actually achieved very attractive pictures, following out the doctrine of truth to nature and of careful, idealistic craftsmanship. This apparently eccentric idea was part of the attempt to recover what they conceived to be the early medieval world, when "artists" (they thought) did not exist. However ill-informed their historical judgment, this desire to recover lost human oneness was important. It endured, in spite of the far more powerful influence of mass-production and standardization, which divorced the product from the designer, and eventually gave the "artist" an elite status even more rarified than it had been at the time of the Brotherhood's formation. Dante Gabriel Rossetti, poet and painter, was a wild, wilful, lazy, tempestuous Italian Londoner. His favourite word of praise was to call someone a "stunner." He entitled a book of his poems "Songs of Art Catholic," using the word in its dictionary meaning and oblivious of possible misunderstanding. He dragged along, in his enthusiasm, the conventionally idealistic and earnest Holman Hunt (painter of the famous "Light of the World"), and the neat, precociously talented Millais, who later forsook Pre-Raphaelitism for more commercially successful forms of art, and produced the famous "Bubbles" used by Pears Soap as an advertisement. Rossetti proclaimed a vague but glorious vision of a union of all the arts (except music, which bored him). He envisioned a community of ascetic and dedicated artists, who would give themselves to art and works of charity, forswearing drink, bohemian clothes, bad language, and (possibly) smoking.

"A group of young fellows who couldn't draw" was Rossetti's own later description of the Brotherhood. Its ideals were based on ignorance and historical naivete, its aspirations were unrealistic, the membership itself so heterogeneous that it could not and did not stay long together. Yet it started something which the times needed, and the enterprise aroused the enthusiasm, the hope and the idealism of thousands. It did so because, however misconceived, it evoked a possibility of a way of life more whole and more meaningful than anything that seemed to be on offer elsewhere. All around them was the euphoric Victorian self-satisfaction epitomised by Prince Albert's grandiose Great Exhibition, that display of human achievement in "art," science, and above all commerce and industry, housed in its vast Crystal Palace to dazzle the beholder both mentally and physically. The effect of it was awe-inspiring to the huge crowds which flocked to see it. At last Man (with a little assistance from the other sex in the form of proper admiration) had the universe well under control and was showing what he could do with it. While this was to most people a reassuring thought, a basis for that mood of extraordinary complacency in Western culture which it has taken over a century to shatter, there were many who found the whole thing infinitely depressing. Some escaped into low life, or cynicism, or travel, or they wrote funny verses, but some were driven to great leaps of imagination in search of something — almost anything — which would be as different as possible from that which was being so splendidly celebrated by the genius of Victoria's "dear Albert." And neo-medievalism supplied this.

William Morris picked up the Ruskin-inspired pre-Raphaelite idea, but in him it developed quite differently. He was a designer rather than a painter (even his best painting shows an insensitivity to the quality of paint) and he seized on the aspect of the movement which, taking its lead from Ruskin, looked to the Middle Ages for an ideal of "craftsmanship for all," a community of free workmen. "Topsy," as he was nicknamed, was a large, vital, intelligent man, full of warmth and enthusiasm and unhindered by doubts about his own abilities, which were indeed remarkable. He took the pre-Raphaelite dream and translated it into fact, first of all in the form of a house and furniture for himself, in which he tried to re-create an ideal of solid, honest craftsmanship, a place which would be beautiful not because it was made by "artists" but because "art is the expression of pleasure in labour," as he said later. It never occurred to him that art could grow from a tortured mind, for his own labour was an immense pleasure to him, and he was an optimist. His heavy oak furniture, decorated with panels depicting Dante and Beatrice or some Arthurian subject, and the tapestries and the blue wall-hanging decorated with little flowers by Janey, his adored but rather over-powered wife, all expressed his sense of the unity of art and life.

To put into practice further his notions of honest, free, craftsmanship he founded a firm that produced furniture, papers and hangings. The furniture is now sold to museums and collectors for enormous prices, while "Morris wallpapers" have become legend. These things really did have some of the beautiful vigour and hopefulness of their medieval models, for they were never copies. Morris wanted each piece to be unique, the true product of its maker's spirit. When he travelled around England, or in France, he marvelled at the splendid diversity of the carvings in the cathedrals and churches. In them he saw many works side by side — the exalted, the earthy, the workaday, the delicate, the bawdy, all co-existing comfortably, just as the men who made them, of many trades and skills, worked together on one building. To Morris, these churches did not express what he thought of as Christianity; they expressed an ideal of human society totally different from the competitive, exploitative one he saw around him.

But the firm of Morris & Co. produced lovely things which only the wealthy could afford, and the contradictions worried Morris who realised, as Ruskin did, that the ideal of "honest craftsmanship" of the Middle Ages only made sense in the context of a society where ordinary people could make, and use, such objects and buildings as a matter of course. Weaving, dyeing, painting, carving and textile design, and writing poetry and fantasy on medieval and Norse models ("A man who can't compose an epic poem while he's weaving a tapestry isn't worth much" he said once) did not, in the end, satisfy Morris's catholic conscience. He wanted to translate this "wholeness" of art and work into what he felt to be its necessary social structures. He became an ardent socialist. In his firm's workshops all worked together. He employed boys from a London Boys' Home, and also local men, one of whom, a glass painter, had met Morris at the pioneering Working Men's College which was one quite undreamy result of the great pre-Raphaelite dream. This kind of experience convinced Morris that art alone was inadequate, and that only political action could bring about a society in which people could be free, self-respecting workmen. He was a socialist of the kind that other socialists found queer company, but his vast enthusiasm gained him a hearing. His doctrine was that society should "produce to live, not live to produce," and he saw the profit system as degrading to free people, whereas most of his fellow socialists simply wanted to transfer the profits from private to public ownership.

Towards the end of his life Morris wrote "News from Nowhere," an evocation of the kind of society he longed to see. He knew very well he would never see it, nor would anyone else, for it involved not only a change of social structure but a change in human nature, eliminating all competitiveness and envy, all violence, or anything which could turn to madness. Yet the book is well worth reading, for what Morris evoked in his vision of "London-as-it-should-be," was a future society closely resembling in its ideals those of a medieval religious order. In it, he imagined himself going to sleep in the dingy London of 1890, after a socialist meeting in a smoky, poky, room, and waking up in the same place, far in the future, in a London whose river water is clear and sweet, flowing between tree-lined or grassy banks, where houses are few and (medievally) beautiful, where men and women create beautiful things for the love of the work since no money exists, and where for the same reason people do "menial" jobs, cooking, hay-making or — he stresses — even garbage collecting, which are equally valued with architecture or painting. Their clothes are graceful and of good, hand-woven stuff, in glowing colours, and all of them look decades younger than their nineteenth century equivalents. Schools, prisons, politics, wars, poverty and marriage are absent.

The whole idyll is impossibly youthful, jolly and carefree. Morris was fifty-six when he wrote it, and was struggling with the gradual but inevitable failure of his own marriage. The socialist, artist, poet, craftsman, unable to bring into being any of his many radiant visions, still clung to a faith that, somehow, human beings must be capable of fullness of life, of a harmony of body and soul, art and work, individual and community. And if his vision was impossibly perfect it was not as utterly impossible as many have assumed, nor were his and others medieval evocations entirely fantastic. In the introduction to Cobbett's "History," which I quoted before, the editor, Gasquet, gives a description of medieval village life as it can be re-created from records of the monastery of Durham, published as the "Durham Rolls." He shows how the dry factual records evoke a world in which each villager had his "toft," a bit of land on which to grow vegetables or "pot herbs." They tell of quarrels and settlements, of the consideration and generosity with which justice was administered and rents collected and adjusted.

"In fact," he says, "as the picture of village life among the tenants of the Durham monastery is displayed in this interesting volume, it would seem almost as if one was reading of some Utopia or dreamland. Many of the things which in these days advanced politicians would like to see introduced . . . were seen in Durham and Cumberland in full working order in pre-Reformation days. Local provision for public health and general convenience are evidenced by the watchful vigilance of the village officials over the water-supplies, the care taken to prevent the fouling of useful streams, and stringent by-laws as to the common place for clothes washing and the times for emptying and cleansing ponds and mill dams. Labour was lightened and the burden of life eased by co-operation on an extensive scale. A common mill ground the corn, and the flour was baked in a common oven. A common smith worked a common forge, and common shepherds and herdsmen watched the sheep and cattle of various tenants . . . on fields common to the whole village community. The pages of the volume contain numerous instances of the kindly consideration which characterized the monastic proprietors . . ."

This account refers to the period just before the Reformation, the period of decline, when the Church was badly in need of reform, when there were grave abuses in administration of Church money, and monastic life was at a low ebb. If this picture, even if not universal, is a fair description of medieval rural society at the time of the Church's lowest ebb spiritually, it is no wonder that contact with evidences of that culture at its best was an intoxicating and utterly convincing experience for Morris, and other artists and men of letters, but even more so for people who were, besides, enthusiastic Christians.

Some of them, inevitably, were Morris's customers. The medieval model which inspired Morris made his firm a success because he was not alone in the re-discovery of the medieval past, and in particular because many of the commissions to Morris & Co. came from clergy and patrons of churches. They were newly requiring decorations — windows, murals, carvings — whose aim was to introduce to Anglican congregations bred on a low-key ethical Christianity some of the rich vitality, the celebratory, inclusive character which its advocates discerned in medieval religion.

They had no desire to become Roman Catholics, because what they had been discovering was that they *were* Catholics. They didn't need to leave their church, they asserted, but only to uncover and display its lost glories.

The original thrust of this re-discovery of the pre-Reformation Church came from people not primarily interested in ritual changes or Gothic decoration. The outward and more ritualistic expression of the movement has been in some ways a distraction, to later observers, for it drew attention away from the deep spiritual roots of the revival. Yet this outward and often tasteless manifestation was part of the whole. It expressed unmistakably a desire for integrity of religion, life and art, after the centuries of departmentalisation, and indeed of suppression of some aspects of life.

The Oxford Movement is the obvious point at which the tendency to recover this catholic spirit became public. The Tracts, which gave the name Tractarian to the movement, were a series of essays written by a group of sincere and devout Anglicans designed to show that the Church was a living organism. They saw it as a whole, human, but divinely commissioned community with a continuous tradition, alive and developing but one with its apostolic beginnings, through bishops who were the successors of those apostles. The Tracts followed each other, spreading across the country a message expressed in quite traditional, academic language, yet the message stirred a tremendous excitement among many of the clergy and the educated laity of the Church of England.

Newman, Pusey and Keble are the best remembered of the group, but there were others joined with them, praying and studying together. From their common dedication to the recovery of the true Catholic faith within the English Church flowed not only the Tracts (which were fairly heavy going) but poetry, scholarship, sermons — all giving a tremendous sense of a fresh power at work in the stiffened body of the Church. Newman's sermons at St. Mary's at Oxford, where he was Vicar, "touched into life old truths," as a listener said. Keble's poems, "The Christian Year," were a revelation of Christian symbolism and celebration.

At this time, most official religion, Protestant and Catholic, was in a state of torpor. It was respectable, undemanding and, on the whole, boring. Real fervour was not to be looked for in the parish churches and their congregations but in the evangelical movement and its Catholic equivalent, the Jansenists and similar groups. The evangelicals, impressive and saintly as they often were, were also narrow and gloomy in their view of human nature and of the Church as a community and a way of life. So the Tractarians, with their emphasis on a Catholic faith, a whole, traditional Church life, integrating art, worship and daily living, offered a new vision to people hungry for one. They proclaimed a *holy* Church, capable of glory, full of the Spirit, as in the beginning.

The response was tremendous. So, of course, was the opposition. When Newman and one or two others "went over to Rome" the opposition felt able to justify its suspicion that at best all these "new" ideas were undermining the Protestant resistance to Popery, and at worst might well be a deliberate plot to hand the Church of England over to Rome. But in one way Newman's conversion was a red herring. He felt obliged to recognize in the Roman communion the authority and continuity which, in the end, he could not find in his own beloved Church, and his conversion had a far-reaching and much needed effect on the Church he joined. The movement as a whole was not a "Romanizing" one, and Anglo-Catholics, as they came to be called, were clear about their position that the Roman Church had failed to maintain a truly Catholic tradition since the Reformation. They were looking for the essential *Catholic* tradition, and they found it, half buried but very much alive, in their own Church's history. They were, they felt, the heirs of the medieval Church which, for all its eventual decadence, had been clearly the Catholic Church, in need of drastic reform but still the real thing.

One of the proofs of the truth and vitality of the ideas of these Anglican clergy is to be found in the lives of those — and they were many — who worked in slum parishes in the huge, new, horrible cities. They brought to the industrial poor a religion whose full humanness, warmth and spiritual courage were expressed outwardly, as they had been in the Middle Ages, in beauty of decoration, in colour, light, and ceremony. These men lived and died, often worn out, among the very poorest, those without any heritage of culture, without experience of beauty or spirituality. Their work justified them, and the Gothic-style churches they built in the poorest areas are still there, in England and in America, now half-empty but testifying to their vision.

These people also saw (and this is why the usual concentration on the Oxford Movement can be misleading) that the glory they had re-discovered was an unbroken tradition in the Anglican Church, although it had been nearly swamped, since the end of the seventeenth century, by the State Protestantism established by William of Orange (a man who was, in private, without religious faith at all), at the request of the English Parliament and for purely political reasons.

The reaction of the Catholic Church centered in Rome to the Reformation turmoil had been a defensive one. Although the "Counter-Reformation" was a tremendous clean-up of abuses, it concentrated on tightening bonds of loyalty to Rome and on putting up a united front against the Protestants. It therefore emphasised all the points on which the Reformers disagreed with the accepted "Roman" theology and practice of the time. Although it remained "Catholic" in doctrine, ideals and intention, it became, in another sense, a sect among other sects. It was no longer *the* Church, faced only by minor heresies and schisms. It was *a* Church and, while it never admitted this, it behaved like one, which inevitably caused a deep loss in the very catholicity which it was struggling to preserve.

But in our own time some of the books, prayers and poems composed by the great seventeenth century Anglican divines have become more readily available to non-specialists. Christians of many Churches have discovered with delight a continuity of truly living spirituality, of strong, honest theology, of tender and yet unsentimental devotion, which had long been ignored except by devout Anglo-Catholics.

Hooker and Laud, Jeremy Taylor, George Herbert and Henry Vaughan — these are names to remember, but only a few among many. There was a firm and conscious tradition. It was a tradition which cherished sacramental theology and rite, and even had a form of religious life in the 'monasticism' in the house of Nicholas Ferrar at Little Gidding. This is the place, remote and quiet still, which inspired T.S. Eliot's poem of that name in his *Four Quartets* and is now the home of a renewed community life of the same type. But the new community is not confined to the Anglican communion, which is as it should be, for the sense of that tradition was seeking a wholeness, and inclusiveness, which it found neither in the fortress-Church of post-Reformation Rome, nor in the Protestant alternative.

Under William and Mary, people who held to this understanding of the nature of the Anglican Church refused to take the oath of allegiance to William, whose power over the Church they considered illegitimate. (But, to keep to historical realism, we have to remember that under William's predecessor, the Catholic James II, they had protested against James's Act of Toleration for both Catholics and Dissenters — that is, non-Church of England Protestants; religious toleration was not a virtue in that period. James brought them to trial for this protest, and they were acquitted, so their refusal of the oath to William was clearly not from motives of love for James.) Many of these clergy lost their jobs as a result of this refusal, and a large number of laymen and women followed them into schism and were known as the 'Non-jurors.' Deprived or not, they remained a small but effective body throughout the eighteenth century, and it was their teaching which eventually inspired the great Anglican renewal which began with the Oxford Movement. It led a great number of people to re-discover a completely different kind of religious experience, one which was symbolised for them by the re-discovered continuity with the medieval world, but which was much more than that.

223

For it was not merely an Anglican renewal. The Anglican re-discovery of the size and beauty of its own heritage spread to other Churches. As time passed, and the bitterness of divisions between the 'parent' Church and the Methodists and other Free Churches died down, some of the newer Churches began to feel the same obscure longing for a more Catholic way of life, to pick up from Anglo-Catholics (often without noticing the sources) a renewed sense of the spiritual breadth of Church life, and within it the importance of the sacramental element as a unifying and deepening one. The Eucharist became, in many cases, more im-portant, more solemn, and more frequently celebrated, worship acquired a greater sense of dignity and beauty in contrast to the spontaneous but often chaotic prayer-services of earlier evangelical history. Even the Chapels had their Gothic windows.

The same kind of development was taking place in the older Protestant Churches in Germany and America. It was happen-ing in the Catholic Church in its Roman fortress, too, for the old Church itself was in equally great need of such a re-discovery. Yet again, it began with a return to the Middle Ages in search of a source of new inspiration and vitality, in music, art and religious life, and it is probably fair to say that it was the in-fluence of the other Churches, and of the converts from them, which helped to make this renewal really effective in the Roman Church, since there it had to work against a deeply entrenched defensiveness and a huge apathy.

This chapter is about the 'Catholic' tendencies among those who did not belong to the Roman Communion. We have seen the craving for a more catholic understanding of life at work in a wide assortment of people, of diverse beliefs or of no particular belief. All of them found in the medieval world the symbol of what they were looking for, and the better-informed were able to make the obvious connection between medieval life and the medieval Church, and to draw certain conclusions from their observations of both. In some the inspiration issued in new ar-tistic principles, in others in new political ones, and in others again the results were explicitly religious, nevertheless including art and politics as expression of a catholic awareness. All of them applied these ideas in their own times, in markedly original and even eccentric ways, quite foreign to the Middle Ages to which they turned as a model. The Catholic enterprise is like that. It has a history and a tradition but it is never purely antiquarian. A true attention to tradition has results which are often far from 'traditional', if the word is taken to mean simple conservatism. The sudden and widespread obsession with the Middle Ages marked a point at which an industrially and commercially oriented world was able to articulate a craving for 'life more abundantly' and saw the signs of that in the past. By doing so it was galvanised into trying to achieve the same abundance to carry it hopefully into the future. The great Anglican tradition has been itself a Catholic enterprise, and in the period which I have been examining this enterprise began to 'feed back' its vision and energy to the parent Church, in the form of converts but also in the form of its own extraordinary witness to a Catholicism which could subsist for two hundred years without a centralised Church bureaucracy and have, at the end of that time, the inner vitality to enter a wholly new expansion of spiritual power and influence.

This raises important questions about the nature of the Catholic enterprise and its future.

Chapter 7
THE WAY OF WISDOM

There is nothing new under the sun, but nothing remains unchanged except what is dead. This book has been much concerned with the past, because that is necessary if we are to understand the present nature, and possible future, of the Catholic enterprise. But not even William Morris or Cobbett thought we could really re-capture the past. Present efforts to do so, among neo-ultramontanes more papal than the Pope, have not only been divisive and anything but Catholic, they have been just as selective, and as uncritical in their historical judgment, as any Victorian Gothic Romantic. The results have been much less fruitful, for recent projects in Catholic nostalgia have unfortunately chosen as their model the nineteenth century, the period of Roman Catholic history when the Church was most defensive and least Catholic.

To look to a particular moment in time as *the* Catholic moment is a waste of time, for there is no such moment. Even the glory of the "High Middle Ages" was a glory more of vision and aspiration than of achievements, great as those were. Yet as the pathways of discovery I have pursued through many strange places come together in our time, it seems that the Catholic enterprise has reached a point at which an unprecedented degree of self-understanding is possible, making possible in turn new developments which may well make the generations to come among its most splendid.

I described in the Introduction the splendour of a human building erected to the glory of God, preserved through many ages and dangers, and renewed to become something it had never been before. Following the clues provided by this parable of inspired human craftmanship, I tried to discover the nature of that Catholic "thing" which produced York Minster and, like it, is now being massively and painfully renewed. It is old and new, scarred by centuries and freshly present, but not quite sure, after all this, what it really is, and what it is for.

So, having come to the end of this long exploration of the Catholic thing (by one of many possible routes) I am left with the most difficult task of all. That is, of course, to offer an answer to the question implicit in the whole book: given that there is this real though elusive thing called "Catholicism", what do we *do* about it?

I put it like that because, in the end, one cannot pursue an investigation like this, even by simply reading it, without being faced with the demand for some kind of definite decision in relation to it. This book is not an account of an historical curiosity, nor a vaguely inspiring record of great deeds, nor an explanation of a philosophical system, nor an introduction to a "spiritual way". It must be, in some degree, a stirring of conscience, a raising of questions which are universal, as the word "Catholic" implies. Therefore I am not asking here "what is the point of the existence of the Catholic Church?" (or, more personally "why should anyone be a Catholic?") but rather, what is the function of this Catholic thing in our time? The answer to that will show us what we have to do, since if it has a function at all, and if its name is not a mockery, it must affect everyone in some way or other. And if it affects everyone, then anyone who becomes conscious of it is faced with the need to take some kind of personal stance in relation to it, with whatever action flows from that.

In searching for an honest and accurate answer to such a question I must turn to the theological basis of the whole thing. To many people this will suggest some kind of evasion, a turning from the confrontation of human reality to take refuge in abstract formulation. But I have, personally, spent some twenty years wrestling with certain fundamental questions about the nature of human experience, and discovered (originally to my own surprise) that what I was unfolding was theology. Theology is not a system invented by religious people and then applied to existing human concerns. It is simply a reflection, in the light of faith, on what actually happens to people — to individual people, and to groups and nations and cultures. Theology is the attempt to find more or less adequate and comprehensible ways of

227

conveying what we perceive of human events as the action of God towards human beings, and the response of human beings to God.

In fact, it *begins* with experience, and then, naturally, reflection on experience — commented on, discussed, handed on — becomes "tradition" for those who come after, and becomes part of their own experience, part of their inherited way of understanding and responding to God. Those who renew this tradition must integrate it with their own new, direct and probably differing experience, and so enrich, and modify, the tradition which they have renewed and must, in turn, hand on.

If theology is this kind of thing then the whole of this book (and of most other books, for that matter) is the raw material of theology, and to turn to a theological analysis at this point is not an evasion but a practical necessity if anything useful is to be done about all this slightly chaotic accumulation of material.

At the outset it must be said that the kind of theological reflection into which I am about to launch would have been most unusual a couple of generations ago. A book on the Catholic heritage written, say, fifty years ago would have had the explicit intention of heartening and encouraging readers who were themselves members of the Roman Catholic Church, and of persuading some others to consider the possibility of becoming members. And there will be Roman Catholics now who will find it hard to see any other justification for such a book. (The book itself would, of course, have been very different, anyway.)

It is true, and I assert this without any apology, that it has been my hope in writing this that readers who are Roman Catholics will indeed be heartened, humbled and moved (as I have been over and over again in writing it) at finding themselves involved, in our muddle-headed and inadequate way, in the incarnate humanity which is the obvious "locus" of the Catholic enterprise. But if this were the only response which such a record could evoke then it would be manifestly built on an inadequate theology. This is not because Catholics of fifty years ago were less intelligent, or less sensitive, than we are, but because the shattering experiences through which Roman Catholic Christianity had passed in the previous two centuries had made it virtually impossible for most Roman Catholics to allow the full implications of Catholic theology to appear. (This is, of course, true at any time — there are blind spots in each generation, and each generation is necessarily unable to perceive what its own particular blind spots are. Those who come after us will know where we, in our turn, have failed to see clearly.)

I have suggested, in various places in this book, that what (not unexpectedly) emerges as characteristic of the Catholic enterprise is its attempt to be truly universal, to reach not only every nation but every aspect of human life and to be engaged (both actively and passively) in its transformation and indeed in the transformation of all created things. This can and did and does often issue in mere arrogance, or in attempts at imposing a distorting degree of uniformity as the mark of unity, or in a lunatic tidiness that tries to legislate creation into some humanly controllable pattern. (It is not only modern science which has thought it could efficiently replace the Creator in running the world). But, somehow or other, that impossible idea of a universal enterprise has never been wholly lost to sight.

It could not be, if Christianity were to survive. For whenever Christians (Catholic in name or not) have, in disillusion and fear, outlawed some aspect of life, at that point they have failed to be Christian. Whenever Christians have treated human sexuality , for instance, as incapable of being transformed in Christ, as inherently tainted, their attitudes and behaviour have become less than Christian, even though in other aspects they might have been saints and sages. When politics also have been put outside the sphere of Christian concern, Christians have failed, at that point, to be Christian, and then politics have fallen into great evil. When beauty — the physical beauty of men and women, or the beauty of pictures and buildings — was regarded as a trap of the evil one, then that area of human life which is concerned with beauty became indeed a source of evil. Wherever Christians have pushed some aspect of their lives outside the boundaries of their Christian responsibility that aspect has fulfilled their expectations and become a point of corruption. Their attitudes have often been quite understandable. Sex, and beauty, as well as money and power, can obviously destroy goodness, destroy *wholeness*, by allowing human beings to mistake the goodness *in* an experience for good itself. The rejection of, or withdrawal from, this corrupting area (it comes to the same thing) is natural enough as a reaction, but it is a disastrous failure of theological insight. It is only by being brought into the wholeness of a potentially transformed humanity that the potentially corrupting influence can become, instead, "a means of grace and a hope of glory."

And it is this realisation, and the work that it imposes, which seem to me to characterize the Catholic tradition. To be aware of the Catholic nature of the Christian involvement means to realise that Christianity *has* to "meddle in politics," and *has* to preach about (for instance) pollution, nutrition, genetics, fashion and housing.

But before I begin to ask more awkward questions about how this works in the historical Catholic Church in relation to other kinds of Christians (not to mention other religions) I want to push the theology still further back, and ask why this should be the essential Catholic task — why, theologically, Christianity as such must fail if it is not Catholic.

At this point I confront the glorious and yet inevitably frightening reality which underlies all I have been saying, as it underlies all of life. I mean the central Christian fact that God became human. Without this fact the Catholic enterprise would not make sense. I say this because it is only the assurance that we know God fully, clearly, and only, in the human fact of Jesus of Nazareth which makes it impossible to reject any aspect of creation as irrelevant to the Kingdom of God. Many great spiritual ways have led towards the experience of God, and clearly they are true ways, they do lead to that ultimate reality. They often assert that material reality is full of signs of God, is the vast array of gifts of his providing, is a manifestation of his Being. But only the revelation of God in Christ asserts the being of God fully and accurately present in one unique human person, who is not simply a manifestation of God, but is God.

The implications of this may perhaps be more extraordinary for us than they were for our forefathers (and therefore perhaps harder to accept) because we have a much more accurate idea of the inter-relatedness of all material reality. The particular human body which is Jesus of Nazareth is inextricably related to other kinds of bodies, inanimate as well as animate. It is related chemically and genetically, in all kinds of complicated ways, to other human bodies in particular, but all those human bodies are modified, indeed in a sense "made", by their environment — by climate, terrain, food. We also know a great deal more than our ancestors about the weird relationships between body, mind and spirit, though what we know now only serves to throw into rather frightening relief the things we don't know. But we do know that people are "made" not only by their physical inheritance and environment but by their culture, and that indeed these cannot usefully be thought of separately, except for purposes of classification. The physical environment poses the limitations for a culture, but also acts as a challenge, to which human beings respond. In its turn, the culture takes charge of the environment and modifies it for its own purposes, and that again produces cultural change.

So the human person is at the heart of an enormously complex, subtle, and varied pattern of inter-related and interdependent being, and beings. It follows that if indeed we can say that, in looking at Jesus of Nazareth, we are seeing the reality of God, then we are saying that all material as well as spiritual reality is capable, at a certain point, of being God. It is, of course, the "certain point" that matters. This is not pantheism but incarnation, the entering into material reality, at a given time and place, of the divine reality which always underlies it. This is the stumbling block for many. They can accept the idea of divine immanence, God present in some sense in all things, but not the scandalous particularity of incarnation, which sees not only material reality in general but history — sequence, development, human circumstance and human response — as divinely significant. So God himself enters into a new relationship with matter at a certain point in time, on a certain spot, and as the outcome of an historical and cultural "process", which is not an imposed plan but the decisions and arrangements (for good or ill) of particular people belonging to a particular nation which had particular experiences, both political and religious.

The Christian assertion is, further, that God thus present lived a human life conditioned by all the things that normally shape a human life — family, neighbourhood, nation, education, job, friends, contacts — both planned and accidental. All the things that happened to him happened within a given situation to which he had to react, with which he had to work, and this includes his own feelings, mental processes and spiritual experiences. His life ended in a death by torture which was a normal Roman punishment, and even this climax, full of awe and terror and glory to the Christian mind, could only occur within the particular human circumstances which were those of his place, people and time. But Christians assert that this life, cramped as it was within historical circumstance, broke through some kind of cosmic barrier and changed not only the course of human history but of the history of matter, by drastically modifying the basic status of material reality. There would be no point, here, in trying to paraphrase St. Paul or re-hash exegetical controversies. If we take seriously the baffling but undoubted inter-relatedness of the spiritual and the material, of culture and environment, mind and body, individual and community, then belief in the resurrection of Jesus is an assertion not only about what happened to this one man but about the nature of reality. It is saying, first, that the ultimate bliss, the goal of all human decision, is not a liberation from material and bodily existence, but a transformation with it and in it. Jesus Christ, "first born of many brethren" broke the barrier, and began a new process which St. Paul refers to as a kind of cosmic parturition.

Yet it is wrong to call the new thing which thus began a "process," although at first that seems the obvious word, because it implies an engineered progression which proceeds according to some kind of master-plan. We can only talk about the "plan" of God if we surround the word with so many reservations and inverted commas that it loses any force. For, once again, the whole thing happens through human decision and human muddle and in and through the given progression of natural growth and change. It is, still, an historical *phenomenon*, worked out not just *in*, but *by*, people — real people in real situations, with normal limitations — genetic, cultural and moral.

Christians also assert (led by St. Paul who makes the most staggering statements as if they were the merest matter of course) that this human transformation is part and parcel of a cosmic transformation. In some way or other human beings are involved in developments within all of material reality. The *fact* of the involvement we find easy to accept, as I suggested, but the kind of qualitative change which is asserted is a much more difficult thing to take seriously.

Yet we have to take it seriously if we are Christians. At this time, too, it seems that many who are not Christians are also groping for some such understanding of the role of human beings in relation to unconscious creation. Many, seeing the appalling things human beings have done to their environment and to other living beings, have wanted, rather, to abdicate a role of responsibility which has been so much abused. This in itself is a sign of remorseful sensitivity to the relationship which is perceived to exist, but the Christian assertion tht Jesus of Nazareth, who died, is risen and glorified, implies that this inescapable relationship is potentially a redemptive one, indeed that if human beings do not take on this role, as redemptive, then the full potentiality of material reality must remain unfulfilled. There is no inexorable "process", there is only an invitation.

This invitation is the basis of the Christian Church. The message is to human beings, but that means to people who are enmeshed in all the rest of material and spiritual reality, and must respond, if they respond at all, in the consciousness of what they are.

What are they? "Co-heirs with Christ," "members of his body," capable of the blissful exchange of love which is the life of God. But also, at the same time, bodily creatures, chemically, genetically, environmentally and culturally conditioned. It is in this situation that the human person hears the invitation to take part in the transformation of the whole affair, assured that such a thing is possible because the way has been opened by a fully human person.

The point to stress is that there is a job to be done. It is not a matter of letting oneself be swept along by some irresistible divine initiative. This is the staggering thing about the Christian notion of the Church. It is the point at which divine love depends on human response. We talk about "Almighty God", but that might is solely the power to go on pouring out love without end or limitation. If Christians are right in saying that in Jesus we see God (and this is, on John's evidence, what he himself said or at any rate that was how his words were remembered by his most constant and intimate and intelligent followers) then we see a God who will never coerce. We see a God who refuses, as the three temptations in the wilderness attest, to use any kind of power at all except the power of utterly self-giving love. It is this God who asks people to take on the job of loving all of earthly reality to such a point that it is transformed into the ultimate wholeness which we call "heaven." This job is to be done in the power of that same love, which will be poured into anyone willing to accept such a frightening gift, and to the very limit of the person's willingness to accept it, but no further.

That is the kind of thing the Church is, and this is of course why it is such a scandal, because its whole basis and raison d' etre is sacrificial love, but, since that love will not coerce them, its members spend much of their energy busily evading the implications of the gift they (usually) genuinely want but of which, also, they are genuinely and understandably terrified.

It must be clear by now what I regard as the theological basis of the Catholic enterprise. It is the attempt to carry out that job of loving everything on earth to the point where earth becomes heaven. Its job is to love *everything* but, since human hearts are constricted by the complex of negatives we call "sin", it is inclined to be selective rather than Catholic in its loving. So the Catholic enterprise is inevitably a failure. The job to be done and the people who are to do it don't match. Yet sometimes it does get done, and this book is a very partial account of how it did and does get done, how things and people are loved to a point where they change and blossom and reveal a glory undreamed of.

At this point I have to move from considering what the job is, which is the reason for the Catholic enterprise, to considering how it has to be done, and here I move away from theology proper and make use of the image which I found helpful first of all in the Introduction

It is necessary to talk about the job to which the Church is invited, and identify that with the Catholic enterprise, but this will not do, just like that, because it is so very clear that, when most people think of the Catholic Church they think of that rather forbidding sister to whom I referred — that domineering, occasionally smothering, always self-assured old lady called Mother Church, with her vast compassion and efficiency and her low estimate of human moral worth.

I hope that the people and adventures and ideas evoked in this book will have been sufficient to show that, much as "Mother Church" may be needed, she can only do her proper work if she acknowledges the equal role of her wayward and exasperating twin. Indeed, it is the ultimate tragedy and nobility of Mother Church that she knows, in her secret heart, that she is mortal and her sister is not. It is at those times when she is able to acknowledge this openly, and live with its implications, that she does her work best, and her best is very good indeed.

In the course of this book I have tried to show the extraordinary variety of human styles, individual and cultural, which have sprung — paradoxically it seems — from the effort towards wholeness, that ideal of Catholicity which seeks to touch every aspect of earthly life with its Christian vision of transformation through perfect love. This, and no other, is the Catholic enterprise. It has led, indeed one must almost say that it necessarily leads, to the grossest failure. It cannot be done, and every kind of evasion and substitute has been explored in the attempt to avoid the implications of being the people whose job is to live by the recognition of universal love. But these evasions have driven many of the best lovers to tear themselves away from the visible unity which seemed to have become simply Mother Church, in one of her fits of broody possessiveness, and when this happens, Sophia, dusted out of the house, has taken refuge in a neglected, bare kind of hut at the bottom of the garden. There the refugees and rebels from Mother Church's household have gone to find her, and to share the hut. And so Mother Church has crept down stairs at night and left the back door open for her sister to come in. Later, with the connivance of Sophia and in a different dress she has gone down the garden and helped to put the hut in better order. Her efforts have usually been received with gratitude, because people realise that even the eternal and ineffable beauty of Sophia is not enough. They need Mother Church just to help them to live sanely with so wild a person as Sophia, and even to celebrate her glory.

As we know, that story has repeated itself more than once, and often the repetition has occurred when the occupants of the hut have, under Mother Church's guidance, so enlarged and beautified their new home that it has become large and solid and permanent-looking, and Sophia has been less welcome in it than at first. (She is always forgetting to wipe her feet on the new mat, and — worse still — bringing home with her the most undesirable visitors). So, once more, she has fled to new homes, and yet she has never forsaken her old ones, even when they have wanted her to. And she always welcomes Mother Church into whatever home she has chosen, though the occupants of some of them prefer Mother Church only to visit at night and incognito, so that her necessary work among them may not be known to the neighbours.

Allegories are all very well, and they can illuminate troublesome areas of life and thought. I am rather fond of this one, and the more I explore it the more it seems to work, but it can't be left in this form. I have to come clean, finally. It must be evident from this whole book, and from my allegory (not to mention York Minster itself) that, to my mind, the Catholic thing from which the enterprise grows is not co-terminous with the visible Roman Catholic Church, yet is intimately and essentially connected with it.

For instance, one of the greatest Christian writers of this century, whose theological insight springs fully and brilliantly from a profoundly orthodox Catholicism is the Anglican poet, novelist and theologian, Charles Williams. There is no doubt of his Catholicism, there is no doubt of his Anglicanism, and he himself was not unaware of the paradox. He felt no need whatever to become a Roman Catholic, yet all his work attests to the source of his sense of Christianity, as a cultural as well as a religious thing, and this source is in European, Roman Catholicism, and not just pre-Reformation Catholicism either. His introduction to the letters of the great Anglican mystic, Evelyn Underhill, shows that she had a similar experience, and he recognized the exact nature of the paradox with which both of them had to live.

Perhaps, to those who belong to neither tradition, the difference between Anglican (or Episcopalian) and Roman Catholic does not seem great enough to be significant as a pointer to understanding the relationship and function for which I am searching. But, to choose another example, Richard Jefferies, the "nature mystic", recorded in marvellous prose an experience of God, immanent in earthly reality, yet unspeakably other, and his attempts to describe his experiences parallel very closely the writings of mystics who understood their own experiences in Christian terms — Ruysbroeck, and Eckhardt, for instance. All of them had trouble with the terminology, and Jefferies insisted that he had experienced something "beyond deity", but so did Eckhardt, in slightly different words, and for similar reasons. The popular images of deity, and the philosophical patterns made to cope with the concept, seemed to all three of them quite ludicrously inapt to describe the ultimate reality. It must refer to something other and lesser and they made efforts to make sense of this gap between "God" and "Godhead". Yet both Jefferies and his specifically Christian predecessors actually present, in different terms, the same theological distinctions which careful and sensitive Catholic theologians have traditionally offered concerning man's possible knowledge of God. Jefferies was truly, and not by any fanciful stretching of his words, within the mainstream of Catholic mystical theology.

Mystics are tricky material, but the Cistercian monk Thomas Merton, who died in 1968 while attending a conference of Christian and Buddhist monks in Bangkok, was a mystic but also a man of enormous culture, wide sympathies and earthy common sense. He was also a man with an unerring eye for the phoney or sentimental, which he did not hesitate to expose —

sometimes, perhaps, with insufficient regard for the feelings of those concerned. This was not a man who would be taken in by the Western fashion for cultivating Eastern types of meditation, a popular quasi-mysticism with much glow and little flame. Yet Merton, in his later years, discovered in Buddhist tradition and practice what he felt to be invaluable food for the growth of truly Christian spirituality. He never ceased to be a Christian and Catholic monk, though his interest in Buddhism gave rise to all kinds of rumours, (among them reports that he had left the Church and even married) which he knew to be inevitable and accepted with rueful good humour. His life as a contemplative was centred in Christ, but he found no contradiction in seeking that centre with the help of an ancient and entirely un-Christian religious tradition, for he recognized Christ present there, transforming and growing, and it seems that some of those Buddhist monks with whom he discussed spiritual matters shared this recognition, though they would have expressed it differently. This is part of what I mean by the Catholic enterprise. It reaches out to all of life, perceiving the seeds of the Kingdom of Heaven, sometimes still hidden, sometimes — as in this case — growing strongly, but each needing, for its perfection, to be fully recognized and celebrated as part of that outpouring of divine love which is also to be discerned in millions of other ways and places, which need to affect each other and to be transformed together.

To do this kind of thing is the Catholic enterprise, and this is not a new idea resulting from Christians being more "broadminded" nowadays. The impulse which sent Thomas Merton, the mature Christian mystic, to sit at the feet of a Tibetan Buddhist hermit is the same impulse which set the jurists of the twelfth century to work to discover and make plain the seeds of the Kingdom of God in human law and custom. They perceived them there, in Roman law, in local custom, but they needed to be identified, and celebrated, as a place where divine love was expended, and by being so identified they would be, and were,transformed. This was the same inpulse that made Dante in his *Divine Comedy* raise up Virgil, the pagan Roman poet, as his guide through the dark regions of the human mind and spirit. Virgil can lead him until that point at which the recognition of divine love becomes so immediate that, in Dante's thought, the pagan religious consciousness, however noble, must itself willingly and lovingly give way to a different guide — to Beatrice, figure of human love and wisdom, so transformed as to be the transparent messenger of ultimate love. The recognition of the divine love in some earthly experience changes it; it becomes capable of a fuller realisation, one whose full meaning it did not know before, though it could, and did, experience it.

This is the impulse that drove scholars and poets, missionaries, builders, revolutionaries, kings, explorers, servants of the poorest and neediest, to discover and love and so transform the created thing. "Nihil humanum mihi alienum est." Nothing human is alien to me, if I am to take the Christian message seriously. Nothing human, and nothing else earthly either. To be Christian, my love and concern must be catholic.

To be Catholic in this sense may indeed mean that my concern is with the preservation and good order of some bits of visible Christian organization. To be "Mother Church" is to be given a great and painful honour, a job full of moral headaches and, by its nature, impossible to do properly, yet essential as long as one human being remains on earth. But to be Catholic may also mean to be driven to explore "the wilder shores of love", to be peculiar and exaggerated and isolated and quite possibly totally mistaken.

In this enterprise, therefore, two things are required. One is recognition of the divine love present in each thing and person and situation, and therefore of the glory that is its "nature" if that love be fully realised in it. It is not enough to be affected, moved, exalted by divine love; it is necessary also to recognize it for what it is — otherwise one cannot act fully, respond fully, to what is going on. The other thing, of course, is to be willing to respond, which is another matter, but not a totally separate matter, because response to a degree, or moment, of recognition brings deeper recognition, and so stronger demand for response. And so it goes on.

But recognition is, among other things, an intellectual process. You have to be able to explain the thing experienced, somehow or other, at least to yourself, and then decide on action that in a particular situation fits the thing recognized.

The Christian body, the Church, has to be so many different things in these many particular situations, because it is the point at which human beings recognize and are forced to wrestle with the extraordinary fact of a God who loves, and to commit themselves to act in accordance with what they perceive. So the Church has to be about any number of different things; it has, in fact, to be Catholic, not only in the sense that its activity must, by virtue of its nature, be catholic, but also in the more difficult and much less obviously appealing sense that the intellectual part of the response, the reflection and attempts at self-understanding which we call dogma, must accurately reflect that Catholicity.

The sticky word is *accurately*. It means there is no room for vagueness or for thinking it doesn't really matter how you express it because love is all that matters. Certainly, love is all that matters, but unless there is an adequate understanding of what is meant by love and how it works then it may well be less than effective in action — a statement which scarcely needs to be supported with evidence here, since the evidence is thrust at us every time we switch on the television or open a newspaper or, indeed, examine our consciences. So an accurate analysis of the nature, activity, source, meaning and results of divine love is required in order to carry out the Catholic work.

Orthodoxy is what I am talking about — that central, vital Catholic orthodoxy which breaks out at intervals into new growth from its tough old roots, and shows up the hot-house, chemically-forced character of so much of the religious thinking whose criterion of value is only its "relevance" and acceptability to a particular group of people.

As I have pointed out, orthodox Catholic theology has a way of appearing like some wily old bramble, in unexpected places — unexpected by Roman Catholics and equally unexpected, sometimes, by those in whose gardens it emerges. It is the sturdy stem of Wesley's theology, as well as that of the Anglican tradition. It has appeared (growing, admittedly, rather wildly and peculiarly but still recognizably) in the teaching of some modern sects which have settled on the religious edge of the hippie world. Indeed Catholic sacramental theology kept on appearing in certain aspects of the youth culture of the sixties, which got some of its ideas from native American religion and some also from northern European legends and lore.

Whenever it appears it has the same effect, of course in varying degrees according to the degree of clarity and completeness with which it is understood. It shows them a world invaded, permeated and called to transformation by divine love (sometimes under other names) and it gives them the job of responding to that love, by recognizing and nurturing it in every place in which it is perceived.

It may seem, after all this, that to call this "the Catholic enterprise" is special pleading. If it can be undertaken by all kinds of people who don't know it as Catholic in any ordinary sense, what is the point of giving it that label? The point is that however many people may get the message without recognizing the messenger, there is a messenger, and it is that historical body called the Catholic Church. Sometimes it has failed to hear its own message, and sometimes others have heard it better and passed it on more effectively, but that is where it comes from.

This is still not the same as saying that the Catholic thing is found in its fullness only in the visible Catholic Church. It would be hard to say, at any given moment, where that fullness is to be found, since it can never be a fullness only of doctrine. No doctrinal formulation, in any case, can every express the fullness of the revelation. The explicitness of recognition, and its accuracy (never it's completeness), matters, but so does the fullness of response to it, which we call holiness from one point of view, and worship from another and there is no measure for those.

Somehow, in spite of all the difficulties of formulation, there is a sense in which there is, there has to be, a center from which the Catholic enterprise springs. Human beings are like that, their enterprises and enthusiasms have centers — symbolic foci, reference points. In one way one cay say, predictably, that Rome is that center, in the sense that Rome has become a word which *means* that center, the touchstone of truth and unity for millions.

(Though it is sometimes only in the negative sense that Roman teaching is what you measure yourself against in order to make sure you teach something different). But in another sense Rome cannot be the center because Rome isn't that kind of thing. This center cannot be geographical or administrative, though of course a geographical and administrative center might naturally and graciously coincide, at times, with the real center, which is, as I suggested, the place of fullest recognition and response. This has to be a place, because people are in places, they don't exist in a sort of spiritual diffusion. But this *place* can have any number of locations. It is spiritual, in St. Paul's sense, which is quite earthly and not at all shadowy.

This place (real but multiple) of fullest recognition and response, must be visible, identifiable, it must be something you can visit and describe and of which, God willing, you can become part. This is why there is an ordinary and commonsense way in which this center is, as I said, inextricably mixed up with the visible Catholic Church. It is delightfully mixed up to the great profit of many people who have no particular desire to be part of the Catholic enterprise, but happen to have been brought up in it, or brought into contact with it, and may find themselves at any moment responding to the recognition expressed in the worship and life of the Church. (This is called conversion).

This center is to be found, as I said, in the visible Catholic Church, and also in other Christian bodies who share the recognition and offer the response, and who themselves are aware of the source of the dogma by which they explain themselves, even if they remain to some extent detached from that source, for various historical reasons. The Catholic Church, in turn, as center, recognizes itself, as center, in other traditions, and each increasingly and delightedly celebrates the others. It is what Charles Williams called the 'courtesy' of Christianity. It is the gay and delighted recognition of the presence of love in the other, and the response to it of veneration and service, yet a veneration which is never stodgy or over-solemn, for it recognizes also the glorious anachronism, the splendid godly joke, of divine life active in such inadequate god-bearers.

There is no group of human beings, however venerable,

however rich in tradition or in sanctity, which can adequately carry out the Catholic enterprise. The idea is ludicrous when it isn't tragic, and in fact those historic Christian bodies which have striven most earnestly to be truly Catholic in the sense described here have always been, by that very fact, frequently tragic in their failures, and frequently ludicrous in the disproportion between their stated aims and their actual performance. One could almost say (but the idea must not be pushed too far) that the ability to make large and horrible and public mistakes, to make itself deservedly a laughing stock to all sensible people, is a fair indication that a Christian body is thoroughly Catholic. On the other hand, to become respectable, to hedge one's bets, to seek acceptability or — worse still — to be unable to find oneself funny is the reverse of Catholic.

For people who like to draw lines, I offer no comfort. I cannot draw a line round the Catholic thing. If it is, as I suggested, a center with a number of locations both in place and time, then this center is above all a source of light. (The Abbe Huvelin, his spiritual guide, wrote to von Hugel, "Truth for you is a radiant point of light which gradually fades off into darkness.") This light must be understood, as well as lived by, and to ask whether understanding or life matters most is meaningless because they overlap and blend, but accurate recognition does enormously matter. The light must also be "serviced," if one may use such a word, so that the means by which it is reflected, stored and transmitted are kept in good order. All this matters, all this is part of the enterprise.

But finally I am driven, for lack of words, back to the twin sisters of my first allegory. And I think it is clear that, if we can shed prejudices and maybe some painful memories, the one I called Mother Church is truly worthy of love, not only because we can never do without her (however much we resist her and even when we only let her in at night) but because she is a very courageous and lovable person, for all her faults. Like most people she becomes more possessive and nastier when she feels herself neglected or attacked, but correspondingly more lovable when she knows herself much loved. Lanza del Vasto, the founder of L'Arche, the lay, rural, peasant-style quasi-monastic community in France which has so impressed visitors by its integral and truly catholic way of life, was interviewed on television by one of those interviewers who are certain that any Christian doing unusual and exciting things must be in a state of revolt against his or her church. But the serene, white-robed founder, looking like a benign Old Testament prophet, proved a disappointing subject in this respect. "The Church is our Mother," he said genially. "All mothers make mistakes." Mother Church is an easy target, and often deserves the missiles thrown at her. Lanza del Vasto was wise and truthful in his reply.

Yet, as I said, Mother Church is mortal. She exists because of sin, in the basic sense of "what is wrong" with earthly life, and so she will die when "all manner of things shall be well". But her sister does not die. (Allegory is necessarily limiting, and mine cannot allow me to explore the glorious oneness which is the reality behind the two-ness of these concepts of the Christian community. To show them as twins, deeply devoted in spite of all differences, is the nearest I can get to suggesting it.) The deathless Sophia, who is the other personality of the Church, is infinitely the more attractive, of course. But perhaps I have been cheating a little, because Sophia is Wisdom, and Wisdom, in her scriptural personality, has more than a touch of Mother Church in her make up.

To read the passages in those later books of the Old Testament which describe the nature and activity of Wisdom is an extraordinary experience and directly relevant to the whole theme of this book. Wisdom, then, will serve to bring the work to its close. In the Book of Proverbs Wisdom describes herself as before all —

When there were no depths I was brought forth,
When there were no springs abounding with water.
Before the mountains had been shaped,
  before the hills I was brought forth;
Before he had made the earth with its fields,
  or the first dust of the world.
When he established the heavens I was there

> *when he drew a circle on the face of the deep,*
> *When he assigned to the sea its limit,*
> * so that the waters might not transgress his command,*
> *When he marked out the foundations of the earth,*
> * then I was beside him, like a master workman;*
> *And I was daily his delight,*
> * rejoicing before him always,*
> * rejoicing in his inhabited world*
> * and delighting in the sons of men.*

But the picture deepens and broadens. Wisdom is no mere onlooker (though even here there is a hint of sharing in the work) but a fellow-worker. The book of Wisdom says things which cause a kind of "double take" effect, for the implications are so startling. Here the author makes Solomon explain why he wants Wisdom as his bride:

> *She glorifies her noble birth by living with God,*
> * and the Lord of all loves her,*
> *For she is initiate in the knowledge of God,*
> * and an associate in his works.*
> *If riches are a desirable possession in life,*
> * what is richer than Wisdom who effects all things?*
> *And if understanding is effective,*
> * who more than she is fashioner of what exists?*

Wisdom, it is clear, is not simply a personification of human wisdom or of an aspect of God, but *is* God, active and original, creating and teaching. Her job is described as a kind of cosmic home-making, creating from within, rather than (as in Genesis) from without. The two concepts are complementary and necessary to each other, but we seldom consider the "inner face" of creation in this way. The author of the book of Wisdom, speaking for Solomon, struggles to explain how Wisdom works, and he uses images that have a familiar ring, not surprisingly, since both St. Paul and the writer to the Hebrews use them, quite deliberately, to describe the meaning and work of Christ, the incarnate Word and Wisdom of God:

I learned what is secret and what is manifest,
for wisdom, the fashioner of all things, taught me.
For in her there is a spirit that is intelligent, holy,
unique, manifold, subtle,
mobile, clear, unpolluted,
distinct, invulnerable, loving the good, keen,
irresistible, beneficent, humane,
steadfast, sure, free from anxiety,
all-powerful, overseeing all,
and penetrating through all spirits
that are intelligent and pure and most subtle.
For wisdom is more mobile than any motion;
Because of her pureness she pervades and penetrates
all things,
For she is the breath of the power of God,
pure emanation of the power of the Almighty;
therefore nothing defiled gains entrance into her.
For she is the reflection of eternal light,
spotless mirror of the working of God,
and an image of his goodness.
Though she is but one, she can do all things,
and while remaining in herself she renews all
things,
in every generation she passes into holy souls,
and makes them friends of God and prophets.

The picture is getting clearer and it shows us creation, not as a long ago event, but going on, from before time and without a break, growing and renewing itself from within through millenia. The same creative power is active in history through men and women who became "friends of God and prophets." In a passage in the book of Ecclesiasticus (which is, like *Wisdom*, among the Deutero-Canonical books, and therefore less familiar to non-Roman Catholic readers than the Hebrew Canon) Wisdom herself is given a voice, and describes her origin:

I came forth from the mouth of the Most High,
and covered the earth like a mist.

I dwelt in high places, and my throne was in a pillar of
  cloud.
Alone I have made the circuit of the vault of heaven
  and have walked in the depths of the abyss.

She also says that "in every people and nation I have gotten a
possession," and it is clear that divine Wisdom, creative and sustaining power, is concerned with all material reality, but
especially with people and societies, in the same capacity. But so
far she is, as it were, anonymous. She works eternally in all
things, but for the fullness of her work it is necessary that she
should also have a house, a recognizable dwelling where men
and women may come in their desire to understand her.

Then the Creator of all things gave me a com-
  mandment,
and the one who created me assigned a place for my tent.
And he said: 'Make your dwelling in Jacob
  and in Israel receive your inheritance'.
. . . And so I was established in Zion,
In the beloved city likewise he gave me a resting
  place,
and in Jerusalem was my dominion.
So I took root in an honoured people. . .

The passage goes on to describe the growth of Wisdom in her
appointed home, "like a palm tree in Engedi, and like rose
plants in Jericho," spreading far and wide the fragrance of her
leaves and flowers. In this passage Wisdom who "came forth
from the mouth of the Most High" and shares in the work of
creation, is herself created, though the first of all. For in this context Wisdom is almost identified with her work among human
beings. She is here the place of recognition and celebration, the
human home of those who, in her and by her, seek to know the
things of God. "I am the mother of fair love, of fear and of
knowledge and of holy hope" she says (at least in some texts,
though not in all) and she gives things to her children.

All this makes it perhaps less surprising that the Church has always been a feminine concept, a figure who is mortal and finite in one aspect, yet eternal in another, the bride of Christ "coming down out of Heaven, like a bride adorned for her husband", the Holy City of a transformed humanity, in which God dwells forever, "and I saw no temple in the city, for its temple is the Lord God the Almighty and the Lamb. By its light shall the nations walk, and the kings of the earth shall bring their glory unto it . . . they shall bring unto it the glory and honour of the nations." There is a tree growing here, too, the tree of life. Mother Church and Sophia are indeed one, and their strange relationship has the fruitful ambiguity of all symbols.

The same ambiguity, baffling and yet enlightening, is evident in another aspect of the same symbolism, for the Word of God is the incarnate Son, a masculine symbol and person, Jesus Christ, but he is, as Paul says, "the image of the invisible God, the first born of all creation," which is Wisdom symbolism. In Hebrew he reflects the glory of God and bears the very stamp of his nature, and he shares God's throne, as Wisdom does. But he is also "the head of the body, the church." He is Wisdom, but in the context of his work in human society "the body of Christ" is the assembly of human beings, and is feminine, and is two-sided, as I suggested: earthly and heavenly, human and divine, finite and infinite, mortal and immortal. But the two cannot be separated. As mortal, she is pledged to an immortal work. As earthly, she is instructed to turn it into heaven. As divine she has to struggle with human facts, and she must neither abolish the humanity nor ignore the divinity. Inevitably, the results are mixed, in every possible sense, but there is no escaping the responsibility.

The Catholic enterprise is Wisdom's work. It is, as she is, infinite in scope, reaching into the depths of the human spirit as it reaches through the heavens and into the abyss. Yet it is localised. Wisdom was instructed to find herself a dwelling. She is not to be found in one place only, but she has identifiable homes, and if Rome is not the only one geographically, the symbolism of that great city tells us a great deal about the way in which Wisdom localises herself. Just as Jerusalem *means* "the dwelling place of God" and also a human city "who kills the prophets";

a city which was occupied by a foreign nation, and was the place where Jesus was crucified — so Rome *means* the center of Catholic enterprise, blazing with the light of apostles, martyrs and saints and the wisdom of scholars, the splendour of great art, but also it *means* scandal, and corruption, brutal oppression, and the most cynical kind of power politics. Here Wisdom dwells as she dwells in other human situations which reflect the same contraries. Here Wisdom has an identifiable habitation to which people may look, a convergence of effort making this particular dwelling some kind of touchstone of truth, although tricky and unexpected in its operations as all touchstones. A people, a visible enterprise — here Wisdom is at home to callers and here, as one text describes it, she gives splendid parties to which all are invited.

Perhaps, in the end, it is by those parties that we may recognize the Catholic enterprise, wherever it is at work, in its various degrees of clarity and consciousness. "She has slaughtered her beasts, she has mixed her wine, she has also set her table. She has sent out her maids to call from the highest places in the town." (*Proverbs*). They call, those indefatigable maids of Wisdom, and her guests assemble at a place they know, and meet people there and celebrate. At these parties there is one symbol and one center — the one we call the Eucharist.

In every age voices from high places have called and those who heard have assembled to celebrate the joy at the heart of reality in a thoroughly Catholic way with everyday food, with music and poetry, with ancient symbols and modern interpretation, with wordless awareness of the presence of divine wisdom, and with very precise words both old and new.

The splendour of saints, the glory of cathedrals, the courage of reformers, the strangeness of myth and marvel, the soaring ecstasies of mystics and the sorrows of the poor — all these are the home of the Catholic enterprise. It begins wherever we are, it continues according to our capacity, it is celebrated as well as we can follow its movements and finds its definition in those feasts which are, if we could only see properly, the universal bridal supper of the human race and its lover.